Homeschooling the Child
with Asperger Syndrome

of related interest

Home Educating Our Autistic Spectrum Children
Paths are Made by Walking
Edited by Terry Dowty and Kitt Cowlishaw
ISBN 1 84310 037 1

Choosing Home
Deciding to Homeschool with Asperger's Syndrome
Martha Kennedy Hartnett
Foreword by Stephen Shore
ISBN 1 84310 763 5

Asperger's Syndrome
A Guide for Parent's and Professionals
Tony Attwood
Foreword by Lorna Wing
ISBN 1 85302 577 1

Freaks, Geeks and Asperger Syndrome
A User Guide to Adolescence
Luke Jackson
Foreword by Tony Attwood
ISBN 1 84310 098 3

Homeschooling the Child with Asperger Syndrome
Real Help for Parents Anywhere and on Any Budget

Lise Pyles

Jessica Kingsley Publishers
London and New York

First published in the United Kingdom in 2004
by Jessica Kingsley Publishers Ltd
116 Pentonville Road
London N1 9JB, England
and
29 West 35th Street, 10th fl.
New York, NY 10001-2299, USA
www.jkp.com

Copyright © Lise Pyles 2004

Library of Congress Cataloging-in-Publication Data

Pyles, Lise, 1955-
    Homeschooling the child with Asperger syndrome : real help for parents
anywhere and on any budget / Lise Pyles.
        p. cm.
Includes bibliographical references and indexes.
    ISBN 1-84310-761-9 (pbk.)
    1. Asperger's syndrome. 2. Asperger's syndrome—Patients—Education.
3. Home schooling. 4. Patient education. I. Title.
    RJ506.A9P953 2004
    371.92—dc22

                                            2003025161

British Library Cataloguing in Publication Data
A CIP catalogue record for this book is available from the British Library

ISBN 1 84310 761 9

Printed and Bound in Great Britain by
Athenaeum Press, Gateshead, Tyne and Wear

Contents

Acknowledgments

If this book reflects truth, and it is my fervent hope that it does, it is to the credit of dozens of families that have been brutally honest in providing me their stories. These good people have filled out distressingly long questionnaires, answered off-the-cuff questions, discussed thorny problems, aired complaints, shared victories, and confessed worries so that other families will benefit. In short, they have provided the guts of this book. I am respecting their need for privacy in not naming them individually here, but I thank each one for the valuable contributions they have made.

As always, I am grateful to my parents, Jay and Estel Larsen, for the life lessons they gave me and for their unwavering support. Also, I thank my two sons who have taught me, each in his own way, what an absolute honor and awesome privilege it is to be a parent.

I'd like to thank Jil Edwards, whose encouraging remarks in high school did more for my budding writing career than any English class, a fact that has given me much to ponder during the writing of this book.

I'd also like to acknowledge Sue Sorensen. Reconnecting recently with my best friend from childhood has been a phenomenal experience. We were on the same wavelength as kids, and now, as mothers to children with Asperger Syndrome, we are still on the same wavelength. I'm starting to understand that true friendship has a great deal to do with wavelength.

Finally, I'm most grateful to my husband, Bill, for giving me the courage to follow my heart and for his help in doing so. In this book, I write about things that 'I' did in homeschooling, but it was a truly joint effort. His constant support, hands-on assistance, and general encouragement have ensured the successes I'm now able to write about. Our homeschooling experience, like parenting, has been a 'we' proposition in every respect, though he seldom gets the credit. So thanks, silent partner. I love you.

Acknowledgements

Preface

When I wrote my first book, *Hitchhiking through Asperger Syndrome* (2001), I covered the issues I thought were important in the thoughtful raising of a child affected by Asperger Syndrome (AS). These issues included education, therapy, diet, medication, general parenting, and, most of all, trying to understand the many challenges that a child with AS faces.

One of those chapters discussed homeschooling, something that we undertook in our family for a few years and found to be profoundly worthwhile. I outlined the main points of homeschooling as I saw them, and included a few practical ideas for how to integrate homeschooling with Asperger issues.

As it turned out, this single chapter was a small drink of water for a thirsty readership. I was not the first to homeschool a child with Asperger Syndrome – far from it. But I had furnished practical words about how other parents might accomplish the same thing, and readers soon told me that they needed to read much more on the subject.

That brings me to this book – an attempt at "more." For this important project, I've enlisted the help of more than three dozen homeschooling families, in order to better capture the breadth of experience. Each parent whose words appear on these pages has one or more children with Asperger Syndrome (or a "near cousin" on the autism spectrum, which I will describe a bit later). We are in various stages, but are all hitchhiking the same road.

If you have a child with Asperger Syndrome or what you suspect is AS, and you have begun to homeschool or think along those lines, this book will reassure that you are not alone. We are all in this together.

Reading this book should also provide a dose of encouragement. The parents you'll hear from have found homeschooling to be not only do-able but a positive experience; that includes those who only did it for a year or two before moving on to other options. Not one person has been sorry for the experience and all felt they'd benefited greatly.

Homeschooling is hard work and not without challenges, but wonderful things can happen for our Asperger-affected kids that might not happen in any other way.

The third benefit I hope you will gain from this book is empowerment. Knowledge empowers, and the practical information and real-life examples are intended to help form a firm foundation for your child's very special home education. It is not the last book you will ever want to put on your shelf, but you will know the basics about both Asperger Syndrome and homeschooling and, most importantly, you will see the two subjects within the context of each other. As you investigate academic topics through the lens of Asperger issues, and vice versa, you will develop a homeschooling philosophy and game plan that keeps your child's special issues – *that keeps your unique child* – always firmly in mind. We have lots to do, so let's get started.

Chapter 1

Should You Homeschool Your Child with Asperger Syndrome?

S hould I homeschool my child with Asperger Syndrome (AS)? That's probably your big question. Homeschooling a child with AS offers the prospect of tremendous benefits, as you will see in numerous examples throughout this book, but it's not the right answer in every case. It's a big decision to make. By the end of this book, you should have a better idea of what such a decision entails, the pros and cons of it, and whether you want to follow this route. Perhaps you will ultimately decide that it is not right for you. If so, then your energy may be better spent working within the educational system to devise strategies that work at school.[1]

Still, you picked up this book for a reason. Even if things are going okay at your child's school, you may be wondering if your child's special needs might be better addressed at home. Perhaps your child is surviving in the classroom now, but not thriving. Perhaps you suspect that the school staff do not understand AS and how to work with the many inherent issues – the communication difficulties, the social deficits, and all the rest. Maybe the staff do seem clued in, but the stress is too great on your child or the benefits are not as great as you'd hoped. Or perhaps an unfortunate event has occurred at school and, even though you may have never in a million years dreamed of homeschooling, the door has now been flung abruptly open. Whatever has caused your interest at this time, you will make the best decision by learning as much as you can about the experiences of others who are already homeschooling their Asperger-affected children. Just how hard is it? How much good is it likely to do? How does one handle special Asperger-related issues? Why have other families turned to it? In this chapter, you will find the following:

- a basic definition of Asperger Syndrome and why it lends itself to a homeschool setting

- what leads Asperger-affected families to turn away from traditional schooling options

- common roadblocks to the decision to homeschool

- a few facts and figures about Asperger Syndrome and homeschoolers.

A definition of Asperger Syndrome

The following definition has been compiled from several sources and "translated" into everyday English. While not every characteristic will apply to every child, as you read the definition below please picture in your mind's eye how each characteristic would affect a child's chance of success in a classroom environment.

Definition of Asperger Syndrome

The child with Asperger Syndrome is socially awkward, has difficulty making or keeping friends and he/she is generally egocentric and lacking, or seeming to lack, empathy or ability to see the other person's point of view. Communication may be literal. Thinking may be black and white and lack imagination (or show unusual imagination). Speech and language skills may seem somewhat odd compared with peers. That is, speech may seem formal or pedantic (teacher-like), or may sound somewhat unusual. Nonverbal communication is lacking, so that the child misses or misreads nonverbal signals (gestures, body language, facial expression) and is ineffectual or limited in sending them. Personal interests (collections, hobbies, preoccupations) may be unusual in subject and/or narrow in range and/or pursued intensely. In addition, the child may gravitate to or take comfort in routines, rituals, and repetition and be upset by surprises. Intelligence, however, is average or better, and initial language acquisition is within norms. There may be abnormal reactions to sensory stimuli (i.e. have unusual sensitivity to light, smells, tastes, tactile sensation, or sounds). There is usually, but not always, physical clumsiness.

We'll discuss a lot of this in more detail later, but it's clear that each trait can represent a separate reason for why traditional school can be torture. Even the trait of normal or higher intelligence can work against an AS-affected child, since our children's intelligence often adds to their frustration over failure in other areas.

Still, thousands and thousands of children with special needs go to school, and special education classes exist for that very reason. So what makes some families reject them and follow a different path? How or why do they seemingly cross an imaginary line and reach the ultimate decision to homeschool?

After interviewing parents of approximately 40 Asperger-affected children who have taken this fork in the road, some patterns emerged. The following four scenarios, illustrated here with the experiences of real families, show the most common decision points.

Four avenues that lead AS-affected families to turn away from traditional schooling options

Avenue 1: An early decision

Making a very early (preschool or younger) decision to homeschool is less common than the other avenues, but it is happening more each year, as early child diagnosis improves and as homeschooling becomes a more mainstream option. Some moms and dads plan to homeschool even before diagnosis. When AS (or autism spectrum) becomes linked to their unique child, however, it becomes a harder decision. They think, "Now what? Is homeschooling still possible?" Jamie T writes:

> I had thought about homeschooling my children…before I had children. When we learned our daughter, Autumn, had autism, I thought, "Well, that idea goes out the window." But after seeing the public school system in my area – what a joke. They could not give her everything she needs to learn. Who am I kidding? They could not give her half of what she needs to learn.

Other parents reported sending their child to school, but immediately changing their minds. From first exposure, they sensed it was not a good fit for their child and brought him[2] back home. Either way, it's an early decision.

Avenue 2: Hitting the wall

The most common decision point for homeschooling seems to be in second or third grade. There might have been a few red flags raised from the first day of kindergarten, but in the beginning teachers usually reassure parents that all kids mature at different rates, and the school experience will soon even out any rough areas of development and socialization. This doesn't happen though, and in about second grade or so, there are no more illusions that things will just work themselves out. Instead, it falls apart. Here is Diane's account:

> During preschool, Allan was very active, inattentive (much more so than other children), somewhat aggressive, and very, very verbal. As he grew older, it became apparent that there were some delays in social skills and writing especially. He would often fly into inexplicable rages.
>
> During first grade, although he did seem to enjoy school, other behaviors began appearing... His health suffered due to lack of appetite because of medication; he lost several pounds during the school year. As first grade progressed, he became more and more resistant to school work, particularly anything dealing with writing or math.
>
> In second grade, behaviors escalated out of control. Major meltdowns at school, incontinence during the day, complete lack of interest in written work, rages at home, and accelerated aggressiveness worried us and also worried school personnel. During the beginning of second grade, he was tested, and it was discovered that he was reading at a third grade, third month level. In the classroom, he was working in books for mid first-graders. It was assumed that because he was behind in other areas, he must be behind in reading, too. No amount of cajoling on my part could get him moved from his classroom placement, and I feel this was due to all the other behaviors present; they simply didn't expect that he could succeed in anything since he was failing in so many things.
>
> I began to be a frequent visitor to his classroom, much to his teacher's dismay. I watched as he would quickly complete an assignment in science, then begin to act out because he was finished and bored. I watched as he fidgeted and stimmed[3] because other children struggled with reading passages he had already read through. Then, when he was called on, he had no

idea where they were in the text because he had already finished it. "He doesn't keep up," "He just doesn't listen," and "I just don't know what to do with him" were his teacher's mantra… I again begged to have him moved but this was all to no avail.

And so things got worse and worse. By the end of second grade, I was really schooling at home, because most of his seatwork was coming home at night unfinished. And, miraculously, he would often sit down and complete it in a matter of a few minutes with focused teaching on my part…keeping him on task and working in a quiet place. We were all frustrated by the end of the school year, his teacher included. The school blamed us at home, and insisted I get him into counseling. I did, but when the counselor reviewed records I provided from school, she agreed with me that school seemed to be one of the things causing the great stress in his life.

I had already decided to homeschool by March, but thought it best to remove him at the end of the year. One evening, while raging about something, he turned to me and screamed, "Mommy, I am the stupidest thing God ever put on this earth!" That was my seven-year-old's view of himself. We both cried and cried that night, and I knew much too much damage had been done to my sweet child. I told him then and there about our decision to homeschool. I talked about why we would do it and what we would do. And I said to him, "Allan, if you learn nothing else next year, you will learn that you are not stupid, and that you can learn anything you set your mind to learn." I think knowing he would be homeschooled relieved some of the pressure. His teacher called me several days later to report yet another outburst in class. She told me that, while screaming at her, he had said, "Next year, my mom's gonna teach me at home, and I'll never have to see you again!" I just smiled to myself, because I knew he was right.

By August after he left school in June, the daytime wetting had stopped. The constant statements of self-loathing had decreased although they were by no means gone. He raged maybe once a week, instead of several times a day. He was off medication completely, and was healthier for having regained his appetite. And, one afternoon, standing at the kitchen window, I heard him laugh for the first time in almost a year. I mean he laughed a big, rolling belly laugh, and I sat in a chair and cried my eyes out,

> thanking God because I knew we were doing the right thing. We have never looked back since. He does sometimes talk about his friends at school, and often remembers the enjoyable things he did there. But when I ask if he is glad he is schooling at home, he always says, "Oh, yes!"

Diane's story is typical. Preschool and first grade may slide by without major turmoil, but eventually the child is completely unable to cope. Whether there is an actual moment of crisis or not, the emotional costs are clear.

Avenue 3: The long goodbye

This avenue is one where the family has already been on a tortuous journey for years through the school system, with a morass of special education classes, special schools, perhaps part-time or full-time aides, extra therapies, and usually enough paperwork to wallpaper China's Great Wall. Parents, teachers, and the student have all played long and hard in the game and have invested incredible effort into forcing the system. And it has worked well enough to keep limping along, year after year, but it is never great. At some point, it is time to give up and say goodbye to public education.

Thus, the decision comes either in junior or senior high years, and it's quite heartbreaking to think about all the effort up until that point that, in the end, didn't make enough of a difference. Ruth's case has a crisis element to it at the end, so it overlaps with the fourth avenue I will discuss below, but her tale is included here because it illustrates a long trail of trying everything else first:

> I had to go through a great deal before homeschooling. My son was in public school without special services besides Ritalin from kindergarten through second grade. Towards the end of the year he had some aggressive outbursts during medication trials. The school insisted that he had to go to a special self-contained school. Back in those naive days, I simply assumed what they said was fact.
>
> In the special school Jordan got occupational therapy (OT), which solved his handwriting problems. They also did some sensory integration (SI) work and I sought additional private OT. The first summer and next school year and summer he had a good teacher and he did well in the smaller calmer class with clear

structure. They assured me he needed another year and given the progress, I was inclined to believe him.

The second year was a disaster. His classmates teased him and hit him and the teacher could not control things. We still did not have the diagnosis of Aspergers and everyone considered him a very ADHD child, and gradually becoming oppositional and compulsive. He was moved to a slow class where the kids were not aggressive. Basically he got no education after leaving public school. I was told that was the only option and since I live in a small metro area I believed them.

Fourth grade consisted of trying to find a different placement for Jordan. By the time I found a good partially mainstreamed program, the year was almost over. That program didn't turn out well the following year. Jordan started head banging, which got him sent home, and then they were going to bump him back to the special school after ten incidents. Jordan seemed able to hold it together [only] two weeks at a stretch, and by November he was halfway to being booted out, depressed and with a workable suicide plan, and I took him home. The day I told our psychiatrist about homeschooling, he raised the issue of Aspergers and everything changed. The diagnosis of Aspergers and what I learned subsequently made it clearer than ever that we needed to be home, and that everything the school had done to handle the situation was seriously misdirected.

Avenue 4: Crisis

The last decision point is one born of crisis (as above) but without all the special services or adult intervention. Basically, most clues have been missed up until that point and certainly no one has joined the puzzle pieces. The child has been holding things together as best he can, internalizing most of it and just trying to avoid the bullies. Working without a net, so to speak, it's perhaps inevitable that he eventually takes a bad fall. The scenarios may vary – maybe you discover your child has been physically harmed at school, mentally abused by bullies, or has resorted to self-harm or violence himself. Or perhaps he's had a blow-up in school, raising the specter of expulsion or worse. Whatever the sudden change, you need to make a move now, before it's too late.

A Texas mom relates: "My son was having a difficult time in junior high because of continual harassment and bullying. We found a loaded gun in his bedroom on a Friday afternoon and on Monday we withdrew him from public school and started homeschooling." This boy had been diagnosed with Asperger Syndrome only shortly before this episode, but had obviously been suffering for a long time.

Other moms report crises of different sorts – about their youngsters fleeing from school or being beaten up. One referred to an arrest being made at the school because a totally avoidable situation had been allowed to escalate without proper intervention. All were last-straw situations where parents turned to homeschooling as not only a good option, but a potentially life-saving one.

In reading the above scenarios, maybe you saw your own situation. Every family writes its own history, but chances are you recognize at least some of what these other families have been through.

The author's experience (Avenue 2 revisited)

Life at school was dismal for my then seven-year-old son. School staff didn't understand his alternately aloof or in-your-face demeanor, his eccentric talk, the odd giggles or otherwise strange or even explosive reactions. The teachers were well-meaning, but rudderless. His only options were a self-contained class for behavioral delays, or a mainstream classroom. Neither fit.

Asperger Syndrome wasn't in the medical literature in 1991, so we were all operating in the blind trying to figure out why John was "different." His medical files revealed a hodge-podge of cryptic abbreviations and conditions – Attention Deficit Disorder (ADD), mild autism, mild Tourette Syndrome, Sensory Integration Disorder, motor problems, language pragmatics issues, and that he was borderline mentally retarded. We seemed to have many jigsaw puzzle pieces for him but no picture. The one diagnosis that might have been helpful was the one for autism, but the outdated research we found at the time only characterized autistic people as nonverbal and in a world of their own. Our son was definitely in our world – it just wasn't going well.

Today, we recognize most of the above conditions as being part of, or commonly accompanying, Asperger Syndrome (all except retardation, which turned out to be a bad assessment – my son's intelligence is actually above normal). Now we know better how to work with Asperger Syndrome, but at the time all we knew was failure. He was still doing kindergarten work in second grade, and having tantrums so uncontrollable that he needed to be picked up from school at least weekly. I dreaded answering the phone. The drug Ritalin helped to improve his ability to concentrate and cope, but we didn't like the side effects. It just seemed that grade school wasn't supposed to be this hard.

Then one day my son talked to kids up the street and learned they were homeschooling. This became his new obsession. Why couldn't we homeschool? After weeks of his constantly bringing up this topic, I finally talked to the lady who was homeschooling. She was encouraging, but since she was also a certified teacher I was still left with the feeling that it was for other people, not us.

Then, two things happened. The school psychologist made a chance observation that John's demeanor at school was akin to a puppy learning to stay. Every ounce of this child's concentration and energy was wrapped up in just *being* in the classroom, so that there was nothing left for anything else. This made so much sense. Even though I didn't understand why it was occurring, I came to at least appreciate the vast energy John expended just to resist his instinct to flee six hours per day. No wonder academics suffered. No wonder he had outbursts or just mentally "checked out." And next year was due to be worse because of a larger class.

The other thing that happened was a wonderful opportunity to move to England. The thought of a new school, new teachers, more testing, and more upset on John's part, though, was more than I could bear. Suddenly, homeschooling looked like a good solution. It was portable, and the way things were going it couldn't be any worse than his school experience. A few days before his eighth birthday, we began our homeschooling adventure.

It was the best decision we ever made for him. He blossomed in a hundred ways. He was allowed time to develop on his own timetable, and it turned out that the real boy underneath all those sensory and other problems was a bright and curious kid. I'm not saying that we didn't have bad days when he couldn't focus and I'd get frustrated. Some homeschooling days make you want to scream – in fact, they make you scream (a little) – but good days outnumbered the bad. I learned to take my cues from him, and he made incredible gains that I am convinced he would not have made in school. We said goodbye to failure (a daily occurrence at the old school) and started enjoying success after success. It was hard work but it was good, positive work, and it has made all the difference.

We homeschooled for three and a half years. In sixth grade (age 11) we fell into a good chance to reintroduce him to the classroom experience in a small school with small classes. With some adjustments, he did okay that year. The following year, we moved to Australia and were able to enroll him in a very small and surprisingly Asperger-savvy private school. That too was a success and he went on through his high school years there and graduated in 2000. Now, at age 19, he's in college and doing well.

Although we only homeschooled for a few years, I know they were the most pivotal years of my son's life. Everything turned around in that time. We had the chance to work all the most troublesome issues, not only academics and behavioral issues, but physical issues. He no longer needed medication to cope, and we were able to pinpoint some dietary issues. Instead of a lifetime of special education, he learned to function in regular classes. Instead of rejecting other people, he learned to make friends. Instead of behavior that included spitting, hitting, and throwing chairs at the teachers, he became a really nice kid. Instead of covering his ears and panicking over bright lights or gooey suntan lotion, he overcame sensory panic. This process took years, not months, but the progress leapfrogged instead of crawled. I reiterate – it all began with homeschooling. That is why I remain devoted to the concept. It is a life passion because it saved my child's life.

As a footnote to this, the stellar success of homeschooling my oldest has recently led me to begin homeschooling my younger son who is just entering his high school years. Although he is not affected by Asperger Syndrome, he is also thriving under the new plan.

Common roadblocks to homeschooling and how to overcome them

Why might you not want to homeschool even if the idea is very appealing? In the next few pages, we'll examine some misgivings that stop people from pulling their child out of school and bringing them home, even if it's what they really think is the right answer. It is a scary step to take, after all, and for a lot of reasons.

Roadblock 1: Homeschooling takes time

Yes, it does, but think of this – so does normal school. Here is a partial list of the things that consume both time and energy when your child is a special needs child going to school. See how many of these are all too familiar to you:

- phone calls to and from the school
- meetings with teachers to discuss problems
- meetings with counselors
- meetings with school psychologists
- being called to the principal's office
- conferring with school therapists (if you are lucky enough to get any)
- having to retrieve a child from school who is in "meltdown" and then handling the ensuing difficult afternoon
- spending hours calming an agitated child after school each day
- daily transport of your child to and from school after he is kicked off the bus
- writing letters to address problems
- training teachers about Asperger Syndrome
- copying pamphlets, book excerpts and so forth for teachers, in order to back up your points
- bringing in your child's medication and addressing medication issues
- trying to handle dietary restrictions or dealing with dietary mistakes
- accompanying your child on field trips, just so he can go, or keeping him home because he can't go
- writing goals for your child's special program. This is called the Individualized Education Plan or IEP in the USA; and Statement of Special Educational Needs or SSEN in the UK.

- writing notes on a near-daily basis about your child's ongoing issues or asking for homework assignments

- fighting over homework or catching up on work your child could not accomplish in a stimulating classroom

- writing formal complaints to school boards when IEPs are ignored

- meeting with child advocates, expert doctors, or lawyers to prepare your case against the school

- crying into your pillow and waking up the next day feeling like you've been run over by a truck.

Are you tired yet? Each of these actions is not only time consuming but also joy consuming, with a resulting drain on one's energy. Exhausted and harried parents reject the idea of homeschooling because they feel they just can't add one more task to an already difficult day. But just think of all the above tasks that you won't ever have to do again once you start homeschooling.

Following this idea further, yes, homeschooling might take a few more hours a week but it also frees up a lot of them. It may be a case of changing several negative hours per week into just a few more positive ones. As Diana R exclaims, "Homeschooling is *so* much easier than battling the schools, and the decrease in stress for our *entire* family is remarkable."

Let's not sugarcoat this, however. You will have to reorganize your days around your new number one priority. It does take commitment, and you may have to delay a budding career, reduce hours spent on other things, or otherwise put your own life on hold. Several moms lamented having to stop their career or go from full time to part time, and the number one complaint about homeschooling is the lack of personal time. More than one mom said, "I never get a break."

We'll talk about coping strategies later in the book (Chapter 9), but for now consider this. Many of our forefathers and foremothers homeschooled their children in a time when the average life expectancy might have been only 40 or 50 years. Today, the average lifespan for people in many countries is well into the seventies or eighties. In the larger scheme of things, concentrating on one's children during those few formative years is not too much to ask. They grow all too fast.

In the end it may even be pretty self-serving. Giving your child the best foundation now may save heartache later. Soon enough, you will have time to go back to a career, take up college, etc. Unless you're training for the Olympics, you can probably wait.

How much time does it take? Most families homeschool three to four hours per day during grade school years. A preschooler doesn't need more than a few minutes of a formal lesson because they are learning things all day anyway. A student in high school might spend more than four hours on his studies but is usually able to work more independently. It doesn't all need to be done in one chunk, either. Sometimes a tag-team effort works where, for example, Mom does language, arts and social sciences with the child for part of the day, and Dad helps out with math and science in the evening.

Further, lessons can often be done at home in half the time they take in school. This point was brought home to me when a friend spent a day following each of her two (non-AS-affected) middle school aged children around their classes. She found that one child was exposed to about 90 minutes of actual teaching throughout the day, while the other received about 45 minutes. The rest of the day was eaten up by passing between classes, getting settled, collecting homework or lunch orders, handing out papers, taking attendance, making announcements, waiting for quiet, dealing with rowdy kids, and getting ready to go to the next class. This mom figured that if she spent even two or three hours with her children daily, it would result in a gain of many learning hours across the year. She homeschooled from that point onward.

Roadblock 2: Homeschooling takes money

Superlative education can be gained with meager expenditure. In *Homeschooling for Excellence*, David and Micki Colfax (1988) detail how they homeschooled four sons (three of whom later went to Harvard) using the most basic of materials. Asperger Syndrome did not figure into their story but the point is clear – a good education need not be expensive. For our kids, you will want to add in some other materials for home therapy but this too need not be expensive.

How much should you expect to spend? Most families I surveyed spend $500 to $600 (US) per year, but often that includes music lessons and other fees they would have spent anyway. The first year is usually more costly because folks are nervous and buy too much. Prices go down during subsequent years, although high school years tend to require more expensive books or outside courses. One family spent as little as $100 by making extensive use of library and internet resources and by buying used curriculum. One family spent $1500, but that included Suzuki method guitar lessons and equipment. Another admitted to a whopping $3000, but this included unspecified field trips (perhaps to far-flung locations), gas, and fencing lessons.

The greater financial burden may be in loss of income. Lucy left a $55,000 per year paycheck that her family still misses sorely, but her presence at home, teaching her junior high son who was in crisis, was far more important than that paycheck. While dollars stretch only so far, it's often a case of priorities. In my own circumstances, we took a pay cut of over 60 percent. We learned to scrimp and rethink a lot of things. See Appendix 8 for more details on how we went from two paychecks to one and lived to tell about it.

For single parents who work, job loss would mean disaster, but still sometimes things can be worked out. A parent may be able to work at home, or combine homeschool efforts with another mom. An older child capable of studying independently can hit the books while the parent is at work, or can perhaps do his studies at a neighbor's house or with a tutor during that time. A common solution is to do the schoolwork in the evenings when the parent is available. None of these may be ideal, but might work in a pinch. You will have to examine your own circumstances to ensure you are within the law, that your child is safe, and that you do not leave yourself vulnerable to attacks from people who don't approve of your homeschooling style. I am not a lawyer, and you truly must evaluate your own situation.

Roadblock 3: I can't homeschool because I'm not a teacher

If you have no teacher training, how can you expect to do it right? One teacher-turned-homeschooler (also a mom of an AS-affected child) replies:

> I was taught how to deal with groups in an educational setting. I learned the different learning styles (verbal, visual, kinesthetic) and how to tailor my instruction... Yes, I know the theory. Yes, I know my subject matter. But it still comes down to there being only one of me, and 25 of them.

Now a parent goes to school to learn about his or her child as well – it's the school of life. From the minute the child is born, the parent is learning about the child: how the baby relates to stimuli; how he or she learns; what makes him or her laugh or cry. The parent is the expert on his or her own child.

You as a parent may not have the four or five years of college coursework to teach you how to teach a group of students, but you do have your child's lifetime of learning to know how to reach and teach him or her. Remember, a lot of what teachers learn is how to deal with different students in the classroom. You as a parent/teacher already are an expert in dealing with your child/student.

In closing, I'd just say, if you'd like to try homeschooling your child, don't let anyone (including yourself) talk you out of it before you've tried it. If you have problems, there are listservs, homeschool organizations, books, and magazines published exclusively for helping you to understand.

Another mom has a degree in special education but admits: "Everything I have learned about Asperger's Syndrome I have learned hands-on from my children, through experience, and through my own reading." She does feel that one aspect of her training that has helped in working with her son is understanding how to take a task and break it down into small attainable steps. She feels that a lot of parents probably possess this ability without training though, or could obtain that training through a course or workshop.

Roadblock 4: I can't homeschool because I don't know what to teach and when

There are lists that provide learning objectives in grade order and they are readily available if you choose to follow them. They are called "curriculum objectives," "scope and sequence" lists, or other fancy names, and every school district or authority has a version. There are also national standards, and even curriculum publishers have their own versions.

When I started homeschooling, I tried to amass a master list of learning objectives. Then I woke up – if each school district has a different idea of what should be taught when (or at all), there is no right answer.

Educator John Holt expressed it this way: "We must ask how much of the sum of human knowledge anyone can know at the end of his schooling. Perhaps a millionth. Are we then to believe that one of these millionths is so much more important than another?" (1982, p.292).

Who knows which millionth will be needed next year or in 20 years? Should I be sad I never learned to use a slide rule? Last decade's push for French is this decade's quest to learn Japanese. Twenty years ago nobody ran to study geriatric medicine, alternative fuels, web-based businesses, or computer security, but today these are hot topics. We evolve. Of course we all need a foundation of understanding about the world about us (and that requires basic facts and skills), but people will argue forever about exactly what goes into that foundation.

Holt also talks about a bright fifth grade he taught, who was obsessed with snakes. (Does this sound like one of our kids?) Holt lamented that the school did not offer herpetology to study, commenting:

> Any time he spent learning about snakes was better spent than in ways I could think of to spend it; not least of all because, in the process of learning about snakes, he learned a great deal more about many other things than I was able to "teach" those unfortunates in my class who were not interested in anything at all. (Holt 1982, p.292)

The message is that the true curriculum a child should follow is one built out of interest and it's the child who decides what's of interest. One thing leads to another, the passion for learning grows, and knowledge is absorbed more completely and with less effort than when any planned and externally enforced curriculum is pressed. In other words, go with the flow, let your child lead and make your job that of facilitator. Help your child get the information that he has determined he needs.

We do this when our kids are little. We divide up raisins with our kids – two for you, two for me – and hardly think about the educational nature of it. Observing bugs on a nature walk is in the same category. And when your child wants to learn more about bugs than you know, you show him how to look it up.

Do things change when the child is older? School has indoctrinated us with fear that only experts can teach, but parents are still well capable. Even parents of older kids traditionally teach a great deal – how to change a flat tire, do laundry, use a checkbook, and various lessons about values, politics, sex, religion, money, and a hundred other things. Why should we be afraid of teaching? We do it every single day. We just don't think of those parent lessons in the same awestruck way we tend to think about school lessons up at a chalkboard. A Texas mom of a 17-year-old explains, "I guess my biggest concern was if I could handle the subject matter. I just studied it a little."

When my family lived in Australia, I met a man who was leader of the local autism/Asperger support group. He frequently praised my efforts at homeschooling and appreciated homeschooling's value, but then he would add that, unfortunately, he felt it was beyond his wife's and his capability. This was astounding. He and his wife had homeschooled their son from age 7 to nearly 13! When I pressed him for an explanation, he apologetically confessed, "But it wasn't formal schooling, and we missed a lot of subjects." I feel he is modest. I am confident that he and his wife expanded their son's knowledge and abilities in myriad, albeit informal, ways. They did so with little help or support though, and I am guessing that, because no tall stack of school-sanctioned textbooks had been absorbed by their autistic son, they felt that it hadn't been "real" schooling. My question is, what would have become of their son if left to the schools that he hadn't been able to cope with in the first place? They homeschooled because nothing else was working, and they did the best they could.

Their son now attends the local high school, and works at a nearby nature park, both because of special programs that were conceived, proposed, and pushed through the bureaucracy by this same modest father. How could he have designed the programs his son needed except through hands-on familiarity with how his son learns? Would his son be in as happy a circumstance if he hadn't been homeschooled, however informally? I wonder. Returning to my original point, I maintain that most of us do homeschooling in many ways, all along, whether we call it by that name or not.

Of course, parents still have worries about diplomas or certificates at the end of the road. External exit exams are the norm for countries such as Australia, Canada and the UK, and 27 US states have introduced them, although only 18 currently require passing them in order to earn a diploma. How do you cope with this? We'll talk about it more later, but in short, you determine for your location what final test(s) may be required, under what circumstances it may be taken, and what objectives are likely to be tested. Samples of past tests are usually available. Or you re-evaluate the importance of that diploma. There are often alternate routes to jobs and college. See Chapter 8 for more on this subject. For some guidance on curriculum goals:

- USA: www.mcrel.org/standards-benchmarks/

- UK: National Curriculum – www.nc.uk.net/

- Australia and Canada: see the excellent website "A to Z Homes' Cool" for individual state or province standards www.gomilpitas.com/homeschooling/materials/Content.html

Melissa has a more general worry: "I mainly just worry that he's not going to get a well-rounded education. That I'm going to leave out important issues, and he's not going to have interest, so we won't spend much time, and later on, he'll need to learn it." The answer to this is simple. If you discover a gap in your child's learning, you work to fill it. Whether it's learning to write a business letter or finally getting around to algebra, waiting until the information is needed can increase your child's interest in the topic. Our kids learn best if they see a need for the material. So don't worry too much about mistakes or artificial deadlines.

Roadblock 5: I can't homeschool – my child does well for the school but explodes or falls apart after school when he's with me. (Or) I can't homeschool – even the experts can't handle him so how can I?

Jenn from Oregon characterizes the after-school hours for her son Manny (aged 6): "My son was doing fine academically, but he was falling apart emotionally. At first his teacher couldn't even tell anything was wrong. He would save it all up and come unglued at home."

Most of the time this is a case of Contents Under Pressure. Our kids are expected to cope with extreme stress throughout the day. They've had multiple sensory assaults, had to try to decode confusing social situations, been forced to try to learn on the same schedule as the rest of the class, and very likely have been bullied or taunted by classmates. They are coiled springs that have been held in a tightly compressed state until they can hold it no longer. Sometimes they explode at school. Sometimes all the anger and frustration come exploding out as soon as they can find a safe place to let it all go – and that's home.

Jenn continues: "One day when I was volunteering in his class, I could tell that he was just hanging on by his fingernails, so to speak. He had that vacant expression and those huge, I'm-not-going-to-cry eyes. It broke my heart. That was his last day in school. We never sent him back."

What if we change things so that the child isn't under pressure? What if he is allowed to feel safe and comfortable and calm, and is allowed to learn at his own rate and in a way that suits him? Under those situations our kids can be very reasonable to live with. There will always be kid issues and behavior infractions and our kids do require a special understanding, but in the calm of one's own home small frustrations stay small for our kids, rather than escalating from having been held in and piled up all day. Maria tells of one of her bad weeks while homeschooling her son:

> I'd love someone to know more about my son than we do. When I'm having a week where I say to myself, "How can I homeschool this kid when I can't even get him to brush his teeth without a meltdown?" I'd love that elusive, wand-wielding imaginary expert to materialize in my living room and hand me the rulebook for my kid.
>
> Really though, my son already has it figured out. During one such week I got desperate enough to say to him, "You know, while we are homeschooling you do occasionally have to do as I ask." Long pause. "If you were in school, you would have to do what your teacher said."
>
> He looked straight at me, fully connected, and very calmly said, "I don't think so."
>
> What a refreshing moment! That's one important reason why we're homeschooling him. He couldn't accept those social norms of "do as the teacher says" just because she said it.

Maria recognizes that her son is better off at home, even on the bad days. She can back off when needed, and the spring never has to get tightly coiled. As a high school English teacher herself, Maria also knows that there is no wand-wielding expert on her son. Although she had some training in special education, she reports that it was minimal (and mostly about the law and liability issues) and it never taught her what she has learned on her own as a mom.

Roadblock 6: My child doesn't want to homeschool

Your child may want to go to school even while it is doing him damage. Our AS-affected kids often have skewed ideas of who their friends are, whether they have friends, and may mistake even bullying and having tricks played on them as friendly attention. They may like parts of school (perhaps science or music) so much that they endure the rest of it, even if they end up raging at home. Or they may simply be comfortable with the status quo, even an awful one.

Homeschooling may sound scary just because it is different. Our kids do not want to go to the dentist either, but we take them because it is in their best interests. With young children, we need to take this approach. Discussing homeschooling in a detailed way may help ease the transition though, as will listening to their worries. If they will miss seeing a particular friend, make pains to invite that friend over to play. With older children, you will have to decide what is to be gained by insisting on homeschooling, even over their objections. It may not be worth it. One idea is to agree to do it only on a trial basis and just see how it goes. Often this is all it takes to make converts out of them. If they are about to fail or be expelled, then their objections are moot.

Roadblock 7: My family (or doctor, or school) is discouraging me

Are you sure? Sometimes we mistake the silence of reserved judgment as criticism, or questions as skepticism. If you truly are getting negative comments, consider that family objections usually stem from fear or concern of facing something new. Most family members soon come around once they see homeschooling in action, and especially when they see the positive changes in your child. Ruth writes: "My extended family was extremely skeptical... However, recently they have seen such positive growth that they are more accepting." And Sharon writes that "skeptical relatives now admit we made the best decision for Sam."

If things don't go that well, consider shrugging it off. One Californian mom declares: "My family are not particularly supportive, nor are they particularly unsupportive – and they live far enough away that it really doesn't matter."

The doctor who scowls at the idea of homeschooling can also be taken with a grain of salt. He's likely been caught off guard. He's used to telling families of newly diagnosed children "Get your child into special education and we'll re-evaluate next year." It's his safety blanket answer, and you have taken it away. Also, if a doctor is familiar with AS but not homeschooling, he may think of the social deficits of AS and feel that keeping such a child home all the time doesn't sound right (as if homeschoolers do that). He rubs his chin and says, "Oh, I don't think so. He should go to school." Next, please.

A similar thing might easily occur when speaking with school officials, only then you also have to deal with professionals who may feel challenged by you. Now, for the good news. Of families I surveyed, at least 20 percent of the homeschooling moms of AS kids were professionally trained in children's development issues. This included several certified teachers, a mom with a degree in special education, an occupational therapist, pediatric therapies, and a PhD psychologist. Obviously, these people know the professional ropes and they have chosen homeschooling. Further, several families reported increasingly encouraging reviews from their doctors, therapists, or school staff. Here are a few comments:

- "The psychologist working with our son has homeschooled her own children and is extremely supportive! ... It means so much as a new homeschooler to have some professional who is in our corner! All of our 'team' is now very impressed with the improvements we have *all* seen in Neal's behavior, anxiety, stress level, etc., not to mention his academic progress since starting homeschooling eight months ago."

- "I informed the IEP team that I had decided to homeschool so I would be declining placement for Jr. High. After the IEP, Sam's wonderful 5th grade teacher asked to speak to me in private. He informed me that he thought I was doing the *best* thing for Sam to homeschool him."

- "Our developmental pediatrician...felt that a place where he could have a consistent schedule year round was better for him. Of course that can only truly be done in homeschool, and she agreed that it was a good placement for him."

- "When I took my son out of school, the principal told me that her sister homeschools and she's seen firsthand how great it can be. She told me she understood why I thought it was the right environment for my son."

- "Even a University of Chicago psychiatrist who saw him commented that Eric really is happy being homeschooled and it really seems to have helped him."

Finally, Dr Tony Attwood, clinical psychologist and author of *Asperger's Syndrome: A Guide for Parents and Professionals* (1998), is on record as being an advocate of homeschooling. He recently encouraged the mother of an AS-affected child with the following comments (reprinted with permission): "I have always found home schooling to be a positive option that has literally saved the lives of many children... I have always been an advocate of homeschooling and have supported a number of families who have considered this option."

Dr Attwood has also worked to educate Australian teachers on the value of distance education programs with regard to Asperger Syndrome. Since he is one of the world's top experts on AS, I believe parents have all the reinforcement they should ever need.

Roadblock 8: We would lose special therapies that we currently get

Some families do lose access to therapy (physical, language, etc.) when they leave a public school. Others do not. It depends on local law and, frankly, often the whim or budget of the school. Several parents have felt that benefits gained from therapy did not outweigh the major traumas going on in other parts of the schooling day, so homeschooling even without therapies was the best solution. They simply made extra efforts to work issues on their own, or sought out therapy through other means. One mom of a young (four-and-a-half-year-old) daughter writes:

> In working with the school district in the last six months for special education preschool, our decision to homeschool has been reinforced time and again. They don't know our child, they will never completely know our child, and they have an agenda that does not always keep our child's best interests in mind. The fight we've already had just for preschool services has been insane and I am not going to work with them any further. Why waste my time fighting for mediocre (at best) services when we can provide quality education at home in the community? We're capable of providing a quality home education and we're willing, so why not do it?

Roadblock 9: Homeschooling might be illegal where I live

As of this writing, homeschooling is legal in all 50 US states, as well as Australia, England, New Zealand, Ireland, Canada, and many other countries. Laws differ dramatically however and knowing law locally is critical.

Within the USA, some states have few requirements; other states expect more. You may need to cover certain subjects and/or submit a plan. There may be actions required at year's end too – possibly submitting a portfolio or having your child take a standardized test.

Some states may have extra requirements specifically for special needs children, although this is less common. In Pennsylvania, for example, any child previously identified by the school district as special needs must have special approval. That doesn't prohibit homeschooling, but it erects an extra hurdle. Some Pennsylvanian families have their child tested privately to avoid opening up a relationship with the school that might turn heavy handed.

Homeschoolers outside the USA often have more bureaucracy, but may also have other interesting options. Sandy in South Australia uses a government-sponsored, long-distance education program. She has to file paperwork every year, but has not had trouble renewing.

Vicki, an American residing in the UK, reports: "I've had no problems. Here in England, I meet with the local education authority (LEA) once a year to review what we have done. He makes notes, sends me a copy and the other copy goes in a filing cabinet where no one sees it." In Canada, too, there is more oversight from the government, but this varies from province to province.

It is impossible to cover homeschooling law for all areas, especially for this author who has no legal expertise, but do consider the following:

1. There is a saying that "all politics are local." The same is true for homeschooling laws. It doesn't matter what the law is elsewhere. Know *your* local law.

2. Be aware of actual law, not its interpretation by your local school body.

3. Contact a local homeschooling group to learn what the climate is for homeschoolers in your area. An excellent website for finding such groups is the following: www.homeschool.com/groups/

4. Contact your national and especially local organizations for autism or Asperger Syndrome. This will keep you informed of rights and resources.

5. Keep homeschooling to a high standard and above the law. Keep all necessary records and file required paperwork *before* the deadline.

6. To help you research your individual circumstances, a list of helpful resources is provided in Appendix 1. A state-by-state overview of US homeschool law is available at this website: www.hslda.org/laws/default.asp

As a final note, when I asked families in the USA to assess their state's homeschooling laws, a couple of moms complained about paperwork or ambiguity in the law, but no one reported any actual problems. Responses came from Alabama, California, Colorado, Connecticut, Florida, Indiana, Illinois, Kansas, Louisiana, Michigan, Nevada, New York, Texas, Oregon, Pennsylvania, and Washington.

Questions on Asperger Syndrome and homeschoolers

How many people are homeschooling Asperger children?

No one knows, but perhaps we can estimate how many homeschooled children there are on the entire autism spectrum at least. According to a US Department of Education report, 850,000 American students were homeschooled in 1999 and, of those, an estimated 8.2 percent of the families reported that their reason for homeschooling was due to special needs or disability, for a total of 69,000 students (Basham 2001, p.8). However, the number of homeschoolers in the USA is estimated at being as high as 2,000,000 by now. If true, the number of special needs kids who have opted out of the classroom might approach 165,000.

What percentage of special needs children has Asperger Syndrome? Within the US public schools, autism spectrum kids represent about 1 percent of the special needs population (National Center for Education Statistics 2000), so one could deduce that the ratio of spectrum children in the homeschooled population might also be hovering at 1 percent.

I suspect the number of spectrum kids being homeschooled might be much higher than that, however, for two reasons. First, I contend that other (non-spectrum) disabilities are better served within a school setting. Hence, those on the autism spectrum might be more inclined to leave the system and not be counted. Second, it's my belief that the percentage of autism spectrum students being counted within the school system is artificially low to begin with. Many Asperger-affected children go for years without being properly diagnosed, so early grades may be especially prone to undercounting. Also, many parents report bringing their spectrum kids into the school with medical diagnosis in hand, only to be stonewalled by school officials who reject the label, insist on their own testing, and/or refuse to count AS into one of their predesignated special education categories (i.e. autism). Whether it is their intent to delay or avoid putting Asperger Syndrome children into special education or not, I cannot say, but the result is clear. Many families are not able to satisfy the requirements of the school to be counted among the special education ranks at all, even when everyone agrees that's where the child fits. Even if parents eventually do jump all the hurdles for proper classification, much time is wasted in the process.

In the end, if we boldly assert that the aforementioned 1 percent is too low and a better guess is 2 or 3 percent, this means that there could be an estimated 3300 to 5000 homeschooled children today who are somewhere on the autism spectrum. That is only for the USA, and does not reflect "kids that don't fit in" but who do not meet enough criteria for diagnosis. Add in the rest of the world, the rest of the "AS-affected but undiagnosed" kids, and the number increases. Next year it will grow again, since these conditions seem to be ever on the rise.

Is Asperger Syndrome under the autism spectrum disorder umbrella or not?

Experts debate this. Is AS the highest functioning end of autism or is it something else? Is it the same as high functioning autism (HFA) or are there differences? The nuances of this debate are beyond the scope of this book (or this author's expertise), but for the purposes of this book and in concert with most current literature, I do count Asperger Syndrome (AS) as being on the autism spectrum. In the above section, I alluded to some school jurisdictions that don't count AS to be part of the autism spectrum and the same can be said for some insurance companies. To my layperson's mind, it looks as though the medical community is largely satisfied that Asperger Syndrome is on the spectrum, but it saves money for the schools and insurance companies to cling to the technical definitions of outdated tomes that still count Asperger Syndrome as a separate pervasive developmental disorder.

The whole situation is maddeningly inconsistent and remains in a state of flux. As for how things are handled in this book, a parent of a child with either HFA or a pervasive developmental disorder that meets part but not all of a spectrum diagnosis (PDD-NOS) will probably find this book useful, but those whose children meet the criteria for more classic autism will not find it a good match.

What types of Asperger-affected families homeschool?

Of the 40 or so such families that I surveyed, most had a traditional make-up with a mom that homeschooled and a dad that went to work. But I also heard from families with less traditional setups – a single mom, a gay couple, a couple living on disability. In some families the mom worked part time, and in one case the dad did the homeschooling. With respect to education levels, parents ranged from barely graduating high school to doctoral degrees. There were other interesting scenarios, such as a family with twins (one with AS, one without), a mom homeschooling all five of her kids, and a situation where a grandmother did a lot of the teaching. I heard mostly from families in the USA, but also from Australia, UK, and Canada. I have to admit an almost total bias toward computer-savvy families, because I conducted my research almost exclusively through the internet. The bottom line is that families of all types, sizes, incomes, education levels, and from various places in the world find homeschooling to be a viable alternative for their children with Asperger Syndrome.

This chapter has been an overview. We've talked about why Asperger-affected children can benefit from homeschooling and common situations that lead families to choose this alternative. We've also talked about what sometimes stops people from doing it, and how many and what kind of families are benefiting from home education today. You may be feeling a bit more encouraged about the idea. You may be thinking that, yes, lots of people do it, and you too might be able to homeschool your Asperger-affected child. But just how does one do it? In the next chapter we'll look more closely at that question.

Notes

1. Those parents who are trying to work issues within the school system may benefit from my first book, *Hitchhiking through Asperger Syndrome*, which contains several chapters on working with teachers and school to provide the best possible environment for their child.

2. I use "he" at times for designating a child with Asperger Syndrome and "she" when talking about the homeschooling parent. This does reflect the most common scenario, and is used for ease in differentiating student from teacher, but is not meant to ignore the many girls out there with Asperger Syndrome, nor the number of dads who take on homeschooling duties.

3. "Stim" refers to self-stimulation or self-calming behaviors that are common among children with Asperger Syndrome. Some examples might be rocking, flapping, or wagging a stick or finger.

Chapter 2

Developing Your Plan

In this chapter, we will be concerned with developing a plan for your homeschooling journey. This is the gestation period, a place to think about the big picture. You're going to consider goals, learning styles, what homeschooling style suits your child, all in the context of all the specialized issues that come along with AS.

Goals – education, not school

Lydia, a mom just beginning her homeschooling journey, wants to know "how to teach these kids, and live with them, help them to cope." It's a tall order, but keep in mind that we do not have to do everything at once. The journey can be, and will be, taken in small steps. For now, we need only think about direction.

When I brought my son (who was attending school at the time) to visit psychologist Tony Attwood, he told us that my son was a hero, because the child with Asperger Syndrome does double duty when he goes to school. One job is academics, and the other job is to cope, to process intellectually all the social things that most children pick up naturally and do not have to think about.

A similar double-duty analogy can be made for our home education plan. One job as teacher is to teach academic subjects. The other job, as parent, is to help our children cope in the world. This is a *key concept*. We do not want to focus on something like teaching multiplication tables at the expense of forgetting the larger aspirations.

How does that fit into day-to-day homeschooling? Suppose you take your child to a science museum and he not only doesn't learn anything, but he has a tantrum and you have to bring him home early. What a disaster, you might think. This homeschool stuff isn't working at all. But please reflect. Think of what else goes on at a museum: noises, smells, waits in line, wearing coats through a hot building, escalators, public bathrooms, velvet ropes, "Do Not Touch" signs, people jostling, and more. If an Asperger youngster lasts an hour or two before becoming unraveled, perhaps it's not a failure but a success. Your child may not learn about the steam engine on display, but if he copes under what are for him difficult conditions, that too is learning. Mark it off as a successful day, and use it as a barometer for what level of sensory stimulation he can handle and what social or sensory issues need more work. Then move on. That is what I mean about keeping in mind the big picture. Progress can be measured several ways, because we are working on several levels. Only one facet is academic progress.

Foundations for learning – a pyramid approach

How do you set up the environment for learning? In my previous book, *Hitchhiking through Asperger Syndrome*, I discussed the works of two men, both of whose work predated knowledge of Asperger Syndrome, but who both reached conclusions important to the discussion of how kids with AS learn.

John Holt (1982) was a primary school teacher who anguished over why his students often didn't learn what he tried to teach them. After years of study, his conclusion was that school presented many hurdles, but among the greatest of these was fear.

Fear is rampant in the schoolroom. Teachers use it to maintain control, the bullying and competitiveness of other children adds to it, and even the learning of new concepts can be unsettling. Fear also feeds on itself. The more distressed we become, the harder it is to learn, and the cycle intensifies. And that is what goes on for normal kids. For children who are wired for AS, sensory, social, communication, attentional, and physical issues only add to the anxiety.

The writings of Abraham Maslow dovetail with this concept. Maslow, a psychologist, is perhaps best remembered for his theory called Hierarchy of Needs (1987). This theory contends that people are driven to satisfy various needs in stages, and one stage needs to be largely satisfied before a new stage can be seriously strived for. The need to learn and perform (e.g. school) must follow the satisfaction of more basic needs. The order of these needs is as follows:

1. *Physiological*: food, water, and air.

2. *Safety*: security, stability, protection, need for structure, and freedom from fear, anxiety, and chaos.

3. *Belongingness and love*: giving/receiving love, friendship, finding a place in a group or family.

4. *Esteem*: competency, achievement, adequacy, self-esteem, and recognition.

5. *Self-actualization*: having the "peak" experience of doing what one is meant to do, reaching one's individual potential.

If the above hierarchy is true, learning doesn't occur until level four, but our children with Asperger Syndrome (and many average kids) who are currently struggling with fear and anxiety in classrooms are stuck at level two. That is, although we assume they've had their most basic food, water, and air needs met (level one), they do not feel safe or secure (level two).

Additionally, our AS kids are rarely made a part of the group. They often set themselves apart, and behave in eccentric enough ways that the rest of the class also sees them as not fitting in. In many ways, the very definition of Asperger Syndrome is not fitting in. Level three of Maslow's hierarchy – to feel acceptance and belonging – is not going to happen either.

Contrast that with homeschooling, where our kids automatically feel safe and they know they belong. Voilà! Levels two and three are taken care of, and on to level four our kiddos go, now at a stage where they are primed to achieve and learn. Homeschooling doesn't "solve" Asperger Syndrome. However, nearly every parent I talk to has commented on the startling amount of learning that goes on when school comes home. It is my personal belief that this is a large reason why.

On days that do not go well, such as the science museum example I gave earlier, it's a good idea to look at it in terms of Maslow's hierarchy. A trip to a busy place may well drop a child with Asperger Syndrome back to earlier levels. It's still a valid experience to expose him to new places, so that eventually he will feel safer and more comfortable in that environment, but in the interim we should not be surprised if not much academic learning happens. To recap then, there are two keys for your homeschooling plan:

1. Think about the whole child, not merely academics.

2. A child must feel safe and accepted before much learning goes on.

Learning styles

Learning style refers to how a child best receives and absorbs information. Educators love to talk about learning styles. My research shows that this topic can be carved up several ways, depending on whose theory you favor. I am no expert in this but the four learning styles that are most commonly proffered are:

- *auditory* (listening)

- *visual* (seeing, reading)

- *kinesthetic* (hands-on)

- *social* (learning by interaction with other people).

Howard Gardner's (1993) model uses visual, linguistic, physical, mathematical, interpersonal, intrapersonal, and musical. Some other folks differentiate between an analytical learner and a global learner, or whether a learner prefers the concrete or abstract, spatial or linear, and probably a lot of other things. Don't worry, you will only get a few basic ideas here, and pointers for you to do further research if you would like.

Educators aspire to change teaching style to match each child's learning style, but with 30 kids in class this is unattainable. Still, the best teachers attempt to teach material in multiple modes, hoping to reach as many children as possible. Teaching techniques might include text, pictures, or videotapes (visual); resources lectures or audiotapes (auditory); lab experiments or crafts (hands-on involvement); and group discussion or small group work (social interaction).

For the parent teaching at home, think about when your child seems most turned on to learning and what he is most likely to retain. Here are the four principal styles, up close.

Auditory learning style

Does your child learn best from listening? A few parents surveyed reported this, or noted that their children have a keen interest in music, concluding that auditory learning is a good gateway for these kids. Well, maybe. Some individuals with Asperger Syndrome may be auditory learners, but my research shows this isn't typical. A recent study in Finland looked at auditory processing in children with Asperger Syndrome and concluded in their study abstract that "auditory sensory processing is deficient in children with AS, and that these deficits might be implicated in the perceptual problems encountered by children with AS" (Jansson-Verkassalo *et al.* 2003, p.197). Testers also discovered that the deficits were more severe for tones than for syllables.

So are parents incorrect? Maybe it's a case of mistaken labels. Some parents may attribute a child's saying everything out loud to himself as auditory learning, but is that the same thing as being able to listen to others? Similarly, learning may accelerate during discussion between parent and child, but learning in this manner is really social learning, and not purely auditory.

Also, a child may do well with an audiotaped book. This is auditory learning, yet not the same as listening to a live person lecturing. The audio book, even though read aloud, has its basis in written word, and as such is much more precise in word usage and literalness than spoken conversation. Also, the tape sounds the same each time one listens to it and can be replayed for clarity. There is absolutely nothing wrong with using audio books if they work for your child, or in listening to information on a computer program, CD, or other resources. My point is only that success with "canned" materials may be a particular brand of auditory learning that may not spell success in other auditory settings.

At any rate, auditory learning is probably not the most successful style for our kids. Interestingly, it is often the teaching method most used in a regular classroom.

Visual learning style

Many parents reported that they felt their child was a visual learner. Sharon H reports that "Sam (15) is very visual and learns the best from reading the material." Susan S in Washington explains that her homeschooling lesson was made immediately more accessible for her daughter (then 9) on the day she introduced pictures to her lessons. That is, Sue drew everything as they talked and the response from her daughter was remarkable.

In addition, a good portion of our kids are of the early reader and/or excellent reader variety, and are naturally drawn to books and text.

Parents of avid readers probably have it a bit easier than the rest of us, since so many education materials are in the form of books. I don't think we have to spend much time on this aspect, since it's pretty self-explanatory. Do look at the section on reading (in Chapter 5) for suggestions on where to find appropriate materials for various reading levels. It should be noted that some children with AS do have difficulties in visual processing. My son, for example, notices the tiniest detail but sometimes misses the larger picture or point. Also, being able to read the words does not mean the underlying concept has been understood.

Kinesthetic (hands-on) learning style

A great number of parents reported "hands-on!" as the way to get and keep their child tuned in. Science experiments are an obvious example of this, and so are things like using manipulatives in math; absorbing a language arts topic by acting it out; or appreciating history by handling an artifact, building a model, or using puppets to act out the historical event.

It is ironic that so many of our kids spark to a hands-on task, yet their hands often let them down due to poor motor skills. It may be more difficult for them to do the very actions that help them learn, but I doubt proficiency has much to do with it. Whether our kids pour a chemical into a test tube neatly or with some dribbles down the side, the action of doing it at all is what is helping them to learn. Our job, then, is to facilitate proceedings so that things are done safely and with minimal frustration. Don't take over the pouring into the test tube for your child, but show him how handy a funnel is, and how to do it over the sink. Don't fuss at him for clumsiness, just hand him a paper towel.

Kinesthetic also refers to movement in general. Jordan, 12, does his best learning as he hikes. He spends time on nature trails, discussing things with his father and learning as he goes.

Speaking of movement, bouncing seems to be a time-honored method with our kids, as well as rocking, flapping, or other stims. It is not always clear what the purpose or need is that is being addressed when these movements occur – that is, whether it is a stress release, a comfortable repetition, a response to excitement, a means of communication, or just what – but regardless of the underlying reason, these movements often help our kids process and cope during a lesson.

Social learning style

Our kids' social awkwardness makes learning through social interaction pretty difficult. Being part of a group project can be a valuable lesson all by itself, but may not be the most efficient means of learning the topic that brought the group together. Some homeschoolers, particularly in the USA, have access to community classes through charter schools, co-ops, or community agencies. The classes are usually smaller and calmer than a typical public school classroom, but they may still be "too much" for younger Asperger-affected children. These can be wonderful options for older kids, especially if you aspire to eventually transition back into traditional school.

Learning through social interaction does work well for our kids in a one-to-one discussion, especially with a parent or other trusted adult. Particularly when the other person is familiar with the communication issues of Asperger Syndrome, it seems to work exceedingly well. Homeschooling parents report spending heaps of time in discussion with their kids – discussing social situations, news of the day, TV plots, jokes, academic subjects, and of course the Asperger child's favorite pet subjects too. (It should also be noted that this same ability to talk seriously to an adult has frequently caused our kids to miss being diagnosed at first. Many doctors who are not truly savvy about Asperger Syndrome may have a focused conversation with the child in question and wrongly conclude that the child must not have Asperger Syndrome at all.)

Learning styles are useful tools, but we don't need to be slavish to them:

1.   No child absorbs by only one method. None of this is all or nothing.

2.   It would be difficult to present material via only one method.

3.   Most teaching naturally touches on a couple of different learning styles.

4.   It's good for our children to be challenged to learn by various methods, although it should be done with recognition that some styles are more difficult than others

for our children. Try not to mix hardest school subject with most challenging learning style.

5. Besides the four styles outlined, some educators talk about *analytical learners* versus *global learners*. Analytical learners like things to be presented in an orderly fashion and tend to see details before the big picture. Facts are of more concern than feelings, and this type of person needs to know what to expect and for things to be logical. I believe that nearly all of our kids might qualify as analytical learners.

6. For more information on learning styles, and how they mesh or challenge the above descriptions, see the following:

    ○ www.geocities.com/Athens/Styx/7315/subjects/learning. html

    ○ www.casacanada.com/whatare.html

    ○ www.learnativity.com/learningstyles.html

    ○ www.challengenet.com/~onemom/page16.html

    ○ www.homeschoolzone.com/add/autism.html

Also see books on this subject. Authors include: Thomas Armstrong (*In Their Own Way*), Howard Gardner *(Multiple Intelligences: The Theory in Practice)*, and Cynthia Tobias *(The Way They Learn)*. A short online test that rates your child according to Howard Gardner's learning styles is available at www.smarterkids.com.

The computer – what style is that?

Most of the parents surveyed emphasized the huge importance of the computer to their child's homeschooling, no matter which learning style the parent claimed their child had. In fact, the success of computer use was often offered as proof of the child's learning style, even though the learning styles differed! Here are some comments from parents of visual learners:

• "Definitely, both my sons (16 and 13) learn better through computer and visually."

- "Peter (11) is a very visual learner… His special interest is computers."

From parents of a hands-on learner:

- "Most books and guides seem to think that these kids are visual, however I tend to think that Scott (10) is more kinesthetic, or hands-on. He definitely prefers the computer over any other medium."

From parents of those with a mix of traditional learning styles:

- "Eric (11) learns best when he is physically active, when music is involved, on the computer (his special interest), and/or when I make a game of it (e.g. 'let's race to see who can finish the math problems first')."

- "Although I have never formally analyzed Allan's (11) learning style, I would say that his mode of learning is primarily visual and hands-on. He is able to learn through auditory means as well, as long as he is allowed to listen *and* do something, i.e. draw while listening to me read, or play games on the computer which have both auditory and visual components."

- "He loves videos, working with science experiments, working on the computer and with his special interests. He has *great* difficulty working with someone who is a 'control freak' and wants to impose 'their' way on him. He can't be forced to do anything!! He loves working with computer-based subjects because he says, 'the computer doesn't argue with me.'"

Finally, and perhaps most importantly, the computer seems to work for those with exceedingly difficult learning styles:

- "Indigo (10) has visual and audio dysfunctions and seems to learn best autodidactically [self-taught] and through osmosis. She can't watch and learn; she doesn't process language correctly so she doesn't get the messages in their entirety; she is overly sensitive to touch so that is not her learning style. The most helpful method is computer interface."

- "Jared (10) loves the computer. That's one of the big reasons we chose a computer curriculum. We talk about things, and I let him process them out loud, and bounce all he needs to, whatever is working for him. He usually chooses how/where/whether to sit/stand/bounce, and I let him read out loud or use a text-to-speech program when he wants to. He processes by talking about everything as he does it. It drives the rest of the family crazy, but I zealously protect his need to do it. I think a regular school would kill the uniqueness that makes him who he is and helps him learn and do things so well."

From these sorts of comments, we see that the computer can appeal visually, aurally, kinesthetically, and also appeals to those who respond to games. The computer allows itself to be controlled rather than control, and doesn't mind if you chatter or bounce constantly in its presence. Because the computer plays such a prominent role in the homeschooling of kids with Asperger Syndrome, an entire chapter is devoted to it (see Chapter 7).

One more style – talking out loud

Many kids were reported to need to read out loud, talk a concept out in order to understand it, say things aloud to memorize them, repeat directions aloud, and so forth. For example:

- "If he reads aloud with me, he does much better."

- "She has to talk herself through the assignments."

- "He would often read aloud."

- "He talks about everything he learns."

- "If she is not very interested in the subject, I've found that I need to have her read it aloud to me and discuss it."

One expert called this need part of a verbal/linguistic style, and another called it auditory. It may have a kinesthetic element to it too (turning something heard or seen into something that the learner does), and for that matter it may have a social element in that something said aloud tends to prompt discussion, whether or not that was the original intent. The label is unimportant. What is important is simply to realize that this "talking out" is beneficial for a lot of our special kids and it usually works much better in a homeschool setting than in a classroom. This is well illustrated by Jared's unique style that was mentioned earlier. His mom explains further:

> He had a very understanding teacher in first grade, and she lost her job, due in part, I'm convinced, to her willingness to allow him to move around when he's learning. Oh, did I tell you how he works on the computer? He talks about everything he learns, and he bounces. I've seen him standing on the computer chair, bent over horizontal at the waist, with his hands on the keyboard typing, as he jumped on the chair. When he's not reading out loud or commenting on what he's doing (right now, he's saying, "Sometimes the best answer is 'All of the above' or 'None of the above'"), he squeals. I guess he'd probably run into some resistance to his current learning style in a traditional school.

Homeschooling styles

Now that we've talked about learning styles, let's talk about various homeschooling styles. How do you want your homeschooling day to feel? Structured? Relaxed? Can it be both? If you've read up on homeschooling at all, you've no doubt run across these terms:

- traditional or school-at-home approach
- unit studies
- unschooling
- eclectic approach.

Let's look at how these work for Asperger families.

Traditional or school-at-home approach

This is the school method that you grew up with, exported into the family setting. Some families like to emulate the school experience and have made over a part of their house into the classroom. School progresses from subject to subject at regular intervals and there is an emphasis on workbooks, tests, and other "schooly" things.

From an Asperger standpoint, the style has good and bad points. On the plus side, it has a structure to it that some kids absolutely crave. The predictability and sameness is comforting, as long as the work isn't too demanding. Often you can buy an entire year's curriculum in one fell swoop, and the planning is done for you.

On the bad side, ordering "fifth grade in a box" from a curriculum publisher offers few accommodations for special learners and there may be no leeway for a child with splinter skills and deficits, who is operating across different grade levels. It may be heavy on textbooks and workbooks, a real strain on kids with reading or handwriting issues. There may be a set schedule to follow, and no way to readily adapt it, especially if you rely on the curriculum provider to do the testing and grading. In other words, some of the hurdles your child had at regular school with style or pace may be transported into your dining room.

If you do desire this approach, do examine materials closely. Is it reading intensive, or will you also receive some lessons-on-tape, manipulatives, hands-on science kits, or computer work? (Curriculum publishers have gotten much better about this in recent years, by the way.) Can you accommodate deficits and splinter skills by swapping out different grade levels where appropriate or supplementing in some other way? This approach can work, but you may need to modify certain materials.

Unit studies

Doing a unit study means studying a topic in depth. You might study trees, for example, and incorporate reading/writing, history, science, PE, math, art, and other things into the topic.

Unit studies can work very well for kids that are resistant to learning about anything but their special topic. Parents can start with the special interest, milk it for all it's worth, and gently widen a narrow topic so as to gradually encompass other topics. A narrow topic on trees might lead to soil, the earth, weather, and so on.

With the unit study, another advantage is that there need not be an abrupt transition from one school subject to the next. English and math go hand in hand under the overarching subject of "trees" and you don't have to really stop one academic subject to go to the next. Children with difficulties in transitioning may do well, and the child that panics when someone says "It's time for math now" will benefit from this less bumpy presentation. The child might happily talk about estimating the number of trees in a forest, or the diameter of a tree trunk, and not mind or even realize that he is doing the dreaded subject of math.

The downside is that it requires creative work and preparation on the part of the parent. Planning a school year (if that's what you want to do) may be tricky because it's hard to know when one is going to be done with a particular topic. You can make an artificial deadline for ending a unit study, of course, but conventional wisdom says that it ends when interest wanes or another topic is picked up.

Still, so many parents have reported good things about using their child's special interest that Chapter 4 is devoted to the unit study approach. In that chapter you will learn how to develop your own unit studies.

Unschooling

This method (championed by John Holt) resembles a relaxed cousin of the unit study, with a different attitude. Unschooler parents make a conscious effort to slide into the passenger seat of their child's education and let their child do the driving. School is not even a topic of conversation, really, nor is it consciously scheduled into the day, unless the child requests it. The world is the classroom and day-to-day life is the lesson. Unschoolers believe that true learning goes on as a natural part of living. A child's best learning happens then, in a way that only the child can determine.

The upside to this method is that it theoretically requires no planning on the part of the parent, although I've yet to meet a parent that didn't still steer their child into the path of learning experiences. Still, ideally it is a joyous adventure of following a child's choosing. It can be a heady experience to see what a child takes upon himself to learn by virtue of his own curiosity, and it's gratifying to see how much learning does go on without anybody really trying. It is a particularly good method for the younger learner (the early years of any child's life are pretty much unschooled). It's also ideal for the school-phobic student, or the strong-headed student who resists lessons imposed by an adult (whether teacher or parent). In later years, an intellectually curious teen can do marvelously with unschooling.

There are downsides, however. Parents concerned with record keeping may need to redefine their methods, and unschooling can be particularly troublesome in locations where authorities demand to see what work has been accomplished. Also, it takes a supreme act of faith on the part of the parent to stick to the conviction that the child will get the education he needs without being forced into it. A lot of families start out with intentions of unschooling but their convictions waver when they reach upper grades.

From an Asperger standpoint, some families who have tried a completely unschooling philosophy lament that their child is at loose ends too often and needs more of a structure. Also, in some kids this can degenerate into the child only wanting to do one thing, such as watching TV. But being unschooled does not mean being undisciplined or without responsibilities. A child can have creative freedom without being allowed to run the household. Why not keep the TV off during the day? Require an hour of outside play activity? Require an hour of reading or a nap after lunch? Have lunch at a regular time and an hour of quiet time when Mom gets a break? You can have a regular family fun night, or a scheduled appointment to go to the library. Family life can have structure without it impinging on one's unschooling philosophy. Sometimes a teeny bit of structure is just what is needed.

For more information on unschooling as a philosophy, I highly recommend any of the books by John Holt. There are also helpful websites, including Unschoolers Unlimited (www.borntoexplore. org/unschool). This website is not written with AS in mind, but it's a great place to understand the concepts behind unschooling and how it can work.

Eclectic approach

The last method is a mix-and-match of the other methods. The strength of homeschooling is in tailoring to suit the child, and taking an eclectic approach capitalizes on this. You may want a structured math program, but prefer a unit study approach to combine history, reading, writing, and perhaps science. You might choose to unschool everything else, assuming that kids will naturally explore art, music, and many other things on their own. Or unschooling might be used as a sometimes thing. Every summer might move to an unschooling philosophy, where you seize on learning opportunities and expand on children's interests, but you don't meet every morning at 9 am to open your notebooks.

When I homeschooled my son, we followed an eclectic approach. We had structure from Monday to Thursday (structure with choices), and

I gave John Fridays "off." Little did he know that "off" meant unschooling. He could do as he pleased except no TV or video games, and I quietly recorded his activities. When he counted his money and browsed a catalog, that counted as math and reading. When he hammered away at a fort in the backyard, I wrote down "gross motor skills." For awhile he got interested in the details of fingerprinting and kept index cards of each family member's fingerprints and practiced lifting them from surfaces – this was science, of course! Once he made a karate video, complete with title cards, background music, written dialogue, and choreographed moves. I filmed while he and his brother performed. Should it count as drama? Music? Writing? PE? Social skills? It was all of that to me, but fun to him.

Putting it together

You have been presented with lots of choices but try not to overthink this. It is mostly a matter of tuning in to your instincts of what you think will work best, and it will evolve over time. The end of your school year will probably not resemble the beginning.

Examples from other families are provided in Chapter 3, but here's how we put together our eclectic homeschooling week when my son was in primary years:

Monday through Thursday

1.   Warm-up (around 9 am). We began with something hands-on to get John involved quickly. This might be a jigsaw puzzle (the USA or the world), checking on a science experiment, or observing/charting the weather. I often asked him quiz questions from a deck of "Brain Quest" questions because he responded better to this interaction than when he was asked to read or write. I could also adjust the questions I asked in order to account for days when he was "on" versus days when he was "off."

2.   After he was warmed up, we discussed what we would do during the day. In typical Asperger fashion, my son needed predictability, so this was an important step. The day also went better if he had some choices. So I let him pick the

first subject to study. He usually chose math or science. I would choose reading or writing or social studies. Then he would choose again and I would choose again. In this manner, all the "heavy" subjects would be covered each day.

3.   Subject of John's choosing (math).

4.   Subject of my choosing (English).

5.   Break.

6.   Subject of John's choosing (science).

7.   Subject of my choosing (social studies).

8.   Lunch.

9.   Afternoons – unschool. No TV or videos. Trips to library, park, errands, house chores, etc. also got done during this time.

Friday – unschool

Although the above schedule looks structured, there were choices built within it. Some days we used workbooks, other days it might be board games or educational computer games. Every day seemed flexible, yet we had a structure that helped John come to the table ready to learn. If I had a unit study lined up, everything would revolve around a particular topic of interest, and division between subjects would be more subtle. We'll talk more about unit studies in Chapter 4.

Asperger issues worked at home

So far, we've taken a look at some generic styles that fit most homeschooling families. Now it's time to put Asperger Syndrome back into the picture. You already know that you need to focus on the "whole child" and not merely academics. But what does that mean in practical terms?

In this section, we will look at some of the challenges of Asperger Syndrome and how that fits into the homeschooling picture. You will get glimpses into many families' homeschooling lives and how they cope with or work with various issues.

Social skills

> The child with Asperger Syndrome is socially awkward, has difficulty making or keeping friends, and he is generally egocentric and lacking, or seeming to lack, empathy or ability to see the other person's point of view.

Social situations are often an enigma for our kids, partly because there are so many different expectations for different social situations and also because people operate in unpredictable ways. The core problem is that our special kids are handicapped when it comes to sensing the social climate, noticing nonverbal cues, and generalizing one situation to the next.

Our job is to "teach" social events to the degree that we can. We don't know exactly how a scenario will go, of course (and sometimes that is the most important point we can impart to our sometimes rigid or rule-based children), but we can talk about certain aspects. We can describe the main parts of a birthday party even if we do not know the order of events. We can talk about what to expect and how we act. As one New York mom describes her methods of working with her seven-year-old, "We deal with social skills in little steps, as if we were teaching him math or science."

Here are some ways that surveyed families have been teaching social skills:

- real life
- group work
- books, websites.

REAL LIFE

Discussion of a social situation before, during, or after an event can be helpful.

Before the event

Vicki writes:

> First, I teach at home, on our own, what's expected in social settings, how to respond, what to say, etc… We used to play-act situations, i.e. the telephone ringing and how to answer it, what to

say. In the past, I have posted notes on the wall beside the phone that said "May I ask who's calling?" – just reminders. Also, we play-acted someone knocking at the door – different scenarios and how to respond for different people whether friend or stranger.

Ever since Stephen was little I taught him that when his sister was crying he should ask her if she's OK, or what's the matter. He still does that to this day and what used to be a rote response has now become a question of concern. He can also transfer this info to others, too.

Vicki touches on an important concept that kids can learn the motions even before they internalize the feelings that go with them, and often for our kids it works better that way.

During the event

A homeschooling parent who is close by during social gatherings can do in-the-moment coaching. A mom writes:

We help remind him when he is being socially inappropriate. We quietly ask him to look around and see what others are doing. "Is anyone else making noises? Is anyone else jumping around? What are the other children doing? What do you think you should do next?" We also allow for his need to "get out" of social situations. Sometimes they become too hard, and he just goes off by himself. We allow this, as long as it does not interfere with his reason for being somewhere.

After the event

Nedra explains that she and her three boys try to do "social autopsies" to figure out any social problems that have happened or are happening. Such discussions could include not only what may have gone wrong but, of equal importance, what went right.

GROUP WORK

Good social skills groups are invaluable for parents who have been able to access them. Elizabeth N takes her son Eric to a weekly pragmatic group. He meets with boys his age (11) that also have AS to work on social skills and pragmatic language skills. MJ, mom to Peter (11), would love to find a social skills group and says, "maybe I'll start one."

Language skills are intimately tied in with social skills, so often a therapist treats the two issues together. Marietta's five-year-old and Cathy's ten-year-old both attend sessions that handle both language and social skills. Other clubs and groups in the community can be useful too, if the environment is safe and understanding. Vicki observes that her 11-year-old son has learned a lot from being in the Cub Scouts – "not necessarily anything positive about *how* to act," she says. "It's more like learning how kids are, and the different personalities that are out there."

Sandy's son Brent attends a youth group with his best friend, who also has AS. Often kids with AS do gravitate to each other, so making that connection is useful. (See also "Working with therapists" section later in the chapter for more info on social skills groups.)

BOOKS, WORKBOOKS, WEBSITES

Homeschoolers have their favorite books for working on social skills. Sarah G uses lessons from *Social Skills Activities for Special Children* (2002a) and *Life Skills Activities for Special Children* (2002b), both by Darlene Mannix, for her 12-year-old daughter.

MJ has purchased *Navigating the Social World* (McAfee 2001) for her 11-year-old son, after it was recommended to her on an email list by another family with an AS-affected child. "I was looking for something beyond the basic 'share your toys, take turns' kind of social skills material that I had found for younger Aspies or those with more of a severe problem than Peter has."

Some parents don't have a formal workbook but simply tackle social skills one at a time, such as Nicki's decision to put special emphasis on table manners right now for her son. Others may wish to refer to Appendix 3 of this book for a list of social skills.

THE SOCIAL STORY

The social story concept was developed by Carol Gray and is a formula-based written story to work through social situations. I have not used these per se, but understand that the format includes the child in first person, along with key points about a social situation and positive statements about the child (the star of the story) doing the appropriate thing. Depending on your child's learning style, I would think you could extend this idea to drawing pictures or cartoons, an audiotape, etc. See

The New Social Story Book by Carol Gray (2000) or her website for sample stories and guidelines (www.thegraycenter.org/Social_Stories.html).

Many older students work on social skills issues on their own. Chapter 8 describes this in more detail.

FACIAL RECOGNITION AND FACIAL EXPRESSION

An offshoot of social skills is being able to recognize facial expressions. Many of our kids do not read faces the way most people do, but have to tackle it in a more intellectual way. Some autism books include a page of cartoon expressions so kids can work on identifying facial expressions. I prefer using real faces and discussing the expressions. Six photos of a face making different expressions are included as Appendix 4. There are also other ways to work this issue:

1.   Watch TV with the child and discuss how the actors look. I like this method because the faces are real, they move as in real life, and there is a social context. A sitcom is often nicely exaggerated, as are children's programs.

2.   Clip out magazine pictures. Discuss them, or make into flash cards for a game (for example, "What emotion is this?").

3.   Play charades. Write emotions down to be acted out.

4.   Cut up photos to separate eyes, nose, mouth. Can you match them up?

5.   Make a bingo game with emotion words (angry, happy, and so forth) written in squares on a bingo card. To play, draw from a stack of magazine pictures of faces displaying those emotions, or vice versa.

Facial expression websites and other resources

1.   Choose the game called "Facial Expression" or the game called "Feelings" (my favorite); the latter shows real people, and the emotions they display change every time you play it (www.do2learn.com/games/learningames.html)

2.   Match face to emotion (www.cultsock.ndirect.co.uk/MUHome/cshtml/index.html)

3.   Create expressions by clicking and dragging eyes and
      mouths onto a blank face
      (www.dushkin.com/connectext/psy/ch10/facex.mhtml)

4.   Take a test to match 17 faces to their emotions
      (www.prosopagnosia.com/interactive/facexpressions2/)

5.   Play six mini-movies of basic expressions being made
      (www.2.cs.cmu.edu/afs/cs/user/ytw/www/facial.html)

6.   Poster/stickers/bingo game – order a "feeling face" poster
      ($5), face expression stickers ($2.50 for 48), or emotion
      bingo ($20) (www.oceansofemotions.com)

Computer programs

"Mind Reading" computer program provides lessons, quizzes, and games
for autistic/Asperger users to learn to recognize human emotions. Try
the sample at www.human-emotions.com and see what you think.

Communication

Communication may be literal. Thinking may be black and white and
lack imagination (or show unusual imagination). Speech and language
skills may seem somewhat odd compared with peers. That is,
speech may seem formal or pedantic (teacher-like), or may sound
somewhat unusual. Nonverbal communication is lacking, so that the
child misses or misreads nonverbal signals (gestures, body language,
facial expression) and is ineffectual or limited in sending them.

Vicki writes:

> We take areas of language as they come. I interpret if something
> doesn't make sense to him. His *Adventures in Odyssey* story tapes
> (which are wonderful by the way) are full of idioms and
> expressions. The funny thing is that he hears them, learns them
> and uses them correctly in context. My job is teaching him what's
> appropriate and what's not, i.e. he might take what the bully says
> in the story and repeat it to his sister – not appropriate; but he also
> might repeat encouragement offered and this *is* appropriate.

Diane takes language issues as they come. She says:

Sometimes I ask "Do you know what he meant by...?" and if he doesn't, we discuss it. Sometimes he comes up with very deep insights or sarcasms, and I wonder to myself why he "got that" and not something else he might have heard. It is truly something that needs to be taught one at a time.

Humor makes these lessons go down especially well. Nicki, mom to 11-year-old Mark, says, "We read idioms and jokes to each other and guess what they mean or why they are funny." Ruth uses humor and daily life to work on language and idioms with her pre-teen. Each morning there is a time for reading the comics and political cartoons and explaining them. She says, "I try to use expressions and teach them. Sometimes we go through the list at the back of *Hitchhiking through Asperger Syndrome*." (Appendix 5 provides a similar list of expressions and idioms.)

Joanna Rae adds: "With two English teachers for parents, there are a good deal of metaphors, similes and wacky idioms flying around."

Sarah C's technique includes purposely stating an untruth in a teasing manner. If she catches herself driving too fast, she might say, "Andy, why are you going so fast?" Since her son knows that she is teasing with these challenges, this has helped Andy to later figure out when someone else is teasing or not.

One mom likes using the book *Teach Me Language* (Freeman and Dake 1997) for her daughter.

ONLINE IDIOM RESOURCES

A fun online game that tests or teaches idioms may be found at www.funbrain.com/idioms/index.html.

A huge collection of idioms (but no game) resides at http://home.t-online.de/home/toni.goeller/idiom_wm/index.html.

Special interests

Personal interests (collections, hobbies, preoccupations) may be unusual in subject and/or narrow in range and/or pursued intensely.

Special interests for our kids can be extremely focused and sometimes an interest escalates into a passion or obsession. Interests might be unusual, such as sprinkler heads or manhole covers, or quite typical kid things such as Legos. The more eccentric interests garner publicity when AS is discussed on television, but although special interests can be taken to negative extremes, they are most often pretty positive.

When special interests do get too overpowering for our kids or threaten to alienate people, we need to step in. Sarah G reports that she encourages her daughter to follow her interests but sometimes needs to "help her understand when she is overwhelming others with information." Sharon writes that for her 15-year-old, Sam, obsessions tend to come and go. Her technique is to put a time limit on how long he can "stick" on something.

Special interests can be a wonderful gateway to learning, however. Jackie's daughter's special interest makes a nice warm-up to the school day. "Nancy is allowed to tell me about her special interest for about 15 to 20 minutes. Then she begins her school lessons."

For Diane, her son Allan's special interest helped a unique learning opportunity unfold before her disbelieving eyes:

> Since Allan was small, he has been intensely drawn to insects, and particularly to bees. He watches insects every day he can, and spends hours searching for them. In the late summer of 2001 we attended our state fair. A beekeeper had a hive of bees in a screened area, and he was explaining about bee-keeping and honey extraction to the crowd.
>
> Allan stood transfixed throughout the lecture. When a volunteer was requested from the audience to help with the honey extraction, his hand shot up. You can imagine my terror when the beekeeper handed over a beekeeper's suit. Allan was ecstatic. He had never volunteered for anything before, but he wanted to be "with" those bees. He donned the suit, helmet and all, and walked calmly and bravely into the enclosure. His job was to smoke the bees. He did a wonderful job! He listened carefully to the directions, and did everything just as he was asked. I kept holding my breath the entire time, sure something would happen, but it didn't. When the lecture was over, he was beaming ear to ear. He was so proud that he had done such a thing, and that he hadn't gotten stung. He was awarded a free cup of honey ice cream, and testified that it was the best ice cream he had ever eaten. He still talks about this experience today. He learned more in that fifteen minutes in a tent full of bees and honey than he often learns in a month of reading books.

As mentioned previously, special interests are custom made for the "unit study" method of homeschooling. Please see Chapter 4 for more on how to use your child's special interests in developing a unit study.

Need for ritual

> The child with Asperger Syndrome may gravitate to or take comfort in routines, rituals, and repetition and be upset by surprises.

Several parents mentioned that things go better when there is structure in place. Even if it has wrinkles in it, having a map is a good assurance of what the day will be like. Conversely, a lack of routine can be stressful for our kids. Joanna Rae writes:

> We homeschool all year round, although when my husband is home (he is a public school teacher) we have tended to have a looser schedule. This probably needs to change. Now that my son is getting older, keeping to a routine beyond sleep and food seems to be more and more important.

Katy also recognizes predictability as important for her 15-year-old's well-being:

> I keep a family calendar... Thomas really likes to know ahead what is going to be happening. He does not like surprise. I spend a lot of time planning ahead... We live about 20 minutes from most of our outside activities, so we aim to leave 30 minutes ahead of time. This gives us a little margin, which helps Thomas stay calm. If he's going somewhere, we rehearse ahead what is going to happen. We have learned habits of putting our supplies into the van the night before and asking everyone if they have everything (in a detailed way) before leaving the garage... I also have a spreadsheet for each day of the week. Most of the school year we try to follow a schedule. My AS son really likes having a schedule, but then we really have to follow it! He does not like having a schedule printed up if it is inaccurate in any way.

On the other hand, too much sameness can sometimes foster rigidity. Margaret W is careful not to let her daughter get too comfortable with choosing the same activities all the time. "We've always tried to keep her from becoming routine-bound by insisting that she take turns with things like TV and computer time. Often other people let her have her way just to have peace. We don't do that as much."

Intelligence

Intelligence is average or better, and initial language acquisition is within norms.

Average or better intelligence is part of the diagnosis definition for Asperger Syndrome and even this can present a challenge, especially when dealing with outsiders such as coaches, group leaders, etc. That is, intelligence tends to raise expectations for other areas such as behavior or social dynamics. ("He's smart. He should know better than to behave like that!")

In the home we're less likely to fall into that trap, but we're not immune to it. As smart as our kids tend to be in academic areas, they still have some profound areas of deficit and even we parents need occasional reminders of this.

Because of behavioral or sensory issues, any IQ or assessment test we give our kids is also suspect. My son's IQ magically gained 40 points over a few years' time. However, it wasn't due to a sudden burst of intelligence as much as maturity in being able to sit through the test at all. The lesson in this is to accept a test score as a minimum score only.

If you wish to administer assessment tests, also consider the test format. When given an oral, untimed test by a kind teacher in the quiet of our home, my son tested at three years above grade level in math. Three months later, when he was given a written test, administered in a cold lunchroom amid a hundred other kids, he tested at the twenty-eighth percentile for his own grade. That speaks volumes about the test and relatively little about his knowledge of math. If you formally test your child during your homeschool adventure, you might ask yourself if the conditions of the test are right for truly getting a picture of what has been learned.

For reasons stated above, assessments may be of dubious validity. Many folks still want or need them though, either to help decide what grade their child is working at or to comply with homeschool law. Approximately half the US states require assessments at regular intervals (typically every two years). See Appendix 7 for how to order the most common assessment tests.

When you receive an assessment or otherwise evaluate your child, it still may not answer your questions though, and you may be amazed and alarmed to see the diversity in scores across a few grades. So what grade is your child really in? Karen Z writes:

> We have considered grade to be just a designation of age. My son is in fifth grade because he turns 11 before September 7. He then proceeds through material in different subject areas at whatever pace makes sense for that subject. So, this year he "completed" 12th grade spelling, 8th grade math, 3rd grade handwriting, and a lot of things that can't be assigned to a specific grade level.

Sensory stimuli

There may be abnormal reactions to sensory stimuli (i.e. have acute sensitivity to light, smells, tastes, tactile sensation, or sounds).

Homeschooling is a haven for kids who find public school to be too noisy, too chaotic, and just too much. Parents can do what it takes to remove sensory input or, conversely, to carefully work sensory input back in. What follows are some examples of sensory problems in a few different areas.

NOISE

Margaret W from Alabama writes:

> We have less distraction at home. Michaela has told me she couldn't concentrate at public school because those other students made too much noise (moving in desks, writing, getting up to walk around the room, not loud talking, just normal room noises). Her sensory problems are in the area of hearing over-sensitivity. The bells at school were torture.

BODY TEMPERATURE

Vicki's son Stephen loves being warm. She writes:

> Many activities are done before our open fire or near the heater or under the duvet. I'm not sure if meeting these sensory needs improves them, but I do know that if they are met, he certainly copes better, listens better and learns more.

BODY AWARENESS

Sarah C writes: "My child benefits from deep pressure, and calming techniques to 'slow his engine down,' refocus and try, try again."

VISUAL PLUS NOISE

Diane writes: "We avoid situations that we know will cause problems. Lots of noise, lots of color, too many instructions given too fast; these might all cause a meltdown."

When it comes to working sensory issues, it's a push-me-pull-me affair. The very sensory input our kids avoid is where they need the work. The trick is to introduce sensory material slowly, give the child control if possible, and find a way to motivate. My own son resisted lotions and also short-sleeved shirts (and short-sleeved pants, as he used to call them). When we filled a backyard swimming pool, my son wanted to swim very much, but this required getting out of heavy sweats and putting on a swimming suit and sun lotion. Since he jerked away when I would try to put the lotion on, I let him put the lotion on himself while I supervised where it needed to go. He still didn't like it, but he did it. Now, he isn't bothered by it at all.

Sandy says: "We really just exposed our son to sounds that used to really bother him, and he has become more tolerant as he gets older."

Wendy finds that she must work on her young son's oral defensiveness:

> Tony has a huge problem with me brushing his teeth. I make the toothbrush talk to his teeth (and they talk back) like puppets. If that doesn't work, I tell him "don't laugh, don't you *dare* laugh!" Of course he can't help but laugh and then I get the teeth.
>
> He also chews on his shirts. I have used plastic craft string and I cut about three inches of aquarium tubing and put the string through to make a chewy necklace.

SENSORY DIET

Nedra keeps sensory things around the house for her three Asperger-affected children, and many other homeschooling parents do as well. A "sensory diet" refers to a conscious use of many things and activities that will challenge our kids' sensory systems. Can you put any of the following into your homeschool day?

Smell sensitivity

Flowers, scented craft dough, potpourri, scented candles, cologne, various extracts, scented pens, and scratch and sniff books can all be used. Make a scent guessing game using little bottles or film canisters, and into them insert cotton balls scented with various extracts or essential oils. Your child can guess the scent, or find matching scents.

Oral sensitivity and oral motor

There are many things that can be used: battery-operated toothbrushes, baby chew toys, lollipops with battery-operated holders to spin them, child's whistles, noise makers, duck calls, bird calls, pitch pipes, harmonicas, kazoos, paper party favors that roll out, blowing bubbles, penny whistles, recorders, drinking straws, pin wheels, any blow-action toy.

Tactile sensitivity

For *hands*, try collages, finger painting, sponge painting, glue work, papier mâché, clay or craft dough, working with cookie dough, mixing meat loaf, doing crayon rubbings using large paper on various rough surfaces. Make a grab bag and sensory book using materials such as burlap (hessian), plastic, wood, feathers, fur, sandpaper, carpet, satin, velvet, corduroy, wool, felt, rope, leather or fake leather, or metal. Play in ball pits, a sand or water table, dig for "fossils" in a box of rice or dried beans.

For *feet*, encourage going barefoot, walking in sand or soft dirt, walking on the grass, or on smooth concrete. Try finger painting but with feet dipped in paint. Make footprints in mud, plaster casts, stomp on bubble wrap, put plastic bags on the feet and slide on carpet. Try foot massages and footbaths.

For *face*, apply "war paint" or make-up, do face painting, soapsuds beards, whipped cream beards.

For *all-over sensitivity*, play dress up or roll your child up in various types of fabric, mats, sheets, bubble wrap, cardboard, etc. Enjoy dramatic scarves and boas, roll in the grass or sand, apply body lotion or sun lotion. Play with Silly String or Fun Foam. Enjoy massage, tickling, and vigorous rubdowns with towels.

Auditory issues

Try using books with sound effects, taped stories, rattles, jingle bells, rhythm instruments, musical instruments, wind chimes, rain sticks, a CD or tape or computer download with various sound effects, music records of all types, making tunes out of glasses filled to various heights with water, squeak toys, talking toys, computer games with sound, rhyming books, Dr Suess, silly poems and songs. Play with tape recorders, talking toys, and radios. Expose child to loud noises gradually and with warning, in small doses, and let the child decide if he's had enough – trains, airplanes, roller coasters, movie theatres, sports arenas. Perhaps have earplugs along to put in when needed or be prepared to leave.

Need for deep pressure

Good firm hugs, rolling a big ball over the child, rolling him up in mats or blankets, sleeping bags, tucking the child tightly into bed, back rubs, draping oneself carefully on the child's back, using a weighted blanket, covering child with sofa cushions. Be careful with all of the above actions, so that you do not injure the child or obstruct breathing in any way.

Knowing where one's body is in space

Encourage your child to try a trampoline, swings, spinning seat toy, hammocks, hammock chairs, crawling through tight places, playing leapfrog, carrying heavy things (backpacks), hauling heavy things. Weighted vests are helpful for some kids. You can order them from specialty companies, or make your own from a simple vest pattern, or just remove the sleeves from a shirt. Then, sew flat weights (washers or drapery weights would work fine, or even raw rice) into the hem, shoulder seams, and into the pockets. Just a little added weight can make your child feel more grounded.

Physical issues

> There is usually, but not always, physical clumsiness.

Physical issues can show up in myriad ways, including poor handwriting, an odd gait, or difficulty in riding a bike, playing a sport, or doing many other activities. Somewhere between 50 and 90 percent of the

Asperger population may have these sorts of physical issues (Attwood 1998, p.103). Luckily, there are many ways to incorporate therapy into the homeschooling day.

FINE MOTOR ACTIVITIES

Vicki from the UK comments on some of her favorite activities:

- Fimo/clay sculptures (or just plain clay play).

- When I do my scrapbooking, I involve Stephen and encourage him to make his own page. He gets to use all the "funky" scissors and needs fine motor to position photos, frames, or stickers on his page.

- Peel clementines and satsumas (citrus fruits). I get him started but he must peel the rest on his own.

- Open potato chip and candy packets on his own.

- Unscrew his own bottles and replace lids tightly. With these two, he usually asks me right off the bat, but I want him to really try first, and then when he gets *really* stuck I help him out.

- Peel-off sticker books. He has to find the edge of the sticker, pull it off without ripping it, and place it in the appropriate space.

- Squeeze (really wring) out the dishcloth (before wiping table).

- Write in shaving cream in the bath or on the table.

- Feel for small objects in a big mound of flour. (Of course these last two items are great sensory fun too!)

- Shell roasted peanuts (and then eat!).

- Blackberry/raspberry picking, either in the wild or at a pick-your-own fruit farm. This requires a firm but gentle tug on the berry so as to pluck it from the bush but without squeezing it to death and losing all the juice.

- Planting seeds.

Vicki's list is wonderful, but other parents had still more ideas. Sarah G works with her daughter Kathryn through a miniatures class, offered by a local homeschool support group. Lucy's answer for fine motor work has been to incorporate needlecraft into her son's arts and crafts lessons. Diane writes:

> Fine motor is a challenge, but Allan is my official coupon clipper, jar opener, pencil picker-upper, and anything else that comes along that can help with these skills. Using scissors is particularly challenging for him, but he enjoys cutting out coupons because he knows he is cutting for a purpose. For Allan, having a reason for doing something is very important. He also loves Legos and plays with them for hours, assembling small spacecraft and robots. He enjoys drawing and usually draws in very small detail. Playing piano has improved his hand dexterity and strength.

GROSS MOTOR ACTIVITIES

Sarah C from Alabama exercises with her children every morning. "If we don't exercise first, we get sad and grumpy over silly things. We whine a lot more, and staying focused is way too hard." They do yoga, especially Yoga Kids (videotape), because the tape encourages acting like animals, which her kids enjoy. They might do Brain Gym (see page 258), walking while pointing to each foot with the opposite hand. Physical activity is also a great break. "Sometimes I have the kids go out and run around or ride their bikes, if they have just finished something new or hard, so they can come back and start fresh on a new subject."

Margaret W reports that her child gets lots more physical activity than when she was at school: "Michaela mostly whined and sat out at PE in school. She was discontinued from PT and OT the year before we began to homeschool." Sarah G's daughter takes gymnastics through their homeschool group.

Lucy writes: "As an occupational therapist, I have done OT with James (now 17) for years without him knowing it. We did lots of gross motor activities. We have a trampoline and a swimming pool. We did scooter board stuff. We did a lot of schoolwork lying on our stomachs."

Wendy also uses the pool, plus a swing set. She says, "My kids' bodies seem to crave these activities."

Sandy W writes, "We make sure Brent gets outside for running or bike riding every day." However, she notes, "He has recently been diagnosed with mild cerebral palsy as well, so clumsiness is pretty much part of the deal."

Nicki's methods for improving gross motor skills for her 11-year-old include horseback riding, yoga (they do it together at home), and skateboarding. She credits skateboarding with great improvements in her son's balance.

Vicki also works on balance by keeping special balance toys handy. "The children's Tilt Walker (Wobble Board) and Kangaroo Hopper are always lying around. That means that whenever the kids want, they can stand on them, balance, play, do tricks. The toys are always there on the floor and they both seem to be great tools to increase balance, even though they are a nuisance sometimes!" (See Appendix 7 for product information.)

While taking classes in things such as karate, swimming, gymnastics, and so forth is pretty typical kid stuff, what is not typical is that our kids may have a disproportionate amount of difficulty with these classes compared to other children who do not have Asperger Syndrome.

When Sim G is asked if she works with her seven-year-old, Alex, on physical issues, her reply is:

> A big resounding *yes!* Every single step needs to be taught; his coordination is pretty bad, although he is physically very tall and strong for his age. He still can't ride a bike without training wheels, and can't do intricate or subtle moves in things like karate or calisthenics. He is pretty good at gymnastics, and was doing well physically, but we are looking for a new program due to a bully and the poor way in which the teacher handled it.

Please see the physical education section (Chapter 5) for more ideas.

Other Asperger-related issues

Stimming

Stimming is a term that means self-stimulation and it refers to the repetitive movements that may occur in our kids – flapping, stick-wagging, or other. Stims may serve a good purpose in self-calming or other ways, but some movements can be harmful or intimidating to others, or simply get in the way of learning and social opportunity. So do we leave a stim alone or reduce or redirect?

Sometimes we need to be careful because when one stim is extinguished, another can pop up. Sarah G helps her daughter control stimming when she can. "I draw her attention to the fact that she is doing it, and I help her change gears so that she can stop." Elizabeth notes that her son has stims that she tries to redirect and give word cues to stop. Both verbal and visual cues can be helpful, along with substituting a different activity.

Diane observes that when her son's anxiety is reduced, the stimming is automatically reduced.

Phobias/anxiety

Diana R's son Neal (12) has been medicated for anxiety since he was six years old. She says:

> As his anxiety from school increased, changes would be made in his medication (after lots of discussion with teachers) but the situations *causing* the anxiety would *not* be addressed properly. As a result, the meds would be increased, the anxiety from unsettled issues would increase, more stress would pile on, and we would get into a vicious cycle. Once we started homeschooling and letting Neal decompress from all the trauma he experienced at school, his anxiety lessened, our household settled down, and Neal's meds were reduced.

Homeschooling won't fix all phobias or anxiety, but it may help reduce stress in general. A sudden increase in anxiety may be a sign that even your homeschool day is too much. Medications are sometimes warranted.

Rage

Elizabeth's 11-year-old, Eric, has had problems with rage, but it's getting better:

> The social skills training helps this indirectly, as some of his rage is due to the inability to understand social cues/settings. As he has become aware that others see this as inappropriate, we have been able to pray together about it and talk about alternative ways to handle situations he finds frustrating. He has made huge strides in being able to recognize that he is getting upset and trying to find

a way to handle it. He has also begun taking medication (an SSRI).

Diane says, "With rages, we try to get him away from the stimulation to a quiet, calm place so that he can get control of himself. We allow as long as it takes for this." She feels the book *The Explosive Child* (Greene 2001) has helped decrease rages for her son, because she has learned how to empathize with him and bring him down to an even keel before the rage is out of control.

Joanna Rae also praises this book and adds: "Structured rewards don't work for my guy as he stresses about what he may or may not earn no matter how petty the thing, so we try to work on small behaviors that he can almost control and praise him up and down when he doesn't do them. This week I've started on the 'no door slamming' campaign!"

A MELTDOWN AVERTED

Diane relates this step-by-step account of how she has applied her book knowledge to handle things in the moment:

> We recently visited our local state museum. Upon entering, Allan noticed the gift shop. Gift shops, for him, are a must-see... He asked about it several times in the space of a few minutes. He became anxious...began his unusual body movements, shaking his head, rubbing his face, growling and mumbling to himself, etc. As we walked further into the museum, he became less communicative.
>
> We were walking down a flight of stairs and I noticed he was not participating in the conversation any longer, and was dragging his feet and lagging behind...I asked what he was thinking about, and of course, it was the gift shop. He was afraid that we would run out of time, forget to go see it, he wouldn't have enough time to explore...the list went on and on. I asked if he remembered what I had said about the shop. He had not remembered that I had said we would visit the gift shop toward the end of our visit. "But why can't we go now? I can't think of anything else until we go."
>
> First, I validated his wish to go to the shop by saying that I, too, wanted to go there. I explained that if he decided to make a purchase, we would have to carry it throughout the museum, and risk losing it. That seemed to help. We then set a time at which we

would go to the gift shop and that helped him relax as well. I reminded him that if I promise to do something, we do it. And so, to seal the bargain, I made a promise to go. Finally, he relaxed and was able to enjoy the rest of the outing. He mentioned the gift shop a couple of times, and I simply had him look at my watch and reminded him of the time we would go, and said I was looking forward to it too.

Because of taking the time to have that discussion early in the outing, he was able to enjoy everything and was able to wait for the gift shop visit. We do this pre-planning with most things…he does not like surprises, and I always answer questions about where we are going, what we will do, etc., to the best of my ability.

Working with therapists

Should your homeschooling world include working with therapists? Here, we'll look at what others are doing, what's out there, and how you might access therapy if you wish. In general, we are talking about social skills training, occupational training (OT), and speech/language training. This is not a recommendation for or against, merely a report of findings.

Why many parents are not accessing therapy

Many parents I surveyed feel comfortable enough to work most issues at home. Their own research has given them ideas for things to do and they see good progress. You've seen many of those ideas already, and more are in Chapters 5 and 6.

Some families don't get regular therapy help but have received minimal consultation. Vicki in the UK received a consultation from an OT through the national healthcare system, then took those suggestions and worked with her son on her own. Families in the USA might do something similar by paying for a one-time consultation.

Other families want regular outside therapy for their child but have been unable to find it. There is nothing nearby, insurance won't cover it, or the school-offered programs are limited. Wendy laments, "School therapy is our only option, but Raymond…didn't score low enough. We were told to have him re-evaluated every year because he eventually will qualify." Families such as Wendy's are thus obliged to work issues on their own, whether they want to or not.

Lastly, some families do not access special therapy of any sort because they've already gone that route and have been disappointed. Either they saw no improvement after considerable time investment, or they felt the therapist was clueless when it came to Asperger Syndrome. This happens frequently. When a parent feels that she can do a better job herself, that's what happens.

Why many people do access therapy

I've outlined the cases where families have not accessed special therapy, but there are certainly families for whom it has been a good option. Of outside therapies available, parents mentioned these as being most helpful:

- occupational therapy (OT)

- social skills groups

- speech and language therapy.

OCCUPATIONAL THERAPY

This type of help received the most favorable comments, possibly because it's generally more accessible, or perhaps because progress is more readily observable than in some other deficit areas. Also, OT issues occur in lots of people, not only those in the Asperger population, so perhaps there's a depth of experience in OT that does not exist in more newly recognized Asperger-specific areas.

Ruth maintains that OT interventions were the first that really seemed to make a difference. Her son particularly benefited by the improvements he was able to make in his handwriting and also with sensory integration. She says, "I'm in awe of how much can be done."

Marietta feels that most of her son's interfering sensory issues have dissipated, partly through time but also from twice-weekly OT sessions. He has now "graduated" out of the sessions. Other parents said that their children had graduated out of OT therapy too, but were not convinced that graduation was warranted. They still saw deficits which they would like to be addressed.

One important difference in the occupational therapy one receives through the schools, versus from a private clinic, is that school therapies will be centered on school-related issues. Handwriting may be of prime concern for a school therapist, for instance, but doing household chores or making a sandwich will not likely be on the list of objectives. A private therapist will usually work with parents to determine which life skills or other goals should be pursued. This is one of those "whole" child issues.

SOCIAL SKILLS GROUPS

Social skills groups specifically for children affected by Asperger Syndrome hold the most promise, because the leaders probably really understand the issues. They know how to interpret poor behavior for what it is (stimulation overload, frustration, or a lack of understanding on the part of the child). They know the right techniques too – to keep things structured and predictable, to break social situations into small concrete bits, and to incorporate rehearsals, among other things. This level of understanding is a relief for both child and parent. The other reason that this sort of group is wonderful is because here is a place for like-minded children to meet and become friends.

If a social skills group includes a wider mix of children (AS plus other special needs kids or plus neurotypical kids), you will want to reassure yourself that your child belongs and will be well treated. Our kids are traditionally victims of bullies so you would not want a social skills group whose original purpose is to rehabilitate bullies. Having your child in the group might be good for the bully as a foil for his social lessons, but it's not good for your child.

Good or bad, social skills groups are rare and difficult to track down. Places to look include the school district, private speech/language clinics, or a medical center or university with specialty for autism. Additionally, some parents arrange their own informal groups.

SPEECH/LANGUAGE THERAPY

Most people think of speech therapy in connection with the more mechanical troubles of forming speech – lisps, stuttering, and so forth. But as outlined in Chapter 1, our AS kids have a different set of speech/language challenges. They need to understand the pragmatics of speech. I think of this as "speech in action" – the art of beginning, ending, maintaining, and repairing of a conversation: how to interpret someone's tone of voice, choose good topics, take turns speaking, understand idioms and common expressions, and more. Context is important here, and because of that there is a close relationship with social skills because the child needs to learn to respond appropriately to social situations. This is why speech/language professionals see the value in social skills groups and are usually the people who run them.

That said, many parents have had the experience of working with a speech therapist who has spent a career working on the mechanics of speech and has little or no interest or expertise in the pragmatics. Parents need to ask questions to ensure the therapist understands Asperger Syndrome and has a plan. After Elizabeth began homeschooling her son, she was offered continued pragmatic language group and speech therapy for her son by their suburban Chicago school district, but she opted to obtain services through a private agency that specializes in AS. It is partially reimbursed through insurance.

For a list of social skills and communication-related goals, see Appendix 3.

How do I pay for special therapy and where do I go?

Therapy is generally accessed in one or more of the following ways:

1. Through the public school system (US): traditionally, public schools in most states have been obligated to test and provide needed therapy when needed for any child, even those being homeschooled. Some states have changed this law in recent years, however, and are no longer obligated. It then depends on available resources or the whim of the person in charge. Make sure you understand homeschooling law before you proceed, however, in case you are in a state where accepting school services comes with strings attached to the way you homeschool (e.g. Pennsylvania).

2. Through medical insurance (US): insurance may cover expenses partly or fully, and usually provides a set number of sessions to be used within a given timeframe. Start with a doctor's prescription or referral and then ensure you have written permission from your insurance provider *before* availing yourself of therapies; otherwise, you could get a nasty bill.

3. Through the CHIP program (US): a national insurance program for children who have no other medical coverage. (See Appendix 1 for further info on CHIP.) Cathy, whose

ten-year-old has had OT in the past and continues to receive speech therapy and social skills training, has accessed these services through CHIP.

4.   Through charity organizations (various countries): the Elks charity helped one Florida family pay for OT. The Association for Retarded Children (ARC) or other charities may pay for programs or offer them at very low rates. Easter Seals is furnishing therapy for another family.

5.   From the National Health and National Autism Society (UK).

6.   From the Autism Society of Australia.

7.   From various local organizations, private companies, or city or state agencies (various countries): some cities offer camps, workshops, clubs, and so forth at very reasonable rates and these may take the place of formal therapy. Margaret W in central Alabama has been able to access a camp for special needs children at a very reduced cost (subsidized by her city).

8.   Some families pay for therapy out of their own pockets.

This chapter has been long and detailed, providing you with ideas about your child's learning style(s), possible homeschooling styles, and ways to work many of the most challenging Asperger issues into your homeschool plan. The goal has not been to prescribe particular things you should do, but simply make you aware of the many issues that you will have the opportunity to address, along with some suggestions on how to do just that. Do not let all of this panic you. In the next chapter, you will see how other families handle things.

Chapter 3

Some Family Models

The previous chapter may have seemed overwhelming, because we've been talking about several difficult facets simultaneously. In this chapter, let's take a breath, sit back, and watch how other folks put it together.

The following families have graciously allowed a peek into their lives. We'll see specifically how these families spend their days and what works, or hasn't worked, for them. These families present a wide array of kids' ages, needs, homeschooling styles, and other factors. Answers were edited where necessary. See Appendix 7 for information on most books, curricula, or organizations mentioned.

Family A

Mom: Wendy P.

Children with AS: Tony, 7 years old, first grade. Raymond, 5 years old, pre-kindergarten.

Location: Florida.

Length homeschooling: three years.

Homeschool style: traditional.

Record-keeping method: notebook.

Time per day spent homeschooling: one to two hours (first grade), 15 to 20 mins (pre-kindergarten).

Does your spouse help?

Occasionally my husband will fill in for me. He tries to do the Bible portion of homeschooling at night for me.

Is your extended family supportive?

Some yes, some do not say anything.

Do you use homeschooler groups?

I have only been involved for support. I haven't been brave enough to bring my kids to activities.

Please describe your homeschooling day

I announce that it is time to begin school. Tony usually comes in with an action figure and says, "Teacher, we have a guest today." I tell him the "guest" can stay as long as he is quiet. We begin usually with a couple of pages of *Explode the Code* (phonics). If he has to write the words, he sometimes flops around and has a quiet meltdown. I point to the words he has to copy and remind him that these activities are tons better than copying spelling words. When finished, we do something more laid-back like reading from a well-illustrated history book. Then we usually do math. I first X out about half of the problems (anything I know he knows inside out). Sometimes he does the math very quickly. Other times he flops around. Recently I had to resort to setting a timer. I tell him math will be over when the timer goes off and if he isn't finished he *will* lose computer time. He *always* finishes. Of course I wouldn't do that with a concept if he were struggling with it. We then do reading (which he loves and is very advanced in) and possibly a language arts page (I do the writing on this), which he actually enjoys. Then he does some work (no more than a short sentence) in his *Handwriting Without Tears* workbook. He is fairly cooperative for this. We then read from a fun, colorful science book or do our weekly experiment and finish by reading a chapter out of a read-aloud.

With Raymond, the younger one, I do nothing formal. We work on phonics for a few minutes. He can now put together sounds and is beginning to read. I might have him do a maze, dot-to-dot, or I'll use glitter paint around the edges of a picture so he can color it with a boundary.

After lunch, I send them outside to play (very important for their coordination which is weak) on their swing set, or if it is hot we swim in our little pool. They both have an hour of computer time in the afternoon, which gives me a much needed break. They both not only enjoy their hour but they enjoy the other hour of watching their brother play computer.

How do you think your children learn best (i.e. learning style) and how do you use that info?
Special interests help a lot. Tony will learn about anything if there has been a Lego book written about it. He loves computers so I encourage educational CD-ROMs. I think both of my boys are hands-on learners. They are not auditory learners.

Do you have special activities during the week?
Mondays, we have therapy. Tony has language therapy and occupational therapy. Raymond has physical therapy. We don't do any school on that day. Wednesdays they have a church group. Thursdays, Dad has his day off and we sometimes go somewhere special. Fridays, Tony again has language therapy and I try to give them both their piano lesson (I am a piano teacher). Saturdays, they go to Special Equestrians. Sunday is church. Their dad is a full-time minister of music so they have a very long day on Sundays. They are involved in Sunday School and children's choir.

Who pays for therapy?
The school pays for Tony's therapies. Raymond hasn't qualified for services through the school at this time, even though he needs help. We did get physical therapy for Raymond from the Florida Elks, which is free to us and lasts for six months.

What do you spend per year on homeschooling?
I spend about $500 on curriculum, I think.

How long do you plan to homeschool?
Through high school. If I can't handle some high school courses there are so many options. There is a curriculum on CD-ROM, videos, and I

plan to send them to a few college courses if there happens to be a community college nearby when they reach high school age.

Overall, how would you describe your experience of homeschooling? Any regrets?

I feel like it may be the reason why they are doing so well. The only drawback is that I don't get a break. I'm satisfied with how much they have learned and feel they have good social skills for Aspies and a very close relationship as brothers (who have very similar Aspie interests).

What's your relationship with your neighborhood school?

The Preschool Evaluation Team is probably glad to be finished with us. They weren't very helpful. Things are going well with the public school OT and LT.

Any other comments?

I think it is fun (now that I'm not grieving the fact that I have two special needs kids) to have my two Aspies at home. They are unique, bright children who do very unusual things. Tony's first imaginary friend (when he was age 3) was Bob Saget (from TV's *Full House*, and host of *America's Funniest Videos*). At age 4, Tony changed the wallpaper on our computer (we didn't teach him to do this). Raymond recently logged onto internet without our knowledge, typed out his name, and sent an email to an old friend of ours. There is just never a dull moment.

Did you notice?

Wendy has come up with effective ways to work with Tony. She alternates coursework so that the writing he doesn't like is interspersed with the reading and science that he does like. Using the timer works because she's got realistic expectations. Although she claims only a couple of hours of homeschooling per day, when you add in the much-needed physical play, plus the socializing her boys get working together at the computer, it's a full day. They also get many social opportunities at church.

Family B

Mom: Sim G.

Children with AS: Alex, 7 years old, second grade (only child).

Location: New York.

Length homeschooling: one and a half years.

Homeschool style: eclectic.

Record-keeping method: calendar plan book, portfolio, and an attendance journal.

Time per day spent homeschooling: on average, at least two and a half hours of direct instruction, an hour of multimedia, from one to two hours of activity outside of the home (field trip, social, physical education, etc.), and at least an hour of self-directed activity.

Homeschool all year or summers off?
We homeschool year round.

Does your spouse help?
Yes, my husband takes over with certain areas that interest him.

Is your extended family supportive?
Many family members were dubious at first, but they have all since commended our decision and have openly stated that they have seen a marked improvement in Alex. My mother and grandmother were supportive right from the start. I find it interesting that the one worry that most had in the beginning was the social aspect, and that is the area in which the same people are applauding Alex's improvement!

What has been your experience with homeschooler groups?
Over all, positive. However, I am very selective with groups and I never tell anyone about Alex's diagnosis. We don't overdo it with field trips. Alex seems happiest to deal with homeschool groups only once in awhile. In these groups, Alex has made friends that he now sees regularly

on a one-to-one basis every week, and it is in this area that homeschool groups have proven most beneficial.

Please describe your homeschooling day

Alex is up and has eaten breakfast usually by 8:30 am. We start homeschooling as soon as possible, because this is when Alex is at his best. I've learned to start the day with math, because Alex seems to really enjoy this. Utilizing various materials and a chalkboard, I teach the lesson or review what was learned in previous lessons. I make the lesson as interactive as possible, or he daydreams. I make sure that he "gets it" on the chalkboard or in other materials or dialogue, before presenting him with work to do on his own. For math, we use both Singapore and Miquon curriculum. If we are using Miquon that day, I usually work with him in his book. If he is using Singapore, he does his work independently. We usually spend one hour on math.

Then I give him a break where he can drift into his own world for ten minutes and draw. Structured academic work of any kind usually brings on bursts of enormous creativity, so this lets off creative steam. I think I should mention that what I find most successful in teaching Alex math is to jump around various concepts during the week, rather than work incrementally with one concept. This keeps it fun and spontaneous for him, and seems to work better for us.

After math, it's language arts. Depending on the day, we either work on writing skills, spelling, reading comprehension, grammar, phonics, reading aloud, etc. We usually spend about an hour and a half on language arts.

Then we break for lunch. After lunch, we usually go on a field trip, library, playdate, physical activity, whatever the weather and opportunity afford. If it's a playdate, we stay out for hours and just have fun. If it's the library, we get books, videos and DVDs. Then, we go home and use them to learn things like science, health, history, etc. If we got out specifically for something like physical education or music, then my husband and I usually work side by side with Alex. Most structured PE programs (karate, gymnastics) have not proven beneficial at this time due to social misunderstandings. Therefore, we are teaching Alex ourselves at this time.

Sometimes we do science experiments or take long field trips, or Alex just takes a day or so to intensely explore areas of interest. His most recent obsession was working on his potter's wheel. He basically taught himself and is doing pretty well. Past obsessions like this included making musical instruments, the cello, making robots that work, and drawing, drawing, drawing, all of the time.

How do you think your child learns best and how do you use that info?
With us, it seems to depend on the day. I never know what to expect. Some days, he races through everything at lightning speed, and will just take the math book and do up to ten pages. Other days, I can't seem to get him to focus at all. The method I have found to be the best is to go with the flow. If he is having a productive, attentive day, we have been known to take it as far as it will go, up to six hours or so of intense instruction. On unfocused days, things are kept very short. On highly creative days, I let him do whatever he wants with or without facilitation.

Do you have special activities during the week?
We like to homeschool all weekend and normally Friday, Monday, and Tuesday as well. However, we switch days to suit whatever is going on. This works for us, because traffic is brutal on Long Island on weekends, and everything fun to do is so crowded.

What do you spend per year on homeschooling?
Homeschooling curriculum costs me about $50 to $100 per year. Our library is wonderful. They have ordered everything I ever asked for. We also utilize the internet a lot. The biggest expenses are when we go into New York City for the weekend to do a whirlwind museum tour or something. Field trips can get expensive too, but most homeschoolers are on a budget, so we all try to look for cheap things to do. Keep in mind that even if Alex were in school, we would still have these expenses, because we would still take him on a lot of these trips.

How long do you plan to homeschool?
I'm taking everything one step at a time, day by day. As of now, the rewards of homeschooling are so great I'd be foolish to discontinue. However, I can't predict the future; I'll cross that bridge when we get to it!

Overall, how would you describe your experience of homeschooling? Any regrets?

Overall, I'm very satisfied with my decision to homeschool. It has taken my son a long time to let down his guard and bond. Why shouldn't he bond with his parents instead of strangers? The benefits: Alex feels safe now. He felt extremely confused and defensive socially when he was in kindergarten. Now, he's a happy, relaxed kid. In preschool and kinder-garten, he did not make one single friend. With us to help him, to facili-tate one-on-one friendships with hand-chosen peers and parents, Alex has a nice circle of friends that has remained consistent.

Alex has always done well academically in school. Now that he is homeschooled, his learning has taken a more personally meaningful road for him.

The biggest drawbacks and regrets are the battles of wills. My son is usually very self-directed and it has been exhausting at times to direct him. Alex is usually happiest when things are unstructured, rather than structured and teacher-led. We have learned to compromise with each other. He is still very happy to be homeschooled, and the best way to get him to behave if he gets belligerent is to ask him if he would prefer to go to school. Then he behaves! "No, I don't want to go back to school. I'd rather learn here."

In many ways, it is a thankless exhausting job. However, the more I homeschool, the more I see the rewards later on. It's just not instant grat-ification (due to the strong will factor and his chronic complaining).

In what area would you like more guidance or help? Any worries?

I guess I would like it if more parents shared pitfalls, so that those of us just starting this journey can learn from them. I also hope I'm covering all the bases!

What's your relationship with your neighborhood school?

Strained. I feel my son's public school violated my son's privacy by leaving his supposedly sealed diagnosis file out where anyone could read it.

Any other comments?

Thank you for writing this book, and for allowing me to contribute!

Did you notice?

Sim has used a non-traditional weekly schedule to advantage. She does some unschooling in letting Alex pursue his interests. Alex has no siblings, but is doing well socially due to making sure his interactions are successful. When they are not, as in the case of the PE classes, she quickly removed him. Sim is protective about Alex's diagnosis and this works fine in younger years when she is always with him. In later years when he is doing things without her nearby, she may find it necessary to discuss any troublesome issues with a few trusted adult leaders.

Family C

Mom: Nicki.

Child with AS: Mark, 11 years old, fifth grade.

Location: Texas.

Length homeschooling: six months.

Homeschool style: eclectic: math – workbook, games, and manipulatives; English – grammar text, journal writing, and *Spelling Power*; history – unit study; reading – books; science – unit study.

Record-keeping method: portfolio.

Time per day spent homeschooling: two to two and a half hours per day.

Homeschool all year or summers off?
We homeschool all year.

Does your spouse help?
My husband does not teach at all.

Is your extended family supportive?
My family is very supportive. My husband is not.

Do you use homeschooler groups?

I have found that in the exclusively Christian groups they are ill-prepared for my son's idiosyncratic behavior. They find him ill-mannered. In inclusive groups of all cultures and beliefs, they have been very accepting thus far. (I am Christian and was surprised by the reactions of some people.)

Please describe your homeschooling day

- 7:30 Wake up
- 7:30–8:00 Free time
- 8:00–8:20 Breakfast
- 8:20–9:30 Chore time
- 9:30–12:00 Lesson time
- 12:00–12:30 Lunch.

How do you think your child learns best and how do you use that info?

My son learns best when he is free to move around, touch, manipulate and create, unhindered.

Do you have special activities during the week?

- 12:30–1:30 Public library (Monday)
- 12:30–2:30 Homeschool library (Tuesday)
- 12:30–1:30 Campfire group (Friday)

We go to co-op on Wednesdays from 10:00 to 3:30. On those days we skip chores and do math and grammar only (before co-op). At co-op, Mark takes science lab, geology, art, drama, and chess club.

What is the costliest part of homeschooling?

The costliest part was jumping into a curriculum that was all wrong for my child. I now buy through used bookstores, used curriculum sales, swaps on the net, and a discount house where I buy grammar and math.

How long do you plan to homeschool?

I will homeschool on through high school. I have already made a class plan of courses to teach. I have even chosen some of the curriculum (not bought it – I can find it used, through the years).

Overall, how would you describe your experience of homeschooling? Any regrets?

My son is much more relaxed now. He seeks out social opportunities. Some days he is distractible and hard to keep on task. But as bad as it gets at home, it *never* is as bad as it was in public school.

I always wanted to homeschool, but my husband listened to the therapist who said "He will never develop normally if you keep him home. He is socially stunted." Every year I begged my husband. He always said, "If it's this bad next year, okay." Well, this year he slipped so far behind academically, I asked to have him moved to resource classes. The school said no. He was too smart. But, they promised they would not fail him. My husband said, "Pull him out. I don't care about failing. Will they teach him anything?" So I pulled him out.

My son, socially, has been a target at school. He's been beaten up (even had his head flushed in the toilet). He has constantly been bullied. This was what was hard for me. But it wasn't until the schools couldn't/wouldn't teach him that my husband agreed it was the best thing.

What's your relationship with your neighborhood school?

My relationship with my elementary school is very good. I was supported by the staff there in our decision.

Any other comments?

I feel as though I have spent the last several years fighting the schools and now I can breathe. I watch my son, now he can breathe.

Did you notice?

Nicki and her son have had a hard time getting to the point of homeschooling. Luckily, even the school supported the decision, ultimately. She is receiving good support from the homeschooling community. Homeschool-friendly states such as Texas are often places where "co-ops" have started up to teach courses or crafts in small groups.

Family D

Mom: Diana R.

Location: Texas.

Length homeschooling: one year.

Child with AS: Neal, 12 years old, seventh grade.

Homeschool style: eclectic. Our homeschooling style is a mixture depending on the subject. We use Switched-on-Schoolhouse for history (all computer based – supplemented with outside books), textbook for Saxon math, which I sit with him and teach step by step (he needs immediate feedback in math), a speech/language pathologist is helping us with language arts issues (*huge* area of weakness and *stress*), and various books, magazines, kits, etc. for science. We also watch a lot of PBS, science and history channel programs.

Record-keeping method: I keep records of *everything*. I log in a calendar and notebook daily and keep all of his work together in binders, file cabinets, file boxes, etc.

Time per day spent homeschooling: we usually spend approximately three hours per day of "work" not including social events, field trips, and therapy.

Homeschool all year or summers off?
We are schooling through this summer, but with some days off here and there.

Does your spouse help?
I do all the homeschooling.

Is your extended family supportive?
Our extended family, I think, thinks I'm crazy, but Neal is *so* much better since taking him out of school. The stress and anxiety are greatly reduced and he is *so* much happier. His psychiatrist, psychologist, speech and language therapist and occupational therapist are amazed at the difference in him! And, he seems to be learning more at home than he did in school.

Do you use homeschooler groups?
We have not joined any groups, but we do see other families that homeschool.

Please describe your homeschooling day
We usually start schoolwork around 11:30 am. We work on one subject for about 30 to 45 minutes, then take a break for 30 minutes, then on to the next subject and so forth. It feels pretty relaxed and Neal has some control over the "times" we work on a subject, but he knows the amount of work to be completed on most days. This usually works out okay. Some days, though, he just "can't work" and he may just spend the day reading or watching educational videos/programs. He is agreeable to make up the time on weekends.

How do you think your child learns best and how do you use that info?
Neal learns best visually. He loves videos, working with science experiments, working on the computer and with his special interests. He has *great* difficulty working with someone who is a "control freak" and wants to impose "their" way on him. He can't be forced to do anything! He loves working with computer-based subjects because he says "the computer doesn't argue with me!"

Do you have special activities during the week?

Every Monday is speech therapy, Wednesday is OT, and Thursday is social skills group with the psychologist. Once a month is a visit to the psychiatrist.

Who pays for therapy?

Our therapies are paid partly out of pocket and partly insurance reimbursement.

What do you spend per year on homeschooling?

Homeschooling costs *so* much *less* than a private school or having to pay our private psychologist to attend school IEP meetings with us to *fight* for an appropriate plan. I'd guess we've spent about $600 on materials, books, etc. That does not include field trips to museums, zoos, etc.

How long do you plan to homeschool?

I plan to homeschool through middle school. I am seriously thinking about some kind of formal school setting for high school but want to keep an open mind about things.

Overall, how would you describe your experience of homeschooling? Any regrets?

I have no regrets pulling Neal out of school. I wish I'd done it sooner. His anxiety and stress were tremendous. Unfortunately, finding the right fit for middle school in our area seems impossible through the public schools and financially prohibitive through the private schools for now. I was generally pleased with the efforts and understanding of the school personnel we had for elementary school, but completely dissatisfied with the transition to middle school. Homeschooling is *so* much easier than battling the schools and the decrease in stress for our *entire* family is remarkable. Neal is much happier and is very interested in learning if given choices and if he feels some sense of control over himself. I tend to spend more time in his areas of interest, but so far, I have found it easy enough to incorporate other subjects into his special interests.

In what area would you like more guidance or help? Any worries?

My main concern now is the language arts difficulty Neal has always experienced. He *hates* to write but *loves* to read. His comprehension is quite good – at least grade level – but his writing skills are very poor. He has had access to a keyboard, laptop, etc. for a long time so he does not have to write with a pen/pencil. He has good keyboarding skills. Putting thoughts, sentences, paragraphs, etc. together is torture. I hate book reports! He has such difficulty with main ideas, etc. I know that *every* fact and detail is important to him as an Aspie, so it's difficult to teach.

I also have concerns that I may not be able to keep up with him in math and science once he gets to high school. He is very bright and needs more challenges than I can offer. I have thought about finding programs that are specific to his needs and then homeschooling the rest. I have to say, though, that I am doing *no worse* than his teachers and he is much calmer and happier now.

What's your relationship with your neighborhood school?
I have no contact with our school district currently.

Any other comments?
I believe homeschooling is a very viable option for some situations. It is definitely worth considering for the mental well-being of the child *and* his family!

Did you notice?

Diana is very conscious of the best ways to work with her sons. This includes quick feedback, acknowledging stressful subjects, allowing him some limited control, taking frequent breaks, and using visual presentation. The payoff for her efforts has been great.

Family E

Mom: Sandy W.

Children with AS: Brent, 16 years old, Year 10. Kyle, 13 years old, Year 8.

Location: South Australia.

Length homeschooling: four years.

Homeschooling style: for the first two years, I created my own curriculum using a combination of workbooks and textbooks. I focused on areas where the boys were having the most difficulty – handwriting, maths, and creative writing. I also made outside activity compulsory, as the boys preferred staying indoors. I did register for National tests in maths, science and computing and the boys were able to sit the tests at home and received certificates.

Kyle asked to return to school after three terms. Now with just Brent at home, he is doing his work through Open Access College – an Education Department school set up to provide education to [Australian] children who are isolated by geography or medically unable to attend school.

Record-keeping method: notebooks, calendars, timetables and a portfolio. I had to present these all to the Education Department on their annual inspection.

Homeschool all year or summers off?
We homeschool according to the "normal" school year. We have younger sons who attend school.

How much time per day do you homeschool, generally?
[The first two years] on average four hours. This fluctuated depending on what subjects were being done at the time.

Is your extended family supportive?
Yes. Initially they were concerned but they now see the transformation in our oldest son especially.

Do you use homeschooler groups?
I have not really been involved with any homeschooling groups.

Please describe your homeschooling day
Initially we set things up so our younger two left for school, then the older boys started their day. The rule was they had to be up, showered, dressed and fed before their school day started at 10 am. The mornings were for handwriting, maths and English. I took the opportunity to teach them how to make sandwiches and prepare food themselves for lunch. Afternoons were for blocks of science, art, or social studies.

Now with just Brent at home he is doing the Open Access College. Our schedule revolves around telephone lessons. He has seven half-hour phone lessons per week [one for each subject]. Friday is his free day to catch up with any work not completed during the week. He is required to do three hours per week per subject, as well as the phone lessons. All the materials are provided now, which makes life easier for me.

How do you think your children learn best and how do you use that info?
The boys definitely both learn better through computer and visually. Hands-on too. We try to restrict special interests as they can take over the whole day. Brent is a computer whiz and would, I am sure, spend 20 hours a day on the computer if we let him.

Do you have special activities during the week?
Brent belongs to a youth group, which he attends with his best friend who also has AS.

What do you spend per year on homeschooling?
Initially there was a lot of expense getting set up. Concerned that I needed to pass inspection by the department in order to be approved for homeschooling, I bought curriculum guidelines and testing criteria – all sorts of things I never used. So the first year cost me probably double what it would have to have the boys in school. Now, using a departmental school, we pay the standard school fees and everything is provided, including the speakerphone Brent uses.

How long do you plan to homeschool?
With Brent in his third year of high school, we plan to keep him home for the remainder of his schooling. He was strictly homeschooled through Year 7 and Year 8 before being accepted on medical grounds into the Open Access College Distance Education program. We have to reapply annually to continue his enrolment, which is an annoyance, as we wouldn't need to do that at a regular school.

Kyle returned to school after three terms at home. As much as we would prefer to have him homeschooling still, it is his wish to stay at school despite the ongoing problems. Currently if he gets one more suspension he will be excluded [expelled] from school and the department will recommend home schooling using the Open Access College.

Overall, how would you describe your experience of homeschooling? Any regrets?
The biggest benefit has been to our oldest son. He is no longer stressed. Despite not having the social interaction of school, he is much more sociable as he isn't so stressed and distressed. Extended family members have noticed that he talks a lot more, is much calmer and confident in himself.

The drawback is the financial drain on the family as I have been unable to return to my career as a teacher and that is now basically lost to me unless I go to further expense to update my training. As much as I love my sons, it has been a strain to have at least one with me 24 hours a day for four years.

Initially I requested Open Access College just to give the whole family some respite from the stress the boys were suffering and bringing home with them. The official from the department said she couldn't see what stress there would be and refused, saying I could take them out of school for one term (ten weeks), then return to school for the second term. She couldn't see that this would create even more stress. Leading up to our decision…both boys had been beaten up at school on more than one occasion. One student was beating Brent every day at lunchtime and swearing him to silence – if Brent told anyone, he wouldn't be his "friend" anymore. When we discovered what was happening, the school counselor wanted us to allow Brent to remain friends with the boy inflicting the injury as "he has problems and I think

it would be good for us to work through them using Brent as his friend."
Naturally we refused and this started our search for safer schooling for
our AS boys.

With Kyle, we are hoping ongoing issues since his return to school
can be resolved for his own sake, as he wants to stay at school having
made friends.

*What are your special worries in homeschooling a child with Asperger
Syndrome?*

As Brent is now reaching adulthood I worry about his lack of independence, but he is currently coping well with work experience, albeit in a
sheltered environment. It concerns me that he still has no idea of road
safety, as he can't judge distance. His lack of knowledge of his physical
surroundings is an ongoing issue – we have lived in the same house for
seven years and he is just beginning to recognize the house from a short
distance when we are coming home. Despite the repeated trips to the
local shop he cannot find his way there alone. So I really fear how he will
cope when he is on his own.

What's your relationship with your neighborhood school?

After my initial concerns, the department representative was really supportive of my decision.

In what area would you like more guidance or help? Any worries?

I would love to see more centralized support overall for disabilities and a
recognition that mainstream school on the whole is not the best place for
these kids. I would love it to be less of a battle to get the support in school
or the support from the department to school at home.

Did you notice?

Sandy has used two sorts of homeschooling – the latter sanctioned program is becoming increasingly available for those with Asperger Syndrome in South Australia. Sandy recognizes that Brent needs help with independence issues but a follow-up with Sandy indicates that the sheltered work experience Brent received (from the Phoenix Society) was not a good fit. Work was not interesting and all other employees were mentally challenged. Once again, kids with Asperger Syndrome seem to be neither fish nor fowl.

Now that you've had a glimpse into the daily lives of several families, you can see that there is no single right way to proceed.

Chapter 4

Unit Studies

Our long experience in homeschooling has shown, time and again, that an intense interest in anything inevitably leads everywhere. (Rupp 2000, p.2)

The unit study, also called thematic unit, allows study of a topic from diverse angles and incorporates many skills. Instead of doing a history lesson on World War II, a science lesson on DNA, and an English lesson on "What I did last summer," you make several lessons revolve around one theme. If you choose "Oceans" as your theme, you might explore fishing as a way of life in different cultures (social studies); dissect a fish or do a salinity experiment (science); and read *Old Man and the Sea* (English). You might investigate scrimshaw carvings or amber jewelry (art from the sea), visit an aquarium, or do any number of other ocean-related things. Incorporating math takes some of us rusty parents a bit more thought, but this might be a good time to discuss volume and liquid measurements, or to look up comparative depths of the world's oceans.

We have already discussed the positive aspects of using a unit study in Chapter 2, so let's move on to how one could put a unit study together.

A sample unit study

When my son was enthralled with Japan, I devised the following unit study.

Japan unit study (John, 10)

- Read a children's book on Japan (reading, social studies).

- Learned to use an abacus (math).

- Decorated a folder with flag of Japan, map, Mt Fuji (geography, art).

- Learned about kite-flying day and made a kite (art, social studies, science).

- Cooked a Japanese meal to eat with chopsticks (home economics, math, fine motor).

- Tried Japanese writing with black poster paint (language arts, art).

- Folded an origami frog (art, math).

- Learned karate from a *Karate for Kids* video tape (PE).

- Watched *Karate Kid* movies (social studies and fun).

While the Japan unit study was quite comprehensive, others we did were more abbreviated and did not necessarily cover every academic subject.

Here are examples of how other parents of children with AS have stretched their child's special interest into a broader learning opportunity. While few of the parents would formally label these unit studies, and you could probably call it unschooling just as easily, the examples are quite inspiring. When a child chooses the topic, the line between unit study and unschooling gets blurry, but in the end it doesn't matter.

Cooking (Michaela, 11)

Margaret W writes:

> Michaela's special interest last year was cooking. She loved Emeril (TV chef) and wanted to cook like him. I had to teach her basic safety skills in the kitchen because if I tried to forbid her to cook she would simply get up when I was asleep and try to cook quietly without waking me up. I would rather have waited until she was a little more mature to cook, but I didn't want to risk her starting a fire or hurting herself, so I taught her how to do it safely. She loves to cook simple muffin mixes entirely on her own, and is very cautious about getting hot pans out of the oven. Cooking has

been really helpful in teaching fractions in math and the effects of heat and cold in science.

Notes

Smart mom to work with, instead of against, her daughter. Maybe Michaela's interest will branch into reading cookbooks, learning cooking terms (lots of French), or taking a small cooking class at some point.

Making bread (Andy, 9)

Sarah writes:

> Andy loves making bread, so for his birthday we got him a breadmaker, so I don't have to worry about him using my mixer and the hot oven (a safety issue). He loves it. When he felt limited by what kinds of bread he could make, he looked into recipe books at Amazon and picked out the two he thought he would use the most, and with Mom's help we ordered them. He has also posted questions to different (computer) bulletin boards and received answers, amazed that people on another computer in another part of the world can help him – people he doesn't even know. Big warning here, though – Andy doesn't surf the web unsupervised.

Notes

Here, cooking has branched into computer research, comparison shopping, and it could start an interest in geography to learn where his e-pen pals live. Writing real letters to real people about a real passion is much more meaningful than composing a fake letter as an exercise.

Whales (Aidan, 5)

Joanna Rae writes:

> Aidan had a whale obsession for a while which led to our local science museum, where they have a life-sized model of a sperm whale that one can walk through. We later met the man

responsible for building "Connie" the whale model. Aidan was unable to talk with him directly as that felt too overwhelming, but we did get business cards from him, which led to Aidan dictating emails to him. He went so far as to draw a picture of a whale as a thank you for having received a book and video about whales – this from a boy who never draws, only "writes" (dictates).

Notes

Wonderful – a scientific interest has expanded to language arts, art, and a reach to communicate between a five-year-old and an adult.

Amphibians (Kathryn, 12)
Sarah G writes:

Kathryn has always been obsessed/preoccupied with amphibians…especially frogs. We have used her interests to follow the life cycle of a tadpole to a frog, by raising 16 African water frogs when she was in kindergarten. Each year in her studies, we cover amphibians at least once, looking at different aspects each time, and each year looking at them more in-depth.

Notes

Some AS children keep a special interest at intense levels for months or years. Topics need not "finish," but can be ever-broadened, so that students can return to the well many times for more learning.

Sports (Stephen, 11)
Vicki writes:

Stephen's interests have included sporting events such as the Olympics, Commonwealth Games, hockey, baseball, FA Cup games, and motor racing. Since he really enjoys calculating too, we found a book called STATS, Math Made Fun by Don Fraser. Taking game summaries from the NHL, statistics were calculated: who scored more frequently, who is a more efficient goal scorer, does the home team have an advantage, does the team who scores first usually win the game, and so much more. We spent all the autumn term for maths doing calculations like this, as well as probabilities and percentages. He learned how to figure percentages using information he found highly interesting.

Notes

Vicki also described how Stephen's interest prompted him to keep charts during the Olympics, tallying how well various countries were doing – who had received gold, silver, and bronze medals. This entailed coloring and language arts. He became familiar with national flags and colors, and some geography. Mom adds that the flexibility of homeschooling allowed Stephen to watch the Olympics in the first place, which in England didn't start until very late. She just altered his schedule by letting him sleep later in the mornings.

What if your child's special interest seems strange or not worthy of study?

There may be a limit somewhere, but I haven't found it yet. When my son seemed only interested in video games, the topic annoyed me. However, it led to many things: library research on how video games worked; phone skills from calling video stores for prices on rental games; math from calculating the best deals (with help). Finally, I will never forget the night my son, a very reluctant writer, stayed up until midnight writing a very long letter to Nintendo describing six ideas he had for new games.

And check out the following weird, but wonderful, study we did.

Graveyards (John, 10)

- We made rubbings of the intricate gravestones, using large paper and the sides of crayons with the paper peeled off (sensory, tactile, fine motor, art).

- Took lengthy walks (gross motor, PE).

- We read dates and calculated how long people lived (math).

- We read poems, quotations, and inscriptions on the tombstones (language arts).

- We observed nature by following a rabbit, and discussed embalming and decomposition (science).

- We observed soldier's graves, sectioned off according to each war, and noticed the many child deaths in the early 1920s, probably due to the great flu epidemic (history).

Building your own unit study

You can buy prebuilt unit studies from curriculum publishers on some of the more common topics, but they tend to be worksheet oriented and rather dry, and probably will not cover the exact topics you want anyway. I encourage you to make your own. With internet, the library, and your child's questions, you'll do fine. Here are a few tips:

1. Less is more. If you overplan, your child may feel overwhelmed and if he balks, you will get cranky. Have a few general ideas and only stay a day or two ahead, rather than a month ahead.

2. Let your child's level of interest dictate how long you stick with a topic.

3. Do some of the research with your child. You do not have to know all the answers.

4. Keep in mind your child's learning style. Favor hands-on or discussion over great gobs of reading and writing, if that's the way your child learns best. However, a reluctant reader/writer may be gently encouraged if the topic is compelling enough.

5. It's okay to handle more than one interest at a time, or to leave it for a while and pick it back up again at another point.

6. To look on internet for unit studies that other people have compiled, use your favorite search tool and a few key terms. For an Egypt unit study, for example, type "thematic unit

Egypt" or "unit study Egypt" or even "homeschool Egypt" to find heaps of resources. If you type "lesson plan Egypt" you will also get lots of resources, but some of the activities will be geared for teachers of entire classrooms.

7. There are entire online sites that feature these sorts of thematic or unit lessons. Try these websites for thematic units, or in some cases classroom lesson plans: www.atozteacherstuff.com/ themes/ and www.thegateway.org/.

Figure 4.1 shows a worksheet to help you organize thoughts and supplies to build your own unit study. You need not touch every base with every unit study! However, it's a place to at least see the potential bases you might want to hit.

Figure 4.1 Unit study worksheet

Do not feel obligated to fill in every blank. This is only a place to brainstorm and write notes. If you write down twenty things, you don't have to do all twenty! Quit when interest flags, and start a new topic/new worksheet. Have fun.

Subject: _____

Reading ideas. This could be a child-level book, a book you read to your child, magazine articles, newspapers, textual websites, etc.

1. _____

2. _____

3. _____

Writing ideas. List essay or story prompts; ideas for keeping a journal; other writing opportunities (research, interview, letter, etc.).

1. _____

2. _____

3. _____

Vocabulary and main ideas. List central points, ideas, or terms important to the topic. Attach a separate sheet if necessary, but don't get carried away.

1. _____

2. _____

3. _____

Math. What about this topic might be measured, weighed, counted, ordered, estimated, calculated, sorted, graphed, mapped, diagrammed, etc.?

1. _____

2. _____

3. _____

Science. Where does science intersect with your topic? Can you bring in an invention, a discovery, an experiment, or some aspect of nature?

1. _____

2. _____

3. _____

Social studies. Think of historical, geographical, cultural, political, economic, or community aspects. Can you involve a map? A poll, vote, survey, or law?

1. _____

2. _____

3. _____

Music. Can you play music to fit the theme or era? Make up a song?

1. _____

2. _____

Art. Find images of your topic in art. Draw it, make a model, or other.

1. _____

2. _____

Sensory experiences. Can you bring some sensory experience into it as you work on your topic? Think especially about deep pressure, tactile, taste, smell, and listening for certain sounds.

1. _____

2. _____

3. _____

Motor/movement. Are there opportunities for gross or fine motor movement? A dance, a game, or physical chore such as hauling supplies, digging, trekking, climbing, etc.? Might there be some fine motor opportunities such as pushing tacks into a bulletin board, doing a science experiment, cooking, or art work – folding, stamping, typing, coloring, cutting, etc.?

1. _____

2. _____

3. _____

Bible, spiritual, or family value lessons. Any morals to the story? Character dilemmas? Lessons learned? Applications to one's religion?

1. _____

2. _____

Life skills/problem issues. Think about cooking, home chores, sewing, using tools, dressing, eating, hygiene, and any other issue you need to plan for.

1. _____

2. _____

Social opportunities. Might the child make a phone call for this topic? Shop for a supply? Request a library book? Read or recite to a family member? Interview a neighbor?

    1. _____

    2. _____

Field trips. Ideas – library, museum, park, historical site, factory tour, or even visit a neighbor who knows about it.

    1. _____

    2. _____

Games/interactive websites/movies. Have a bit of fun!

    1. _____

    2. _____

    3. _____

Chapter 5

Where Academics Meets Asperger

This chapter details how to present academic subjects to our kids. It is a reflection of my own experience and what other families have reported, and is not a full survey of what's out there. If you are using a particular program not mentioned here and it's working, keep using it!

Math

When I homeschooled my son beginning in grade two, I turned to humble materials such as household objects, dime store workbooks, and games to teach math. We eventually added computer games and, starting in grade five, an old but serviceable math book (free from my school district's "book morgue"), which we worked through at a steady two pages per day. When he reentered the school system the following year, he tested well and continued to do well through high school.

I mention this because there are so many textbook vendors out there, each hinting that unless you make the right choice, you might miss a concept or teach something out of order. It can be overwhelming.

Relax. Don't rush into a math program out of panic that you must get on the train before it leaves the station. Take the time to figure out how your child learns best, and realize that it's natural to have a few false starts before you settle into something you are both happy with.

Early math

Early math is well handled through games, counting songs, and whatever math comes up in life. Jamie T is taking a low-key approach by working with her three-and-a-half-year-old daughter on shapes (circle) and numbers (one to ten). Manipulatives are great, but do not have to be specially built for the purpose (e.g. Cuisenaire rods, although they are nice). Legos, blocks, or other countable, sortable toys also make early math tangible and fun. Adding little dabs of nontoxic colored glue or puff paint to craft sticks can make "counting sticks." Dividing up a pie and talking about it as you go can help to introduce early fractions, and using measuring spoons and rulers are other everyday methods of talking about numbers. There are heaps of learning toys (mostly battery operated) that help with early addition and so forth, and even many traditional family games (cards, dominoes, board games, darts) are wonderful for encouraging mental math. There are very simple and fun early-grade worksheets, but if your young Asperger child balks at putting pencil to paper, don't turn it into a nightmare control issue. Use another approach – perhaps internet computer games.

Math curricula (from vendors)

At some point, though, parents do start shopping around for organized sequential math material – usually a textbook or a series of workbooks. Whatever one you try, you may need to adapt it to make it work for your child. A few popular series are evaluated below, but it's more important that you be able to spot potential troublespots so that you can make your own choices. Here are some common problems families have noted, along with suggested solutions when it comes to math books and kids with AS.

COMMON PROBLEMS WITH MATH CURRICULA FOR OUR KIDS

- *Problem*: the child gets upset because there are too many problems, too many colors, or too much chaos on the page. *Suggestions*: cross out problems, or cover all but what is being worked, or transfer problems onto plain paper, or choose a different program.

- *Problem*: there is too small a space in which to write. *Suggestions*: have child dictate to you, or use separate paper or whiteboard.

- *Problem*: child enjoys or needs more review than book provides. *Suggestion*: supplement. Use online math sheets or make up problems in order to provide extra review.

- *Problem*: child balks at doing review problems. *Suggestions*: if child truly understands the math, ease up on review work. If you suspect he needs review, try to make it fun. Race with him or use a computer game or perhaps a reward system.

- *Problem*: child has trouble lining math problems up on the paper. *Suggestions*: graph paper, or turn lined paper sideways to make columns.

- *Problem*: child needs you with him constantly during math work. *Suggestion*: this may be a general trait of your child, or maybe work is too difficult. A computer curriculum may give him the feedback he needs, or he can be taught to check his own work.

- *Problem*: child does not want you around or gets upset when you correct a wrong answer. *Suggestions*: a computer program may give feedback he accepts better, or give him the answer key to check, or teach him to check his own work. Also, work on perfectionism (see Chapter 9).

Favorite math programs

Here are some math programs that met with approval. Your views may differ.

SINGAPORE MATH

Parents like the cleanly presented pages and more opportunity to do some of the work in one's head than with other programs. This can be a boon for kids who hate showing their work every time. British spelling, metric system, and Singaporean money are used. American moms I consulted did not feel that those factors detracted from an overall good program.

SWITCHED ON SCHOOLHOUSE

Presented via computer CD, this program pleased many computer-happy kids. Quick feedback and keyboard work rather than pencil work are two reasons kids liked it. It's also easy on the parents. Bible-based curriculum may be a problem for some (Grades 3 to 12).

MIQUON MATH

A K–3 manipulatives (Cuisenaire rods) approach, built on the premise that a child can make math discoveries on his own (although it requires an involved parent to aid in this). Surveyed parents who used it liked it mostly as a supplement to other programs.

SAXON MATH

Some folks in the survey liked Saxon Math for its incremental approach and copious review. However, just as many parents felt it "bombed" for their kids with AS. It may be best suited for children that enjoy drills and worksheets (some of our kids do). The predictability of presentation may appeal to ritual-based kids, but volume of work overwhelms others. It's interesting that so many families used this program, possibly because it's extremely popular among "regular" homeschooled kids, but comments were definitely mixed. Look at sample pages or try before buying, if possible. If you can order through a school, look into the Saxon adaptive workbook.

HORIZONS MATH

Used by a few parents of our kids with good results. The major criticism was (again) that it featured too many math problems per page for some. It is for grades K–6.

OTHER MATH PROGRAMS

Other programs mentioned favorably were *Ray's Arithmetic, A Beka* (Bible based), and *Touch Math* (you touch numbers as you work with them). *Math-U-See* was mentioned twice but neither family stuck with this program. See Chapter 8 for notes about math for the older student.

Miscellaneous math comments

Marietta writes: "Math has been a fairly constant special interest in my son's life. I fill him up with math books, math computer games, handheld electronic math games, etc., as well as talk about math a lot in our everyday life. He enjoys math games on the Cyberchase website" (Robby, 5).

Jenn: "We use math worksheets or math computer games. Manny's obsession is *Star Wars* and lately *Spiderman*. I sometimes incorporate them into his math story problems (which he loves). They are more the carrot dangling on the end of the stick when he has trouble focusing and wants to quit!" (Manny, 6).

Lise: "My son had difficulty with estimating. To his way of thinking, saying anything less than the right answer didn't make sense" (John, at 9).

Melissa: "He hates writing down the problems. He does them in his head, and doesn't want to have to show his work" (Scott, 10).

Elizabeth N: "We used Singapore math last year. Math is something we both enjoy, and it worked well for us" (Eric, 11).

Jackie: "We used computer-based curriculum for all subjects this year. I did have to do a little modifying and some writing of math on paper. Nancy's special interest at this time is a TV show on PBS called *Cyberchase*. It is a cartoon show to teach kids about math concepts, with many interesting characters that she likes. I am trying to make a schedule for this special interest, otherwise she will just start in talking about it any old time she feels like it... Mostly [this past year] I would incorporate it into her math lessons for any concept that overwhelmed her when she looked at it on her own. I would break down the steps into a story problem involving the characters from *Cyberchase*. This usually helped her" (Nancy, 11).

Nicki: "I found a discount house where I buy grammar and math. We use a worktext, games and manipulatives" (Mark, 11).

Margaret W tells first of her 11-year-old daughter Michaela's experience in public school and then describes how homeschooling and adapting work for her daughter has made a difference:

> She was making As and Bs, but her math scores were often 50s and 60s. I...realized their idea of adapting for her Aspergers was to cut the number of problems without spreading them out on a page, and add points to her scores so her grades were high. She was supposed to do math in a resource room, but often said she had to sit through the other children's lesson. She began to think she was stupid. I reached the end of my rope with the school system.
>
> We use Saxon Math with the Adaptation Workbook (available through a school. I used my umbrella school)... This workbook leaves more room for problems, provides reference sheets...and does things like draw guidelines to keep columns straight. My child needs these adaptations for math, her most challenging subject. The repetition of Saxon is good, but sometimes I have to

highlight which problems to do because some days she simply can't handle the volume of Saxon. Her public school teachers were planning to give up entirely on division. I let her do it on our whiteboard, lots of blank space and *big* numbers. She can do problems on the board that she cannot keep straight on paper.

Diana R: "We use a textbook for Saxon math, which I...teach step-by-step. He needs immediate feedback in math... I have to say, though, that I am doing *no worse* than his teachers and he is much calmer and happier now" (Neal, 12).

Nedra: "We have tried about everything for math... I like Singapore Math the best because the pages aren't cluttered" (Will, 11; Jake, 15; and Mike, 17).

A unit study / special interest approach to math

Don't forget that a special interest (snakes, dishwashers, whatever) can be measured, weighed, or compared, and collections of things can be graphed and values estimated. Events can be timed, places mapped, mileage calculated. Movie/TV heroes can be used for story problems.

Unschooled math

"Schooled" math seems so orderly that it's hard to think of unschooled math. Yet the following offering, written by an unschooling mom, may be all you need to spark a lifelong love of unschooled math.

"A FEW WORDS ABOUT UNSCHOOLING MATH," BY LUZ SHORE

Freedom to choose: fingers and toes, pattern blocks, two by two, 4×4, narrow gauge, ruler, tape measure, scale, model, profit (loss), earn, spend, save, interest, checkbook, recipe, batting average, Captain May I? Soccer, baseball, basketball, love, fault, birdie, strike, spare, first and ten, penalty box, map, compass, Pokemon, Candyland, Monopoly, Go, Chess, Sorry!, dominoes, dice, poker chips, Bridge, Crazy Eights, Go Fish, graphs, charts, Origami, mileage, knit 1 purl 2, weave, weigh, motor, engine, pulley, ratio, odds, chances, statistics, average, more or less, even, odd, yards, N scale, circumference, volume, area, score, speed limit, braking distance, fourth dimension, sixth sense, Indy 500, build, plan, rate, estimate, predict, revise, garden, yardage, height, depth, angle, trade, straight, curve, spiral, high tide, low ball, tempo, quarter note, half pound, temperature, weather forecast, bargain, budget, price, half off, plus tax, sequence, seven percent solution, hundred percent markup, latitude, longitude, light years, escape velocity, precession of the equinoxes (oh Best Beloved), range, set, stitch, sort, size, tally, calculator, plot, dozen, gain, lose, exactly, approximately, income, borrow, allowance, loan, design, diagram, knots, beads, gear ratio, minutes, degrees, timer, computer, fathoms, grid, meters, Anno, The Number Devil, half pipe, quarter turn, double time, full bore, safe speed, turning radius, blocks, stacking, nesting, measure up, scale down, abacus, credit, debit, limit, infinity, first class, third rate, equal share, short shrift, waxing, waning, phase, rhythm, balance, cycle, magnitude, perspective, value, graph, apogee, perigee, frequency, rotation, revolution, dollars, cents, pennies, wooden nickels, full deck, full house, double helix, time zone, millennium, program, binary, generation, epoch, era, nanosecond, code, puzzle, calendar, fiscal year, progression, midpoint, watts, lumens, horsepower, Ohms, Great Circle Route, '52 Pickup, '55 Chevy, Hundredth Monkey, altitude, make change, Lego, shopping, Tangrams, Battleships, Fibonacci series, checkers, speed, width, length, volume, sphere, output, displacement, schedule, time limit, collection, add up, count down, age, four score, last full measure, census, Are we there yet? Dance, a bushel and a peck, postage, efficient operation, elegant solution, gigabytes, google, Powers of Ten, increase, decrease, supply & demand, links, contour lines, Great Divide, Bingo!, group, air pressure, count down, stock market, daily log, rent, bills, discretionary income, arc, Dewey Decimal System, #510 Stone Circle, dosage, grams/ounces, meters/feet, 16 mm, 22 caliber, shutter speed, f stop, 20 pound test, dot-to-dot, orienteering, yield, squared, low bid, etc. etc. etc.

(Printed with permission. For more on unschooling, see website: www.borntoexplore.org/unschool)

Some favorite math websites

- www.homeschoolmath.net/123-math.html

- Online math games: www.primarygames.com/math.html

- Math Fact Café: http://mathfactcafe.com

- Worksheet creator for math:
  http://superkids.com/aweb/tools/math

- Free Math Help: www.freemathhelp.com/worksheets.html

- Free math worksheets: http://interactivemathtutor.com/

- Math lesson plans: www.col-ed.org/cur/math.html#math1

- Math proficiency tests:
  www.hsas.org/faculty/ozdemir/optpractice/

- Math Nerds free math help: www.mathnerds.com/

- Algebra Help: www.algebrahelp.com

- Changemaker: www.funbrain.com/cashreg/index.html.
  The game depicts coins for USA, UK, Australia, Canada,
  Mexico (you choose).

- Specifically UK math sites: www.primaryworksheets.co.uk/
  and www.teachingmoney.co.uk/

Other sources

- *Math games*: Rack-O, Yahtzee, Monopoly.

- *Homemade math games*: Math Bingo, Math War, Fraction
  pizza, Clothesline math, Egg Carton math, etc. (See Chapter
  6 for instructions on all of these.)

- *Computer games*: Math Blaster (Davidson), Math Workshop
  (Broderbund), "Tycoon" games (various) and other
  simulation games.

- *Math-related TV shows*: Cyberchase. See the website
  http://pbskids.org/cyberchase/

- *Fun math books*: STATS, Math Made Fun, by Don Fraser.

- *Math texts mentioned in this chapter*: see Appendix 7.

Social studies

In this section, we'll discuss the sorts of social studies taught in younger grades (see Chapter 8 for older grades):

- The community
- Other cultures
- Current events and historical events
- Geography.

The community

In primary school years, our kids typically discover their community and the people in it. Children's books feature policemen, mailmen, grocery stores, etc., but Asperger kids also benefit from actually being out in the community. This brings us to a mundane but surprisingly pertinent topic – doing errands.

THE ERRAND

It's tempting to leave difficult kids home with a spouse or sitter in order to do errands in peace. Harried parents do deserve a bit of peace. But errand running is a huge piece of what coping in society is all about and it should be part of homeschooling, especially for our specially wired kids. We all hope and expect our kids to become functioning members of the community as teens and adults, so that means being able to cope with ordinary daily living. This means things like shopping, renting videos, sitting in traffic jams, choosing from 30 kinds of cereal at the store, dropping off laundry, pumping gas, picking up prescriptions, returning a purchase, crossing a busy street – all need to be taught. It means that parents need to model, discuss, and rehearse. With the social and sensory challenges that our Asperger-affected kids have, it is also a bigger job than one might suspect, which is why I so strongly advocate making tiny inroads of progress now. I know more than one teenaged or young adult with Asperger Syndrome who refuses to go anywhere, can't navigate a city street, won't leave a message on someone's answering machine, or gets upset in a shopping mall. Do not just assume that one day your child will "get it." It comes from gentle and repeated exposure and patient practice.

Kids may resist, for reasons of sensory overload or the memory of a bad day – having panicked, acted out, and gotten yelled at by someone during past trips. To change this outcome, try to change your perspective and turn it from an errand into a child-focused life lesson. Try these steps:

- Go out when your child is fresh.

- Make the trip about your child, not the errand.

- Remember to explain to your child beforehand what to expect and stick to your plan. Explain as you go, also.

- Don't cram in too many errands at once.

- Keep your child's sensory limits in the front of your mind.

- Leave before a problem starts, so that the trip, as a lesson, can be successful, even if you didn't finish the errand itself. Keep it positive.

- Make the trip worthwhile from the child's viewpoint. A treat or park break is great, and don't necessarily save it until the end. Use it as replenishment rather than a maddeningly elusive reward.

Chances are, after working in this manner for a while and building on small successes, you will have the reward of a functioning child (and you'll get your groceries).

As a last step, write it down in your school records as "social studies" or "life skills" or whatever seems to fit, and celebrate the valuable lesson it is.

Other cultures

After learning about one's own community, next comes studying other people's culture – food, clothing, family life, geography, animals, customs, art, music. This is handled well through unit studies. Our kids often already have a special interest that is a location – I've mentioned my son's love of Japan. Other AS-affected kids have been enamored of such places as Australia, London, Canada, Egypt, or other.

If your child does not care about a particular country, perhaps an event, animal, or thing can be used to spark interest in another culture. An obsession about the Olympics could lead to a study of Greece. One boy's passion is lizards – why not study how these creatures are protected in one country but eaten in another?

TEACHING SOCIAL SKILLS THROUGH OTHER CULTURES

When talking about customs of other lands, it's a great chance to slip in lessons about manners in your own country. For example, in some cultures it's impolite to show the bottom of your foot to anyone. Perhaps a parallel might be that westerners consider it impolite to point one's finger at a person. Some cultures use fingers or chopsticks to eat, but we only use fingers for eating certain things, and so forth. Other topics include:

- differences in body space

- clothes

- greetings

- eye contact.

In this way, you can impart social information in a neutral, non-threatening way. In doing this lesson, you may be surprised to find out how much your child doesn't know about his own society's expectations. That's okay. Finding out this sort of thing is one of the reasons you're homeschooling him. Just start where he is and move forward.

Current events and historical events

The subject of social studies is more than "who did what and when." It also is a study of "why" and that's the hardest "W" question for our kids. People and their motives are eternally baffling. Societies differ in their views on things too – who is correct (and why)? Often two or more sides to the same story or issue emerge. Why do countries go to war? Why is this leader bad but that one good? Why should this country be allowed to fish for whales but not that country?

Because so much is subjective, there is a grayness of issues that can mystify the black and white thinking patterns of the child with Asperger Syndrome. It forces discussion of why people think the way they do. With the theory of mind issues (difficulties with understanding what other people think or know or feel), such thinking is strenuous exercise.

The success of our kids in life will depend in part, though, on being able to put themselves in other people's shoes and recognize other people's wishes, thoughts, feelings, and reasons for doing what they do. Our special kids are not likely to "pick up" this realization by osmosis or intuition, but certain improvements in this area can be made by working on it intellectually. My own son at 19 years old is much more able to do this than as a youngster. I like to think that it's at least partially because of the many conversations we have had along these lines.

Of course you don't have to work on theory of mind issues in this way. Working them in everyday life is even more important. But if it seems reasonable to you, you could try one or more of these in the course of your social studies work:

1. *Role playing.* After studying an event, role play it with your child. For example, you could re-enact the first American Thanksgiving, taking turns being the Pilgrims and the American Indians.

2. *Role play by proxy.* Turn popsicle (ice lolly or ice block) stick armies against each other; enlist help from puppets, action figures, and dolls. Or follow history by moving small markers around on a map. Nedra tells us that much of the history she has taught her three boys was via little Lego people. The exact characters are up to you or your kids. Use whatever captures interest and prompts discussion.

3. *Impersonate history.* Have your child focus on one person. Let him wear a piece of clothing or hold a prop to make the lesson more meaningful. Ask him questions that he might answer as if he were that character.

4. *Debate.* After you've studied an issue, let your child choose a position and defend it. Now, switch positions. Again, this is hard. Keep it short and gentle but make sure the message gets across ("Now think like the other guy").

5. *Lists.* Listing the pros and cons of an issue helps your child see more than one side. Let your child dictate while you write to keep the focus on the social studies, not handwriting issues.

Keep in mind that for our kids, adopting the mindset of another person is an invitation for them to give you a blank look or even shut down. You may be disappointed at the lack of success in this area, in fact, because it is one of the subtle but debilitating parts of Asperger Syndrome. Try to keep any such exercise light, short, and fun, and be willing to do the motions yourself so that you can model the thought process needed. With patient work and sufficient information from us (as opposed to just asking leading questions), our kids can start to develop a useful intellectual procedure for thinking beyond themselves.

Geography

Geography is a passion for many of our kids. At least one of the families surveyed had a child participate in the National Geography Bee. My own son absorbed phenomenal amounts of geography as preteen, playing Microsoft's Flight Simulator computer games. He not only learned where countries were, but cities, mountain ranges, rivers, and various landmarks, not to mention the locations and runway orientations of individual airports. When he re-entered the classroom in junior high, his geography teacher asked me, "How does he *know* all this stuff!" In fact, she asked me twice. I think it bothered her that he knew so much.

The computer game "Where in the World is Carmen San Diego?" is also a great game for learning about geography. We found that it required the use of atlases, almanacs, and mom's help at times, but that's okay.

Geography can also be an interest in maps, trails, and so forth. Ruth's son Jordan, the avid hiker, is keen to discuss maps and map reading with his father as they hike. Marietta's son's special interest in hiking trails, trail signs, and maps allowed her to introduce him very early (age 3) to map reading and topography. Vicki S plans to turn this year's family vacation into a learning experience by having her son follow maps through Colorado and chart mileage and estimate distances. Our kids often learn best when there is a real-world reason for doing it, so this is a great exercise.

Another way to use maps is to start simple and build. MJ adds blank maps to her social studies program. Her son Peter fills in features and place names as he learns about them. This is a better technique than giving a child a very busy and cluttered map.

Map reading is another intersection where academics and life skills meet. Sometimes our kids can have extraordinary difficulties without this skill. When my son returned to school in grade six, I thought he would have no trouble navigating the small school, which had only two main halls. One day, weeks after start of school, he was found by a teacher, inexplicably lost. It turned out he'd been following one particular boy from class to class all this time, and when the boy was absent, he didn't know what to do. After that, I helped him practice reading both his class schedule and a map of the school. I also informed him that it was okay to ask any adult for help.

Remember Sandy's son's problem in navigating his neighborhood, despite years of living there (Chapter 3)? She worries because he is still unable to get to the local shop and back. It's hard to know what is going on but a few possibilities occur to me. Perhaps she assumed, as I did about my son and his school, that he would pick it up on his own eventually, and she is now alarmed to see that he still hasn't. We often find out the hard way that a certain lesson has not been learned by osmosis. If that's the case, he may need direct teaching to help him identify landmarks, and/or work with a paper map of the neighborhood.

He may also have a mental map that needs to be corrected. Perhaps he pictures parallel streets but reality has literally thrown him a curve, so intersections don't work out as he thinks they should. Seeing it on paper may help. Or perhaps he's tried to navigate by landmarks, but chose ones that changed. "Turn right at the blue car" doesn't work if the car has moved. For three years, I used a mailbox as a signal to turn into a friend's street and when it was moved, I became disoriented. Where do I turn? Our kids can be very detail oriented and when details change it's hard to recover.

Maybe this boy hasn't thought about any of this. He assumes he will always have someone to walk with or to go to the store for him, and so why worry? The status quo is comfortable. His mom may need to push things a bit. If mom "forgets" to buy this or that for him, the benefits of being able to go to the shop on his own will be clearer. A few of us have been amazed at what our kids can do when we find ourselves laid up or sick and our kids must do things they would not otherwise do. Perhaps mom can take to the bed for a few days and let the groceries run low?

I am only brainstorming here and have no special insight, but I do hope this mom continues to encourage her son and work with him.

What survey families suggest for social studies

1. *Textbook, computer research, props.* Margaret W uses the A Beka (Christian) program for her daughter but the 11-year-old daughter loves to look up various research topics on internet or on her computer encyclopedia: "This year we're doing world history. She's really enjoying looking up different countries. She was born in Germany and we have souvenirs of a couple of European countries around the house. She did the lesson on the Netherlands wearing wooden shoes."

2. *Good reference book.* One mother writes: "I didn't have to do anything for history, his *Usborne Book of World History* is tattered with use. The child knows more about world and US history than I do!"

3. *Field trips, unit study.* Sarah has been using a formal computer curriculum for most subjects this year, but next year plans on getting away from that for science and history to make room for field trips and more child-led interests.

4. *Wide reading (especially biographies), notebooks.* MJ prefers "real books" to textbooks. Her 13-year-old son enjoys being read to, and she encourages him to keep a history notebook. Vicki, who favors an eclectic approach, worked on American history this past year via assorted workbooks and reading books. She says that she probably spent more that way than with a single textbook, but that was okay with her. LeAnn presents history to her 13-year-old son via biographies and historical fiction. Reading the biographies of historical people who were different in some way can be very helpful when it comes to talking about your child's own differences. Rather than feeling "defective," your child may feel a kindred spirit with other bright and intelligent people – scientists, writers, artists, mathematicians, etc. – who were misunderstood or in some way did not fit in. We all need heroes. Thomas Edison resonates for many kids because he was a different sort of thinker. His teacher called him "addle-brained" so his mother homeschooled him.

5.   *Timelines.* You can add structure to the whole thing with a timeline. Sources for timelines include internet (see History Mole website, below), books, buying a pre-made timeline, or building one as you go. Some ideas for building your own timeline are in Chapter 6.

6.   *Movies.* No survey family mentioned using movies but there are lots of good historical ones out there.

You never know where an interest in history will lead. Marilyn's son (17) has a special interest in history, as does Lucy's son (17), who has made a love of military history into a career goal. Some more history resources for older students are included in Chapter 8.

Favorite social study websites

- Kid-safe encyclopedia, almanac, dictionary, and atlas: www.factmonster.com/index.html

- Blank outline maps of all the countries and continents of the world: http://geography.about.com/library/blank/blxindex.html

- Australian history: www.kidcyber.com.au/. Also click on "People and Places" for simple biographies and social studies information on other countries.

- Australian maps: www.ga.gov.au/map/images.html

- Easy-to-understand explanation of European Union (EU): www.kidcyber.com.au/ (click on "People and Places")

- History with a UK flavor to it (includes history from all over): www.schoolhistory.co.uk/images/schoolhis.gif and www.spartacus.schoolnet.co.uk/

- What happened in history? Calendar: www.readwritethink.org/calendar/index.asp?date=7/1/2003#

- Online games for learning US states and presidents: www.primarygames.com/social_studies.html

- The History Mole – fascinating timelines cover themes such as botany, chemistry, various wars, and lots of British history. Each event is linked to more info: www.historymole.com/

- Historical movies, lists names of movies according to subject: http://mentura.com//DVDRentals/Homefires.html

- History of the US in ten minutes (short animation): www.animatedatlas.com

Favorite books

- *Usborne Book of World History*, by Jenny Tylor and Gee Robyn.

- *The Little House* books by Laura Ingalls Wilder.

- Biographies of all sorts.

- *Collins Atlas of the World* (high quality, modest price).

Computer games

- Where in the World is Carmen San Diego? (Broderbund)

- Oregon Trail (Broderbund)

- Amazon Trail (Broderbund)

- Museum Madness (MECC).

Science

Science – wildlife, nature, weather, geology, the elements, etc. – is all around us. Look up and you see clouds, look down and you see the earth in its glory. You may live near a lake, the ocean, a forest, or a mountain. We all live in our bodies. You just can't miss science, and kids are curious about it. Easy, right? The early years of science are filled with discovery, observation, and wonder. Parents can homeschool effectively with just a few basic supplies.

Once you decide to do anything very in-depth, however, it quickly gets more challenging. There are technical terms and procedures for each science specialty, as well as big numbers, higher math, memorization, and challenging concepts. How does that affect our homeschooling efforts? It perhaps explains why parents typically use field trips and unit studies and an eclectic collection of workbooks and hands-on experiments during the younger years, but turn to a more textbook approach in the upper grades.

How we proceeded (early years)

I used basic reference books, activity pages I found here and there, and a book of experiments by Janice Van Cleave. She has written several kid-friendly experiment books. Beyond that, I bought kits from the toy store. We had a volcano kit, a radio-building kit, and electronics kits. I noted with satisfaction that my son, who had performed way below grade level in the first half of grade two in school, was able to master electronics kits with no trouble as soon as we began homeschooling. He followed schematics, learned about diodes and resistors, and patiently worked through the delicate wiring (astonishing for a boy with poor fine motor skills). Enthralled and left at peace to follow his interest, he completed every experiment in his 30-in-1 electronics kit. He was particularly pleased at having built a motion-detector burglar alarm. When my napping husband woke up and opened the bedroom door, we all found out how well it worked.

When John reached fifth grade (our last year of homeschooling), he requested to study chemistry. I found an elementary book on chemistry and we read it together; made up "molecules" from toothpicks and balls of clay; and I purchased an elementary chemistry set for him. He also continued with Van Cleave's experiments throughout. There were days when the kitchen counters were strewn with homemade litmus paper – tiny strips of paper dyed with purple cabbage juice and left to dry.

Ironically, one reason we elected to have John re-enter a traditional school was my increasing fear that I was short-changing him in science. His interest was pronounced, and what did I know about it, anyway? What about equipment? We toured the local school and found that it had an array of high-tech goodies with which we could not compete – not only a science lab, but banks of computers, a satellite system, weather equipment, and a greenhouse. For that reason, as well as others, we did decide to enroll John into the school. The reason for bringing this up here is to point up my mistake. I fell for a shelf of techno-toys, most of which John never got to use, touch, or even see while he was in that school. In fact, he was in tears after his first science lab where their task had been to put celery into dyed water. He had done that experiment years earlier! This boy had taken science seriously while we were homeschooling and had embraced it for the sheer joy of exploration and learning. No wonder he was distressed to see the plodding and joyless nature with which science was presented at school. Also, the teacher postponed tests repeatedly because the class wasn't ready or he wasn't. My son wanted to get on with it.

So, as you plan your homeschooling adventure into the world of science, do not sell yourself short just because you do not have the knowledge or equipment of a scientist. Educator John Taylor Gatto castigates schoolroom science as "memorizing science vocabulary, repeating well-worn procedures certain to work, chanting formulas exactly as they have been indoctrinated to chant commercials from TV." He continues: "Anyone who thinks school science is the inevitable precursor to real science is very innocent, indeed" (Gatto 2002, pp.67–8). He notes that the origin of most major scientific discoveries have not been in academic or government laboratories, but in people's garages, basements, and attics, with cheap, simple equipment.

From this, I maintain that at worst we homeschoolers can admirably keep up with science teachers in having our kids memorize science vocabulary and conduct a standard set of traditional experiments. At best we can fire the imaginations of our kids and give them the time, freedom, and passion to grab one or more of the sciences by the collar and shake everything they can from it. After all, we've got garages, basements, and attics too.

The Asperger angle for science
INTENSITY AND SAFETY

Our kids can get very hooked on science topics, and we should be ready. In their single-minded enthusiasm they may end up going at a faster pace than we planned for, perhaps doing three experiments in a day instead of one, or taking things into unknown territory by changing the variables of an experiment. Since I tended toward caution and followed the book whenever we had a book to follow, uncharted territory was uncomfortable. I had to remind myself that it isn't always important that the experiment works but that it teaches something, whether through its success or failure. But we do need to be aware of safety in all of this. A visual checklist of safety steps is a good idea for our kids, and do stay close by. Even a barometer had potential for problem in our household. I thought it was great when my AS son put a barometer into a large sealed cardboard box, made a plastic "window" in it so he could read the barometer, and sucked air out of the box with a vacuum cleaner. He turned on the vacuum and was thrilled to see air pressure drop inside the box. A little later, though, he'd convinced his little brother Jay to join the barometer. He did have a safety procedure set up, however. His little brother was to keep tapping on the box until he passed out! I doubt that Jay was in truly serious trouble, but one never knows.

BRINGING IN OTHER ELEMENTS

Science can become a gateway to math, reading, and writing. It demands fine motor work in many cases and even offers sensory experiences. The study of science also has social implications. (Are we better off with certain technologies?) Therefore, as with other disciplines, we parents should be ever conscious of opportunities.

FEARS AND PHOBIAS

Science crosses into scary areas at times, such as bacteria, viruses, AIDS, cancer, diseases, natural disasters, dangerous insects or animals, chemical or biological warfare, nuclear weapons, organs and surgery, or mortality in general. This can be an area of concern for all children, but there is a somewhat higher incidence of anxiety, phobias, and obsessive thinking among those on the spectrum versus the general population. From my observation, it is generally, and most logically, "real" fears that seem to bother our kids the most – not aliens, ghosts, or monsters, but things that really can harm people. Their method of dealing with it is typically to get "stuck" on the topic, and ask a million questions (or the same question a million times). Somewhat paradoxically, it might become a special interest.

Parents should just be aware of this. For example, if you get involved in a discussion about the dangers of tornadoes, also be ready with safety measures and statistics on how rare they are. Knowledge is power for our kids. Also, ask if a certain subject worries them. Our kids can worry and not tell us. Alternatively, you can avoid certain problem topics entirely. Sarah C's son loves his science book, but Sarah tapes the edges of certain pages together if she feels he's not ready for that topic (the topic of sex fits in here, too).

Science curricula comments from surveyed families

No commercial science program got high marks. Two moms did seem well pleased with the computer curriculum *Switched on Schoolhouse*. One noted that it has been helpful since a lot of science was beyond what she had had in high school. Of the folks who didn't like it, one parent found the computer curriculum too rigid for her nine-year-old. Another mom found that her daughter struggled with the science, although other subjects in this curriculum had gone fine. Jackie said, "I discovered she needed more hands-on instruction and discussion in science. Plus, I had to find a way to make what we were studying in science interesting for her."

Sonlight Curriculum got mixed reviews as well. One family was happy with it, Elizabeth N noting that the science portion came with a musical CD for learning various systems of the human body. "This appealed to my son's musical interest and his ability to memorize the song words easily." However, another mom tried Sonlight some years back and found it too demanding. She is happier with *Apologia Science*.

Lastly among the published courses mentioned, Margaret W has used an *A Beka* science course. She found the language used in the book a bit over her daughter Michaela's head, even though her daughter had had the subject matter the year before.

Please note that all of the above curricula have a Christian focus. Those who prefer a secular approach will need to make adjustments or look to other publishers. Core Curriculum homeschool supplier sells material from many secular publishers (see Appendix 7).

Other comments from parents about science homeschooling experiences

Wendy writes: "We read from a fun, colorful science book or do our weekly experiment."

Vicki: "Stephen's dad would do science every Friday with him."

Jamie: "We use everyday things around the house. We watch a spider in my kitchen spin webs, feed it, etc. Other examples are apples, nutrition, and teeth."

Melissa: "Pokemon characters (a special interest) were very scientific, and we discussed a lot of the principles of science when discussing those cards."

Sim G: "Sometimes we do science experiments or take day or weekend field trips... Most of the time, Alex (7) loves to do science experiments and make things."

Margaret W: "Michaela (11) is frightened by storms, but loves to do the weather forecast with the local meteorologists, and has put together a weather station to keep up with the temperature and rainfall amounts. During the height of this interest I found it easy to teach her anything that related to the climate of the earth."

Diane R:

> We use various books, magazines, kits, etc., for science. We also watch a lot of PBS, science and history channel programs. Neal (12) learns best visually. He loves videos and working with science experiments.
>
> Neal's special interests revolve mostly around science topics. He loves and reads about rocks, minerals, chemistry, biology, animals, natural disasters, geology, insects, marine biology, dinosaurs... He loves *facts* – anything in the *Guinness Book of World Records* is *important*! "Did you know...?" is a very often-used phrase around here. When we work on science experiments, I have him work out the math...and have him write his observations and predications. With the experiments, there are lots of opportunities to use pragmatic language skills and logic. We also work on being able to "work as a team" and plan things out. Lots of times we can incorporate some historical facts into the lesson.

A few families have found support for science in their local homeschooling organization. Nicki's son Mark takes a science lab and geology class (among other things) at his local co-op. Ruth's husband leads a homeschooler science group that her son attends. Lucy's son James has also attended a science club at the local homeschooling group. The children would take turns performing an experiment, explaining it. Lucy says that James likes hands-on activities in science as it made it less boring.

There were a couple of moms of younger kids who admitted to doing very little in science at this stage, partly because they have been emphasizing reading, writing, and math, and partly because of the intimidation factor of science. One mom confesses: "We don't do science…but I hope to change that soon… I really need to work on incorporating that into the curriculum next year. It's not natural for me. I'm a 'word' person (reading, writing)."

This mom needn't fear. At her son's age (six), just exploring and having fun counts as science. There are many things she and her son could do: take care of pets; visit a pet store; go on a nature walk; collect stones and try to identify them; count tree rings on a stump; collect different leaves; overturn a water glass over a flame and see what happens; take apart an old appliance; identify a constellation or two in the sky; pour vegetable oil onto water; watch nature shows on TV; plant a seed; chart the weather; notice a puddle get smaller on a sunny day; make a weather vein; examine an old bird's nest.

Favorite websites for science

- A good kid-safe encyclopedia: www.kidcyber.com.au/ (Aus). Click on "animals," "planet earth," "food and my body," "technology and inventions," and "space." The web page "classifying animals" could easily provide the backbone for a great unit study.

- Games, activities, and experiments:

  www.primarygames.com/science.html

  www.questacon.edu.au/html/activities.html (Aus)

  www.questacon.edu.au/html.star_lab_activities.html (Aus)

  www.questacon.edu.au/html/100_years_of_innovations. html (Aus)

  www.abc.net.au/science/play/ (Aus)

  www.csiro.au/helix/experiments/index.html (Aus)

- Science coloring book pages: www.enchantedlearning.com/ coloring/ (US). These can be used by older students, too. Clear pictures, labels, and information about heaps of animals, insects, habitats, life cycles, migratory patterns, and more.

- Science animations: www.brainpop.com/ (US).

Favorite books for science

- *Guinness Book of World Records*
- Dorling-Kindersley books
- *Magic Schoolbus* books
- *Big Book of Questions and Answers*
- *How Things Work*
- HarperTrophy's "Let's Read and Find Out" Science Series.

Favorite computer games

- Thinkin' Things (The Learning Company)
- Gizmos and Gadgets (The Learning Company)
- Museum Madness (MECC).

Favorite science suppliers (kits, microscopes, etc.)

- Edmund Scientific (see Appendix 7)
- Home Training Tools (www.hometrainingtools.com/).

Handwriting

Handwriting is a frequent stumbling block in three ways:

- *Neatness*: "Her handwriting is too big and messy to handle the close confines of most worksheets."
- *Speed*: "His handwriting is slow but neat."
- *Reluctance*: "Handwriting is still a huge obstacle for him." And "If he has to write the words he sometimes flops around and has a quiet meltdown."

Means or an end?

Our AS-affected kids often need to "draw" their letters in a conscious way long after it has become automatic for peers. For an inordinate length of time handwriting remains the end product of a big struggle, rather than a useful tool for creating some other end product (a short story or poem, for example).

Sometimes the unrealistic drive for perfection gets in the way. If a perfectionist child doesn't perform to his exacting standards, he might rip up the paper or become distressed (see Chapter 9).

A highly recommended program

There has been a diversity of opinion as to the best curriculum for many other subjects covered in this book, but on the subject of handwriting there is broad consensus. If you want to purchase a good program to help with your son or daughter's handwriting, the recommendation I heard over and over from parents was to use a program called *Handwriting Without Tears*. Developed by an occupational therapist and designed to work with multiple learning styles, it has earned praise from parents surveyed (see Appendix 7).

Cursive writing?

Our experience was that John's teachers told me they did not plan on teaching him cursive writing at all, because his printing skills were so poor. I didn't argue, but a couple of years later when we were homeschooling, my son asked to learn cursive. I picked up a basic hand-writing exercise workbook at the grocery store and he practiced a few lines of copy work every day. Since this was his idea, he led the way on this project, which helped his attitude immensely. I also let him judge his own work. I gave him a highlighter to color the letters, words, or sentences that he felt looked good, or sometimes I let him use metal-rimmed bingo chips that he could clear away with a magnetic "wand." (One could use paper clips and a magnet.) He enjoyed working with those things so it was an incentive to do his best work. So we proceeded, and gradually he learned cursive. These days, I would favor a handwriting style that simply joins printed letters together, rather than a true cursive or manuscript style.

Keyboarding/typing instead of handwriting?

Keyboarding is covered in Chapter 7. Keyboard ability has growing importance in today's computer age, but we can't assume it will take the place of all handwriting any time soon.

Ways to improve handwriting

- Have your child make loops and curves in the air. Large muscle control precedes small muscle control.

- Give your child water and a paintbrush and let him make letters and designs on a fence or sidewalk.

- Encourage your child to use whiteboards and markers, or blackboards and chalk, or large paper and pencil.

- Provide daily *short* practice with a simple workbook on handwriting or through journaling a sentence or two.

- Use a pen rather than a pencil to minimize fatigue, but some kids need a pencil so they can feel it moving against the paper. Pens are too "slippy" and do not provide enough nerve feedback for the child to feel what he is doing. Experiment with this.

- A short stub of crayon or pencil forces the proper grip.

- I recently read that the thinner the pen, the easier it usually is for young hands to handle. So why were we given pencils the size of tree trunks when first learning to write in school? I'm confused, so I will just say "experiment" with both fat and thin pencils. If thin works well, a Magnadoodle writing toy is a good purchase.

- Experiment with different widths of lined paper. Sometimes narrow paper and small writing may be easiest for our kids.

- A triangular rubber pencil grip, or piece of rough material wrapped around the pencil, can help keep it from slipping.

- Writing on a slanted surface can help. Prop up the writing surface with a board, or clip paper onto a closed binder that is slanted toward the child.

- One mom has started a "30-second writing" exercise that has proven useful. She challenges her child to write as many of a certain letter or word in 30 seconds. It's fun, she gets the writing in, speed is improved, and perhaps that "automatic writing" trigger will switch on sooner from such an exercise.

- Don't let handwriting problems stop the learning. In other subjects (science, language arts, etc.) work around the issue. Let your child do an oral report, let him dictate to you, do his work on computer, or other.

Handwriting resources on the net

- Handwriting worksheets:
  www.crosswinds.net/~rozalski/Handwriting_Worksheets
  . html

  www.handwritingworksheets.com/

  worksheets.teach-nology.com/language_arts/handwriting/

- Handwriting animation that shows the strokes involved: www.handwritingforkids.com/handwrite/cursive.html

Creative writing

We've talked about handwriting. Now let's talk about the creative process of forming reports, essays, and stories. Handwriting and creative writing are best tackled separately if either one is difficult for your child, and my research suggests that both may be difficult in younger years. To reiterate how difficult this process is, I think back to a college Russian class where I endeavored to write in this foreign language. Forming unfamiliar Cyrillic letters, worrying about spelling, keeping grammar in mind, all the while trying to actually say something, was a horrendous experience and caused me more stress than any other coursework.

It's much the same for our children. The mother of 11-year-old Nancy writes: "I think it was too hard for her to think about forming her letters and making her handwriting legible and focusing on the answers to her school work at the same time."

Even when you take handwriting (and spelling, etc.) out of the equation and move to such methods as keyboarding or dictating, the creative process of writing is difficult for many kids. Especially with fiction, they don't know what to write. I remember my son being asked to write something from the point of view of a horse. He wrote, "I don't know what a horse thinks because I am not a horse." That was the end of it.

We did work on creative writing though, and found a few things that helped. The most helpful lesson I learned was not expecting him to create something out of thin air. He needed some ingredients with which to work. If your child is like this, the following ideas may be helpful:

- *Fill in the blanks.* Use "Madlibs" or an equivalent. This is a book of pages where the structure of a story is provided but the child needs to fill in blanks (nouns, verbs, adjectives). These can yield quite humorous results and can be read as a story once completed.

- *Computer games.* We used to have a very old and no longer available computer game that allowed the creation of a comic strip. The child could choose the characters and background, then fill in speech bubbles to make a story. Reader Rabbit 2 is another game that encourages writing activities.

- *Magazine pictures.* I kept a box of magazine pictures I thought my son would find funny or interesting. He would choose one and talk about what might be happening, and then I would help him write it down.

The message here is that our kids can work to a structure much better than to a blank page. As a child progresses and becomes older, the structures can become more demanding. Perhaps the child can progress from filling in only a few words to filling in most words. Traditional techniques for brainstorming might also be used, such as creating a "web" of smaller ideas radiating from larger ideas, or listing out many small points and then clustering them together. These are used traditionally for non-fiction writing (reports, essays, and the like), but fiction writing may improve from these techniques too. Do not be afraid to treat this process in a methodical way at first. A story might be created by asking for one sentence about the time of day or night, another about the setting, another sentence describing the character and action, and so forth. It may sound as charmless as directions on the back of a cakemix box, but it's really not a bad way to start and your child may be grateful for some concrete guidance. Once your child has been successful in this "cakemix" way of writing, he will likely be able to loosen up and make the writing his own.

I did have the good fortune to talk with the mom of one 15-year-old teen with AS who is a very good writer. Since so many families confessed that this is a very difficult area for them, I'm afraid I pestered Sharon quite a bit, asking her for whatever ideas she had. She offered what clues she had and also asked her son Sam for his opinion on what helped him to enjoy and become good at writing. Here are the comments I received:

- "He has really always liked to write, since very early – about second or third grade. What I have noticed is that he writes about cartoon-like characters (talking animals, etc.) in 'social situations.' I really believe he uses his writing to work out 'social stuff.' (Another mom reported her son having written a puppet play for this reason too.)"

- "*Writing Strands* and *Learning to Write the Novel Way* helped Sam with organizing his writing. Early on it was very disjointed. These two curricula helped him. He even had his 'novel' copyrighted."

- "He has always of course been more interested in non-fiction. However, he does like fiction and actually wrote fairly good pieces in school."

- "I was *very* concerned about ninth grade English (distance ed program). The literature book had what I term very classic stories and difficult questions. However, the curriculum workbook took the kids, step by step, in how to read and analyze fiction. He has learned so much and is actually doing very well."

- "He has to write three reports per semester for US history. Topics are challenging. However, I think the above-mentioned resources helped him so much that, so far so good. His reports are not only put together well (he loves grammar so no trouble with mechanics!), but he actually understands analyzing!"

- "Homeschooling truly gave Sam the opportunity to write at length and I think that has been the key…time!"

- "Also I forced him to read fiction and to write book reports (instead of question and answer stuff) for me every year of junior high homeschooling. He had to read novels as part of our language arts block. In his spare time he almost always chooses non-fiction. Again, he read so many more novels than he would have ever read at school."

- "I think Sam's personality is really the heart of his desire to read and write. I guess the AS didn't totally take over what seems to be a natural trait. I actually asked him the question for you – when and how did he learn to write and why he likes it. He couldn't give me an answer except to say 'I guess it's just my personality.' However, I asked him about *Writing Strands* and *Learning to Write the Novel Way* curriculums and he said yes they helped – he liked the *Novel* one the best and felt it helped the most. So there you have it – straight from Sam."

Thank you, Sharon and Sam. One's affinity toward writing might indeed grow from one's personality, but early successes and good experiences as Sharon described probably helped sustain Sam's enjoyment of creative writing.

Personality is beyond our reach, but the rest of it might break down into these five components:

1. A sense of personal purpose.

2. Directions.

3. Time.

4. Practice.

5. Exposure.

A SENSE OF PERSONAL PURPOSE

Sam worked through social issues in his writing. Can you help find reasons meaningful for your child? (I'm again reminded of how energetically my son wrote to the Nintendo company with his ideas for video games. The ideas were fiction, but his purpose was real. He also composed many letters of complaint with the same vigor.)

Diane also mentioned that her young son needed a reason to write. She tries to come up with real-life reasons to write, but also had results with a simple reward system she used in the beginning. For 15 minutes daily, she asked for just one sentence in a journal. If completed, a sticker was placed in the book. Her son could periodically cash in stickers for money, and could earn extra stickers for more sentences. The technique is perhaps a step removed from finding a personal reason to write, but it can help a child over the initial hump of reluctance. Diane discontinued the reward system when it was no longer needed. Reward systems don't work for every child, but if it works for yours, her low-pressure example may be a good model.

Other possible reasons to write might include: a letter to a friend or relative; writing to a company with suggestions, complaints, or requests; entering a contest; submitting to a children's magazine for publication; or writing a letter to the editor.

DIRECTIONS

Sharon and Sam have suggested their favorite writing programs, but whatever materials you consider or devise for yourself, aim for concrete language and clear, precise directions. What do concrete steps look like? In grade 12, my son received low marks for "simplistic writing." The teacher suggested he try for more eloquence and sophistication. This meant nothing to him! He did not know what to do. I read over his paper and said, "You wrote 'big' six times in this paper, and that is boring for readers, so use 'big' only once and find five different words that mean 'big.' Do the same with the other adjectives and adverbs you have re-used. That will make your writing more interesting." Aha. A plan. With the precision of reducing fractions in math, John adeptly made the changes. His teacher was thrilled and his grade went up.

TIME

Time is homeschooling's best gift to our kids' writing. We don't have to rush our children to finish before the bell rings. We can ease off on difficult days, yet on another day when the creative juices are flowing, we can allow a child to write for hours uninterrupted.

PRACTICE

As in other areas, our kids gain from the chance to rehearse what they are learning. Present many chances to write and be successful.

EXPOSURE

Pleasurable reading, and eventually analyzing the works of others, is helpful. In-depth analysis is best left to older students. For younger kids, read to them daily.

THE FORMULA

So perhaps that is the formula: purpose + directions + time + practice + exposure = success in writing. We mustn't forget about personality, which may flavor the whole experience too. You may be noticing at this point that this all looks suspiciously like hard work, and yes it is, with few short cuts.

Grammar and spelling

Grammar doesn't seem to cause the angst for our kids that writing causes, possibly because it's rule based and regular for the most part, and usually there is a worksheet of sentences to do, so it's easy to see both what is required and when the work is finished.

One small warning: make clear to your child that some grammar is opinion. Where to place a comma is often debatable, for example. I know of one girl with AS who became very upset over exclamation points. She thought there were must be absolute rules about when to use them. Once she understood that their use is subjective and up to the writer, she was able to relax. Or maybe I should say, she was able to relax!

Spelling also tends to be a strong suit for most, possibly due to good memorization skills. Even in the relatively small sample of families I surveyed, a few revealed that spelling is a special interest for their child or at least he or she does well with it.

Favorite writing/grammar/spelling curricula mentioned by families

- *Learning to Write the Novel Way,* by Carole Thaxton

- *Writing Strands* (National Writing Institute)

- *Easy Grammar,* by Wanda C. Phillips

- *Spelling Power* (Castlemoyle Books; one parent advises that this is heavy on drillwork)

- *Harvey's Grammar,* by Thomas Harvey

- *Painless Grammar,* by Rebecca Elliott.

Note: most of these are available for multiple grade levels.

Favorite writing websites

- Wacky Web Tales (fill in the blanks to make online stories): www.eduplace.com/tales/

- SuperTeach grammar (has online exercises): http://webnz.co.nz/checkers/grammar2.html

- Mini-movies online, on topics of grammar and letter writing: www.brainpop.com

- The Five Paragraph Essay (for grade five through early high school): www.geocities.com/SoHo/Atrium/1437/

- Creative writing projects: http://faculty.washington.edu/chudler/writing.html (this site's writing ideas all center around the brain, which might please young science types)

- Kids Online Magazine – safe online mag where your kid's stories can be published (no pay though). It also has contests and accepts artwork: www.kidsonlinemagazine.com/index.html

- A collection of writing-related sites for kids: www.greatsitesforkids.com/gsfk/homeworkhelp.asp

Reading

Learning to read

The message is clear from reading experts and homeschooling parents alike – systematic phonics instruction should be part of any reading program. Phonics shouldn't be done in a vacuum, however, and it shouldn't be laborious or dull. Many phonics programs throw too much at you – too many lessons and rules, too much bookwork. As with math programs that you've learned to adapt, you can do the same with phonics. Doing zillions of incremental pencil and paper worksheets is not as important as simply learning the rules and patterns, in whatever way is most palatable.

One important thing to know is that the words most likely to "disobey" the rules of spelling and pronunciation are our most common words – sight words. Rule-bound kids (and that means many of our AS-affected ones especially) may encounter terrible frustration if the rules they've been told to use don't work. So it's important to present this concept and identify words that you just have to memorize rather than decode. I used to tell my son "that word is trying to fool us!"; the idea that he needed to outsmart these gangster words that won't follow rules appealed to him.

When I worked with my son on reading, my materials were simple. I had a paperback book by Rudolph Flesch called *Why Johnny Still Can't Read*, which furnished incremental word lists in the back. There were no pictures here and no story, just word lists. We went through a partial list daily. It took two minutes. To that, I added Reader Rabbit computer game, a couple of activity books purchased from Kmart, magnetic letters for the refrigerator, and a lot of reading aloud to him out of Dr Suess and other children's books. That's it!

Most of the ideas for encouraging reading are well known, so I'll just mention a few of them.

1.   Read to your child every day.

2.   Model real-world reading (street signs, recipes, directions, labels).

3.   Let your child see you reading.

4.   Take trips to the library.

5.   Give books as gifts.

6.   Don't be impatient. Early readers and late readers can all be good readers.

Other Asperger considerations to reading

As you read to your child, you may notice:

1.   *He may listen differently.* He may appear to not be listening, while in fact he may be hearing everything. Staring away from people often helps our differently wired kids to listen better. Pausing to chat about different elements of the story will let you know what is being absorbed. Even if little is being absorbed on a particular evening, it is still worthwhile. There is comfort to the ritual that will help your child enjoy reading.

2.   *He may obsess over the same book night after night.* Repetition is comforting, but if it becomes too rigid and unproductive, don't try to stop reading the old book cold turkey. Start also reading something else and do both for a while. That may help fade out the first book.

3.   *Something to occupy hands or bodies can help.* A bit of clay to squish or bendable figure can keep hands busy, while a beanbag chair, hammock, or swing, rocker, etc. can help work off any excess energy in a quiet way.

4.   *Encourage visual perception.* Play with puzzles and books such as Where's Waldo (UK Where's Wally), hidden picture activity sheets, or spot the differences between two pictures. Play "I Spy" with things you see around the room or during a nature walk. Enjoy optical illusions and 3D art. Also see some of the websites below.

OTHER IDEAS TO HELP READING

- A ruler or index card helps a child find the line he's on when reading.

- Experiment with colored acetate (plastic) over the reading material. A color such as green or yellow can cut the glare a child experiences from black print on white paper.

- Take turns reading, by the sentence, paragraph, or page.

- Have your child read short, fun things – a note on their pillow, a scavenger hunt clue, a joke or riddle.

Favorite books from surveyed kids (in age order, young to old)

Pat the Bunny, *Berenstain Bear*****, *Beowolf* [sic], *Ferdinand the Bull*, *Arthur* books, Richard Scarry books (*Best Book of Words Ever, Book of Things that Go, What Do People Do All Day*), *Illustrated Encyclopedia of Trains, Leo the Late Bloomer, Monster Mama*, Dr. Suess books****, *Your Potty, Blue's Clues* books, *Lego Readers, Are You My Mother?, Where the Wild Things Are* (and others by Sendak), *The Cat Who Wore a Pot on her Head, Terrible Toy-breakers, Thomas the Tank Engine, Hank the Cowdog, I Love You Forever, Goodnight Moon, Brown Bear, Mr. Penguin's Poppers, Aardvarks Disembark, Read-Aloud Treasury* (nursery rhymes), *My Bible Friends, Andrew Lost* series, *Curious George, Charlotte's Web, Zack Files, Calvin and Hobbes* cartoon books**, *Amelia Bedelia*******, *Little House* books (Wilder), *Madeleine, Henry Huggins* and *Ramona* books** (Cleary), *Crow Boy, Pippi Longstocking, Wayside Stories* (Wayside School series)*, *Boxcar Children***, HarperTrophy's Let's Read and Find Out Science Series, *Encyclopedia Brown, Heidi, Phantom Tollbooth*, Dorling-Kindersley books (non-fiction), *Five Children and It* (E. Nesbit), *Indian in the Cupboard, Chronicles of Narnia**, *Harry Potter*, Pick-the-ending mystery stories, Mythology***, *Star Wars* books, *A Wrinkle in Time, The Hobbit, Hardy Boys, Lord of the Rings*, Dave Barry humor, *The Lost World* (Conan Doyle), *Big Book of Questions and Answers, How Things Work*, Bug identification books, Comic books, Text books, Encyclopedia**, Julius Caesar, Short stories by Edgar Allen Poe, Various military history books, *Atlas of WWII*, All things scientific – especially weather, human body, dinosaurs, robots.

Magazines

Your Big Backyard, Zoobooks, Wild Animal Babies, computer magazines.

Bible choice

Marie recommends New International Readers Version (NIRV) of *The Bible* for its short words and sentences that makes it very understandable.

NOTES

- * indicates a book having been named multiple times, once for each *. *Amelia Bedelia* was the most popular book, followed by *Berenstain Bear* books, Dr. Seuss books, and mythology.

- Note how many of the books listed are straight non-fiction, or have non-fiction or academic elements to them, such as the *Little House* books, the Bible, and Greek mythology books. This preference is typical for our kids. Even *Encyclopedia Brown* has a non-fiction, crime-solving element as well.

- Social stories figure prominently. *Berenstain Bear* books, *Arthur* books (also the PBS show of the same name), *Amelia Bedelia, The Cat Who Wore a Pot on her Head*, and *Pippi Longstocking* are full of social missteps, lessons, and literalness our kids seem to love. Mythology is full of social lessons as well. Many parents felt their child identified strongly in books such as *Leo the Late Bloomer*, and the boy in *A Wrinkle in Time*. One mom feels such a connection between books and her daughter that she asks everyone who meets her daughter to read *Crow Boy* and *Ferdinand the Bull* to understand her better.

- *Pat the Bunny* is a sensory treat (soft fake fur).

- Reading choice and chronological age have no relationship to each other. Six-year-olds are poring over encyclopedias, and 16-year-olds still chuckle over a children's book. One three-year-old threw tantrums until his dad read him *Beowolf* every night and by the tender age of five has already worn out an illustrated encyclopedia of trains.

- Repetition works. One boy has read *The Hobbit* 27 times; another is on his third copy of *The Atlas of World War II*, having worn the other two out. A five-year-old's history book is in tatters. There were many other comments of re-reading the same books many times and the comfort of a book in times of stress.

Reading comprehension is covered in Chapter 8.

Favorite early reading websites

- This Little Explorer Dictionary of phonetic sounds, illustrated and linked to activity pages: www.enchangedlearning.com/phonetic/

- Online animated easy reader books with sound: www.starfall.com/

- Free phonics worksheets (UK spelling): www.copiable.com

- Alphabet letters to cut out and use: www.activityvillage.co.uk/ alphabet_and_number_strips.html

- A sampling of free worksheets keyed to UK Key Stage 1 literacy (basic phonics): www.firstschoolyears.com/literacy/litsheets.html

- Alphabetization: www.learningplanet.com/act.abcorder.asp

- Literacy lessons, UK Key Stages 2/3 (years 4–7): www.literacylessons.co.uk/

- Activity ideas incorporating phonics: www.literacyconnections.com/WordStudyActivities.html

- Online games for kids learning to read: www.primarygames.com/reading.html

- Some links for lesson plans (grades 1–8): www.enchantedlearning.com/siteindex.shtml

Physical education

I was puzzled by a report I read several years ago that, if true, indicated that a fair percentage of AS kids actually enjoyed PE (at school!), sometimes even rating it as their favorite class. How could this be, I wondered, when PE is a sensory assault on every level, with whistles blowing, projectiles flying, and jostling, screaming, sweaty kids involved in complicated team play – in short, all the worst things? PE class is notoriously the cause of meltdowns and raging for our kids, where aides are needed the most, and where our kids shut down, act out, get sidelined, or get hurt. What on earth could any of our kids like about it? But PE does have three things going for it from a child's perspective:

- physical movement that all kids seem to crave

- learning a new skill to master

- being able to play with other kids in an environment that is safer and more organized than the bully-prone playground.

From a parent's perspective, there's no reason why we homeschoolers can't provide all of these good parts of PE for our kids, while happily avoiding the worst parts. In addition, we can add in another component of physical education that is important for our child's future – improving deficit areas that are part of our child's special wiring. Depending on the individual child, those issues could include clumsiness, muscle strength, balance, or other.

This section will talk about these things and how to provide them. It is somewhat of an extension of Chapter 2 where we discussed accessing outside physical therapy and also how to address some fine and gross motor issues via everyday life activities. But in this section we take a closer look at establishing a proactive physical education plan in your homeschooling day. Read from Chapter 2 and this section for the fullest picture. Here we'll cover:

- physical education activities families have found most successful

- possible problem areas for the AS-affected child

- specific deficit areas and how to work with them

- other tips, notes, and resources.

Physical education activities families have found most successful

1. ACTIVITIES WITHIN THE FAMILY

- Trampoline
- Swimming
- Playing catch
- Batting practice
- Shooting baskets
- Calisthenics

- Yoga
- Brain Gym exercises
- Playing on a swing set
- Bike riding
- Baby splash pool
- Skateboarding

These homespun activities were by far the most popular among families surveyed. Each activity takes only one or two people and involves no complicated game rules or group dynamics. The child may go at his own pace and spend energy on the activity itself rather than on the environment. Any social interaction is likely to be comfortable and within the family.

Joanna Rae describes her physical education plan for five-year-old Aiden and I include it here because it has such a lovely, relaxed feel to it:

> We do lots of playing outside – balancing on the rocks that line our gardens, throwing anything, [playing] catch, tag, hide and seek, writing with chalk on the driveway…found a pedal go-cart, which is working much better than a trike or bike with training wheels as it is impossible to fall and he is less anxious while he works out the mechanics of pedaling.

2. LESSONS OR LOCAL COMMUNITY ACTIVITIES

- Karate lessons
- Gymnastics lessons
- "Sport Tikes" class

- Swimming lessons
- Bowling leagues
- Running (track) club

Although taking lessons has a social component, most of these activities are still rather individual – that is, not a team sport. Bowling requires teams but the players on the team do not interact physically. Karate lessons have physical contact that can be a problem for some kids, but much of it is learning ritualized moves without contact.

3. ACTIVITIES ORGANIZED FOR HOMESCHOOLER GROUPS

- Weekly skate nights or open bowling
- Homeschool non-competitive ice hockey
- Homeschool general PE class
- Homeschool gymnastics
- Homeschool skiing.

Although these activities are not formed for special needs kids, they often work well for our kids because the activities tend to be closely monitored by parents, are non-competitive, and include kids of all ages and abilities.

4. OPPORTUNITIES SPECIFICALLY FOR SPECIAL NEEDS KIDS

- Therapeutic horseback-riding (hippotherapy)
- Martial arts class for special needs kids (AS and PDD-NOS)
- Little League Baseball (Challenger Division)
- Special Olympics.

See further discussion of some of these options under "Other tips, notes, and resources."

Possible PE problem areas for the AS-affected child
THE FAILURES

The lists above show some things that have been successful for our kids, but by no means is each activity suitable for every kid. Many of us have had PE "flops." Sim G reports that her Alex (7) was unsuccessful at both karate and gymnastics: "Most structured physical education programs have not proven beneficial at this time, due to social misunderstandings. Therefore, we are teaching Alex these things ourselves at this time." (My son did well on his own at home using karate videotapes, but when he tried an organized class, he became upset by the body contact and had to quit.)

Our kids are often reluctant participants. They may have difficulties with the activities and often don't like to take risks or put themselves through a new sensory experience. If you don't explain what's going on to a coach or instructor, this can set the child up for failure when he is asked to exceed his limits. However, when you do explain things it doesn't always help either. Some parents have felt their child was made a scapegoat, or the coach backed off the child entirely so that he was never encouraged to really try. However, a good and compassionate coach that is tuned in to your child (whether or not he knows about AS specifically) can bring out the best in him.

SENSORY/SAFETY

Specially wired kids can have difficulty monitoring or "feeling" their bodies. If your child wears sweats in hot weather, or runs around in summer shorts in the winter, you may have such a child. When it comes to sports, parents of these kids need to pay special attention to the following:

- They can get overheated or chilled and not notice.

- They may not drink and eat enough. Two parents commented that their kids often needed to be reminded to eat.

- Your child may not sense overexertion.

- Your child may not notice that he is even injured.

AS children can have a surprisingly high pain threshold. More than once, I have been appalled to see broken blisters on my son that looked so painful it was amazing to me that he hadn't felt them earlier. Sometimes he's been surprised to see blood oozing through his sock where his shoe had rubbed his skin away. Thomas's mom reports a similar lack of sensory awareness in her son. She writes:

> Sensory issues for Thomas (15) mostly involve temperature and learning to plan to take a jacket along. The other issue is that he becomes hungry or fatigued, and doesn't realize it until it is at a crisis point. So we are trying to teach him procedures to follow, such as, "you need to eat every few hours during the day" or "after a strenuous activity comes a rest/relaxation time." He's at an age

where we are trying to allow him more freedom to plan his own day. We're trying to prepare him to eventually live independently.

Specific deficit areas and how to work with them

As a reminder, I am not a physical therapist. Please consider the following as only suggestions by an interested mom who reads a lot and confers with other parents. Please do your own research and consult a professional if you deem it necessary.

HYPOVESTIBULAR ISSUES

When a child doesn't receive or process enough information about the pull of gravity on his body, he isn't able to sense what he needs to do to maintain equilibrium. Someone with these issues generally has low muscle tone, low body awareness, poor balance, clumsy movement, and lack of success in sports.

The good news is that the very movements the child seeks out – such as spinning – are what can help the situation. You can help or encourage your child with the following:

- spinning – try a merry-go-round, Sit-N-Spin toy, spinning in the yard

- swinging – swing set, tire swing, glider, or hammock

- jumping – trampoline, mini-trampoline, or jumping jacks

- changing directions – play tag or do an obstacle course that changes direction

- rolling – rolling downhill, being rolled in blanket

- tumbling – somersaults, monkey bars

- rocking – rocking chair, rocking horse

- accelerating/decelerating – sprint races, one-on-one basketball, tag.

BALANCE ISSUES

If your child seems to have problems with balance, try some of these:

- walk heel-to-toe as on a tightrope

- do above action backwards

- try above with eyes open, then closed, arms out, arms above the head

- walk a pattern made from chalk on the driveway – circle, square, zigzag

- play hopscotch

- play Twister

- walk the edge of a wooden planter box or along a curb

- make a low balance beam from a 2x4 piece of wood on two phone books

- use a Kangaroo Hopper or a Tilt Walker/Wobble Board

- play Follow-the-Leader weaving around stuffed animals, rocks, books

- balance (sitting, lying) on a large ball

- balance on one foot, eyes open, then with eyes closed

- find a tile floor and step on only a certain colored tile.

PROPRIOCEPTIVE SYSTEM

This is the part of the body that tells you what your muscles, tendons, and joints are doing. Children who have trouble judging how much force is needed to do something may have proprioceptive problems, as do those who have no hand or foot preference for doing activities, aren't aware of space, run into things, or have trouble doing two-handed things. Compression helps children with this problem to better feel things within the body:

- have your child carry heavy books, groceries, yard refuse, carry out garbage

- have your child push strollers, wheelbarrows, carts

- roll your child snugly in a blanket
- let your child sandwich himself under couch cushions, mattresses, heavy blankets (ensuring there are no breathing restrictions)
- lay carefully on top of the child as a part of roughhouse play
- wrestle playfully.

Other tips, notes, and resources

BIKE RIDING

Teaching your child on grass rather than sidewalk or pavement is helpful. Falling onto grass is less scary, and the bumpiness provides more body signals to the child so he can better feel the action of the bicycle.

HIPPOTHERAPY

For hippotherapy (therapeutic horse riding) in the USA, contact the American Hippotherapy Association, PO Box 4053, Scottsdale, Arizona 85261, tel: (800) 874-9191, email: ballen@americanequestrian.com.

In the UK contact the Riding for the Disabled Association, Lavinia Norfolk House, Avenue R, Stoneleigh Park, Warwickshire CV8 2LY, tel: (024) 7669 6510, email: rdahq@riding-for-disabled.org.uk.

LITTLE LEAGUE BASEBALL

Little League Baseball, Incorporated has a Challenger Division for players of varying disabilities, ages 5 to 18 (homeschoolers welcome). Generally, the parent decides whether or not the child should be in the Challenger Division. To learn more about it, see www.littleleague.org/programs/challenger.html. Little League Baseball is played in numerous countries. To find teams, see www.eteamz.com/llb/sites/finder/ or write to PO Box 3485, Williamsport, PA 17701, or call (570) 326-1921.

SPECIAL OLYMPICS

Special Olympics has been a wonderful outlet for one young lady whose homeschooling day includes participation on a Special Olympics swim team. Her mom writes:

> Tuesday and Thursday Michaela goes to swim team practice. We couldn't make this if she were in public school. Michaela is a very good swimmer. Her team competes in Special Olympics meets and she has qualified for the State Games this year. I almost hate to have her IQ re-evaluated, because she might not qualify to compete in Special Olympics anymore. Her IQ was barely low enough on her last evaluation. That team is very important to her. It's the first time she has found anything at which she isn't always last.

Eligibility for Special Olympics predominantly focuses on mental retardation or cognitive delays, or a "closely related developmental disability." While I was unable to uncover a specific ruling about Asperger Syndrome, if parents are interested in becoming involved they should give it a try. Contact Special Olympics, 1325 G Street NW, suite 500, Washington, DC 20005, tel: (202) 628-3630, website: www. specialolympics.org/Special+Olympics+Public+Website/default. html.

Music

Only about 25 percent of the AS-affected children reflected in my study took any sort of music instruction or participation, and the lion's share of that was through music lessons or choir. Part of the relatively low activity may be because the child shows little interest or even objects to it. My son's sensitivity to noise discouraged interest in music until he was well into his teens. Some sensory defensive youngsters get very upset at the sound of singing or certain instruments.

A second possibility is that homeschooling parents are more concerned with academic subjects. One mom admitted that she had been occupied with reading, writing, and math, and hadn't gotten around to music, although she indicated a hope to introduce it next year.

A third possibility is that the numbers indicated by my survey are misleading. Since a lot of music lessons and church choir take place outside a normal school day, it's possible that some families doing musical things didn't mention it as homeschooling.

Some AS-affected children do express an interest in music even from a very early age. Marietta writes:

> At age four, Robby's interests were math and computers and music and music history. I was able to incorporate math computer games, audio biographies of various famous composers, books about the orchestra, and musical instruments in general.

Joanna Rae's son (5) takes Suzuki guitar, and Elizabeth's son (11) plays trumpet and piano and attends church choir. Wendy teaches piano to her boys and they are in a church choir. Cathy would like her ten-year-old to be involved in music but is facing some challenges:

> With Jared's wiggliness, his constant narration of what he's doing, and his warbling, the only class I've enrolled him in is a younger kids' music class. The teacher said he didn't look that much worse than the other kids his age. Of course, he's 10 and looks 7, so she may have been comparing him to 7 yr olds. This coming year he's old enough to be in the select choir, but I plan to have him use the regular (open to everybody) choir as a transition because I don't think he could hold still enough to do select choir and its performances.

No one mentioned "music appreciation" as a subject, although it might be a nice addition to a homeschool day. Why not play music over lunch or during personal reading time? This could serve double-duty in exposing music of different types to the student, and also make a relaxed atmosphere. Some studies show that baroque music seems to enhance learning by increasing certain brainwave activity.

There are also ways to use music to learn other material. It was mentioned in the science section that one family has enjoyed learning about parts of the body through an educational music CD. Vicki has used a musical American history tape that highlights important dates and events through American history in song. She notes that her son Stephen seems to learn well through song. She adds: "And, of course, it's the kind of thing I can turn on anytime for some background music. Repetition is key."

Interesting music websites for kids

Warning: Turn down volume on your computer. Many of these sites feature a wide variety of sounds, some of which are squeaky, raspy, or in other ways harsh.

- Hop Pop Town – a great collection of music games for young kids: www.kids-space.org/HPT/menu.html

- Creating Music website – terrific (rhythm band site is fun): www.creatingmusic.com/

- An excellent collection of kid-friendly songs – lyrics and some tunes: www.kididdles.com/mouseum/traditional.html

- Another fun site – hear all the parts of an orchestra: www.playmusic.org/

- For a survey of classical music try: www.classicsforkids.com/

- Music site for young kids (UK): www.bbc.co.uk/tweenies/songtime/

- Printable staff paper for budding composers: www.freestaffpaper.cjb.net/

Art

Art offers our special kids outstanding opportunities for improving visual, fine motor, gross motor, tactile, and pragmatic language deficits, and has the added bonus that art can key in with any number of special interests and be accessed on any level.

Textbooks are not necessary. Working with the hands-on child, you can just enjoy doing arts and crafts of various types, simultaneously introducing one or two art terms or artists as you go along. For the book-lover child, libraries are great sources of gorgeous art books. Just enjoy the paintings.

SOME TERMS FOR YOUR HOMESCHOOL ART STUDIES

Color, primary colors, secondary colors, color wheel, tone, shade, intensity, texture, palette, easel, sculpture, still life, oil paints, watercolor, pastels, charcoal, pencil drawings, perspective, vanishing point, cartooning, light and shadow, shading, matting, etching, subject, background, foreground, pigment, wash, blend, landscape, impressionism, realism, cubism, renaissance, collage, primitive, medium, composition, Dutch Masters, abstract, draftsman, bronze work, art nouveau, art deco, stained glass, glass blowing, tessellation, Chinese Art, African Art, cave paintings, dada, Egyptian Art, Greek Art, romanticism, rococo, surrealism, symbolism, contour, pointillism, stippling, artist colonies, fresco, chisel, portraiture, patron, pen-and-ink, chalk, mosaic, wax-resist, folk art, casting, firing, kiln, thrown pottery, *scherenschnitte*, mural, panorama, Japanese anime, graphic art, comic book art, sketching.

ART EXPLORATION IDEAS

Sponges, string dipped in paint, wrinkle the paper and then paint the lines you made, stamping, printing, collages, tracing, see the effects of painting on different things (onto paper bags, cork, bark, corrugated cardboard, wood, canvas, etc.), using different other objects in place of paint brushes (rags, feathers, putty knife, sponges, sticks, squirt guns, spray bottles, rubber stamps, toothbrush, your fingers). Create your own rubber stamps using a craft knife and a pencil eraser (rubber). Explore sculpture using clay, sand, craft dough, bread dough. Try painting or sculpting with your eyes closed. Explore intricate paper cutting. Try pointillism with the eraser end of a pencil dipped in paint. Sprinkle sand over parts of a wet painting (or use glue). Try fresco painting (painting on wet plaster). Break tiles or dishes and make a mosaic of the pieces. Make pictures from dried seeds, pebbles, nature. Try carving from wax, balsa wood, or soap. Do beadwork with soft seeds, seed pods, shells, pasta, or beads you have made from clay, paper, etc.

Special AS considerations
VISUAL

Our kids can hyperfocus on small details and miss the big picture, quite literally. Enjoy that your child notices a tiny mouse in the corner of the painting, but also encourage seeing the whole picture as a scene. Discuss what is going on, what everyone is doing in the picture, and the overall effect.

SENSORY

Things that are messy – fingerpaint, glue, chalk, waxy crayons, charcoal, and clay or modeling compounds – can be either good therapy or a source of panic, depending on where your child stands on tactile issues. If you wish to avoid sensory panic but still do art projects, make some adjustments:

- Use paintbrushes or Q-tips (cotton buds) to paint.

- Try dot painting or pointillism with a pencil eraser or other object.

- Gradually, increase your child's tolerance of tactile substances. Let them deal with one or two fingers getting messed up before expecting whole little hands to be involved. Anyway, your literal child may point out that they wouldn't call it fingerpainting if they meant for you to get your whole hand messy!

FINE MOTOR

Start with bigger motions, and move to little. This applies to painting, coloring, scissorwork, etc. If doing beadwork, start with big beads and move to little.

FINGER STRENGTH

If your child has trouble using a pencil or if his hands tire when hand-writing, doing sculpting or molding can help increase finger strength.

OBSESSIONS

If your child draws or paints pictures by the hundreds (it happens with a special interest!), you may have a display or storage problem.

- Encourage giving away pictures instead of keeping every one.

- If your child draws something small on a large piece of paper, cut the drawing out and keep it only.

- Display pictures from hanging clipboards or clothespins attached to the wall, so changing pictures is easy.

- Encourage using a whiteboard, chalkboard, or Magnadoodle that can be used over and over.
- Take a photo of your child with his latest art project. After the thrill has worn off, keep the photo and give away or toss the actual project.

Other notes

1. *Cheap supplies*: calendars bought in February or March are extremely cheap and good sources of lovely artwork. They often feature the work of one artist, style, or theme (flowers, marine life, etc.). Yard sales, library sales, and secondhand stores are great places to find art or coffee table books.

2. *To view thousands of paintings, know your Google*: on internet, use google search capability (www.google.com) as follows. Click "images" icon before you type your seach term. For example, click on "images" and then type Monet. You will be treated to all the Monet paintings you could imagine.

Favorite art websites

- At least a dozen fun art games here: www.albrightknox.org/artgames/index_launched.html
- Great resource for kids to learn about artists (color your own Picasso): www.enchantedlearning.com/artists/coloring/
- A venue for publishing one's artwork online: www.kidsonlinemagazine.com/
- Explore Leonardo Da Vinci's studio: www.bbc.co.uk/science/leonardo/

Favorite craft websites

- Aunt Annie's craft site: www.auntannie.com/
- Easy Fun School – craft projects: www.easyfunschool.com/IndexArt.html

Foreign languages

Some of our kids can do surprisingly well in foreign languages, their difficulties with speech pragmatics or other communication issues in their own native tongue notwithstanding. Many kids, including my own son, have done fine in junior high or high school language courses. This seems especially true in the first two years of learning a language, where emphasis is on memorization of vocabulary, short canned phrases, recited scripts, and regular verb conjugation. None of these present hidden landmines for our Asperger-affected kids and, indeed, some of our kids genuinely enjoy their language work and excel at it.

Foreign language coursework may bog down in later years, when emphasis shifts to spontaneous speech and depends less on scripts. It's difficult for all kids, though, and in general our kids still can cope, even if their grades may dip a bit. In general, though, foreign language study as provided in the schools seems to work in schools.

Providing language study in the home environment has its own problems, however. I've seen less evidence of successful language training in home education than any other subject, although admittedly I'm working with a small sample and much of that sample represents children in younger years. It may not be fair to say that foreign language is the weak link in the chain for our group – but it could be. Things have probably improved somewhat since the Colfax family documented their homeschooling adventures in *Homeschooling for Excellence*, but their conclusion was: "If there is a lesson here, it would seem to be that there is no easy homeschooling road to learning a foreign language" (Colfax and Colfax 1988, p.93).

One problem seems to be that while it's easy enough to find resources to gain a very rudimentary exposure (some are provided below), it's more difficult and expensive to find good thorough materials if one is very serious. The most readily available and least expensive programs that you find in bookstores are generally for travelers and are unsuitable. My son and I naively launched into such a course in Danish, but I lost enthusiasm when I heard my son dutifully repeating the phrase for "May I have more ice in my Martini, please?"

The seriously academic programs that do look good often cost hundreds of dollars, well out of the reach of a lot of families. When budget is tight, French or Spanish lessons fall off the end. There are a couple of exceptions though, and I would call these "best bets."

- The computer-format course associated with Switched on Schoolhouse, which provides Spanish or French lessons at a reasonable price.

- The Ultimate French, Living Language Series by Barron Publishers. The set ($75) includes a 400+ page textbook and eight language CDs.

- Power-Glide language lessons have received favorable views from a lot of homeschooling families (not specifically AS related). This is a more expensive option, however.

If I were homeschooling a young child again on a budget, my personal tactic would be to make use of internet websites that offer some nice early language lessons, flashcards, and exercises. This can keep you going for quite awhile. After that, I would try one of the above options. Also see Chapter 8 for options for older students.

Favorite foreign language websites

- The Little Explorers Dictionary:
  www.enchantedlearning.com/Dictionary.html
  Picture dictionary that features several languages: German, French, Spanish, Swedish, Italian, Dutch, Japanese, Portuguese, and phonetic.

- Page of various foreign language activities:
  www.enchantedlearning.com/themes/french.shtml

- French lessons:
  www.frenchtutorial.com/education/french/index.html

- Spanish lessons: www.studyspanish.com/freesite.html

Chapter 6

Making Your Own
Learning Tools

This chapter is about creating homeschooling tools on a budget, using humble materials and a modicum of creativity. Many folks have to quit jobs or reduce work hours to stay home and homeschool a special needs child, and they often have extra expenses as well – things such as medication, doctor's appointments, therapies, and so forth. It doesn't leave a lot of extra money for buying extra things to supplement the homeschooler's day.

This chapter is also about getting used to the idea of making things up as you go along, using whatever works and discarding the rest. If you can make a little learning exercise out of a dime's worth of craft paper, you won't mind throwing it out if it's less than successful or if your child outgrows it in a week. You can also customize it often, every day, if you want to. You don't get that kind of flexibility if you've just spent $40 on some board game from an educational toy company, however. That game will be harder to bend to your own needs, and also a lot harder to abandon. This chapter contains ideas for the following:

- learning games
- items for sensory or physical therapy work.

Learning games

Learning games have much to offer the homeschooler. The prospect of a game can entice a school-phobic kid out from under the bed; can reinforce new learning without the tedium of yet another worksheet; and can liven up a rainy Monday when it's hard for parent and child alike to wake the brain up and start moving. Board games, card games, and other types of learning games can be made with humble supplies. The trick is not to stress over making it "look nice." Your homemade version will not look like a fancy commercial game, but kids honestly do not care about that. You can even employ them to help make the game, which can be a learning exercise in itself.

If you are thinking about throwing out old or incomplete board games, stop! Save the spinner, dice, and game pieces for use in your homemade games. You can even re-use the game board, by gluing down a new playing surface. Also, keep your eye out at jumble sales or yard sales for old board games. For a few cents, you can procure supplies to help in making your own games.

Card games
WAR

This classic card game is for two players. Each player gets half of a deck of cards. Turn over one card each, both at the same time. Higher card takes lower card. Repeat to the end of the half deck. Shuffle whatever cards you have "won" and go again through the cards. Eventually one person wins all the cards. If you both put down the same value card, this is "war." You lay down two more cards face down, and one face up. Whoever has the higher card face up wins all eight cards from that war.

- Addition War – played as before, but each time two cards are laid down, the winner must add the two numbers and recite the sum before picking up the cards. (You can remove face cards if that's easier.)

- Subtraction War – same as Adding War only you subtract the lower number from the higher before collecting the cards.

- Multiplication War – same as Adding War but winner multiplies the two cards he's just won.

- Negative Number War – same as Adding War but winner subtracts the higher number from the lower.

- Division War – same as Adding War but winner must add the cards together. If the sum is evenly divisible by a predetermined number (for example, three), then winner gets an extra card from loser.

MENTAL MATH CARDS

This is a sort of solitaire. Remove face cards from deck. Lay out five cards. Using mental math, see if you can do various operations on the first four cards, in any order, to reach the value of the fifth. It's a challenge!

CONCENTRATION

Pull out 12 pairs of cards and lay all 24 cards individually face down in a 4 × 6 pattern. They should not be in any order. To play, player one turns up two cards. If they match, he keeps them and takes another turn. If they don't match, turn is over and next player tries. The idea is to try to memorize the locations of certain cards to optimize chances of making a match. Person with most pairs at the end of the game is the winner.

- Phonics variation – use homemade cards and write simple words on them. Child must read each word turned over.

- Other word variations – instead of exact matches, go for pairs of cards that rhyme, opposites, states and capitals, or other sorts of pairs.

- Emotion Concentration – match pairs of faces that depict basic emotions. Use comics, hand-drawn, or copy the photo faces in Appendix 4. A pair might be two exact copies of the same face, two different faces but with the same emotion depicted, or a face paired with the word for that emotion.

Clothesline learning

Use clothespins and a clothesline to make a lesson more hands-on, as well as increasing finger strength. Review is easy – just take the items off the line and put them back up again. Here are ways to use the clothesline:

- Number line – write numbers onto wooden clothespins and put them randomly onto a string or narrow clothesline. Let your child put the clothespins in number order.

- History timeline – collect items that have to do with a lesson in history. Read the lesson and, when appropriate, hang the item on the clothesline. If talking about Ben Franklin, the items might include a newspaper (he was a printer's apprentice), and eyeglass case (invented bifocals), a bookmark (organized the first library), etc. Small or odd-shaped items can be placed into a plastic bag first, and items that can't be hung at all, such as a Franklin stove, can be represented by a drawing or card with the word printed on it.

- Other sequences of events – anything that can be presented as a sequence or series will work for the clothesline technique, for example books of the Bible, sequence of events in a novel, amendments to the Constitution, etc.

Games from paper or discarded items

The inspiration for many of these games comes from a well-loved book, *Garbage Games*, which, sadly, is no longer in print. Once I learned that games can be made from almost anything, it became easy to think up games out of whatever I had on hand. Here are some ideas to get you started.

CONSTRUCTION PAPER MATCH-UPS

Onto squares of one color paper, write vocabulary words (for example) and onto circles of another color, write the meanings of those words. Lay them all face up and let the child match up each square with its corresponding circle.

- Younger child variation – match animal names (cat/kitten, dog/puppy, etc.), rhyming words (book/look), opposites or homonyms (up/down, there/their).

- Older child variation – match states/capitals, countries/capitals; make compound words (milk/shake, mail/box); find equivalent fractions (2/3 = 4/6, etc.); or match Spanish vocabulary words with English meanings.

- Variation – cut paper shapes into something more interesting than squares and circles. Make pot/lid pairs, a stopsign to go onto a signpost, or other shapes (bat/ball, star/moon, clouds/lightning bolt, bowl/spoon). Your child could make "lollipops" if you use colored paper circles and wooden craft sticks (write the word right on the stick).

MENTAL MATH SNAKE

Cut a long straight "snake" from colored paper. Shape one end into a snake's head and taper the other end into a tail. Now, fold it up accordion-style. Open it back out and on each of the folded sections write a single-digit number, the sum of which will be the answer, which you will write on the tail. Your child will receive the folded up snake from you and unfold each section, adding in his head as he goes. At the end, he'll see if his adding is correct. You can easily make several.

FRACTION PIZZA

Cut five circles all the same size (approximately five inches across) out of different colors of paper. Leave one circle whole, cut one in half, cut another in thirds, another in fourths, and another in sixths. Mark each piece with the appropriate fraction amount on it, and let your child explore. How many half pieces make one whole? How many quarter pieces make one whole, or make one half?

"EGG-CELLENT" READER GAME

You will need an egg carton for this. Cut 12 egg shapes out of cardstock or paper. On one side of each, write a different word with a long "e" sound and on the other side write a word with a short "e" sound. Mix the eggs up and give them to the child. His task is to read each word and find the short "e" side. Then it goes into the egg carton until he has a full carton of eggs.

COOL FRACTION PRACTICE

Use an ice cube tray (or egg carton) and 12 small items (coins, pebbles, or other). Ask your child to fill up a fraction of the tray. Or you fill up all the compartments and have the child take out a fraction of them. Possibilities include 1/2, 1/3, 1/4, 1/6, 2/4, 2/6, 2/3, 3/4, 4/6, and more.

QUESTION BINGO

Make bingo game cards by drawing 5 × 5 grids onto cardstock. Cut out each grid. Each player gets one game card and enough small markers to cover up all 25 spaces. Use Cheerios, raisins, buttons, washers, or other. As questions are read out, any player with that answer on his card gets to place a marker onto that square. Play until someone gets five in a row, or play "black out" whenever grid square needs to be covered.

MULTIPLICATION BINGO

Multiplication answers (25, 36, 16, 10, etc.) are placed onto the game cards. A deck of homemade cards has the simple multiplication problems (5×5, 6×6, 4×4, 2×5, etc.).

- Dice variation – use answers of 36 or less on the game card and shake two dice to make the math question.

- Playing Card variation – use answers up to 100, and a deck of cards with no face cards. Draw two cards to provide the two numbers to be multiplied. Leave a joker in the deck to be a wild card.

- Fraction variation – equivalent fractions. Put fractions such as 1/2, 2/4, 4/8, 6/12, 1/3, 2/3, 6/9, 3/9, etc. both in the deck and on the game card. When a fraction that is called out is equivalent to something on a player's game card, he can cover that space.

- Rhyme variation – word called out must rhyme with something on the game card.

- Opposites variation – word called out must be opposite to something on the game card.

EMOTION BINGO

Write the following expressions onto random squares of a 3×3 bingo game card: Happy, Sad, Worried, Excited, Afraid, Embarrassed, Disgusted, Angry, Proud, Tired.

Match these with pictures of people who have these facial expressions. Use comics, hand-drawn pictures, magazine or newspaper pictures, photos, etc. You can also find clip art on internet.

This game is harder than it looks for our kids. You may be surprised to find out how much difficulty your child has with looking at a facial expression and matching it to its name.

Board games
GAME BOARD ONE

For an easy game board, color a path onto cardboard, paper, or a folded out manila folder. The path should be one to two inches wide and should be marked with several (perhaps 20 or more) lines across the path to make spaces in which the markers will move. Try one of these themes:

- Highway theme – make the path light gray, and lots of lines across that will be "mile-markers." Number each space. Use toy cars for markers, and make a small deck of "road signs" that tell player to move ahead, go back, etc. Directions could reinforce math facts ("multiply 2×2 and move ahead that many spaces").

- Racetrack theme – make an oval racetrack path, use small race cars as markers. Use spinner or dice for moves. Onto each space write a simple word that uses a short "e" – let, bend, pet, men, etc. The player must read aloud the word he lands on in order to stay. Make another racetrack of short "i" words, short "o" words, etc.

GAME BOARD TWO

Onto a large piece of cardstock or folded out folder, draw small circles. Connect these with a line, or number them, to make clear in what direction players are to move. Use dice to determine the moves, but each player needs to correctly answer a question from a deck of homemade cards before rolling the dice.

- Dinosaur theme – instead of circles, draw various rock shapes in neutral colors. Use plastic dinosaurs for the game pieces.

- River theme – use a blue background, then draw details that will turn the circles into turtles or fish. Do not connect circles. Use numbers.

GAME NOTES

You can make a game board appropriate for any learning situation by using a spinner or dice plus a deck of homemade question cards. Player spins or shakes dice, moves, reads a question from the deck, and if he can answer, he gets to stay. Or he could read first, then spin. Each child can have questions appropriate to him – early learners draw from a deck of simple words to read or easy math, etc. Older learners draw from a deck of harder questions. These cards can change all the time.

Miscellaneous activities
LEARNING JAR

For odd moments when you have nothing specific prepared but would like to keep your child engaged, have a cookie jar ready with slips of paper in it. On each slip, you will have written some activity appropriate to your child's level. Here are examples:

- Put one shelf of books in alphabetical order.

- Measure the area of our kitchen.

- Measure the length of your stride.

- Mix some juice.

- Call the local shop and ask what time it closes.

- Count the money in your piggy bank.

- Look up "cranium" in the dictionary.

- Call the pet shop and ask what an iguana eats.

- Guess how tall you can stack Legos before they fall, then stack them and see how close your guess was.

- Use the kitchen scale to weigh our dictionary.

- Count all the money in a game of Monopoly.

- Find Nigeria in the almanac.

- Find out what the Italian flag looks like.

- Practice eating dry cereal with chopsticks.

- How much does your cat weigh? Find out.

JOB JAR

Require your child to do one or two short life-skill jobs each day – sweep kitchen, clean a window, water plants, wipe counters, put clothes into the washer, vacuum, shake rugs, polish furniture, dust shelves, fold towels, organize one drawer. These should not be big, repugnant jobs but something that can be completed in a few minutes. If your child has difficulty using two hands at once, this is a good chance for some impromptu therapy.

Low-cost therapy items

Sensory "dig"

Fill a dishpan, baking pan, sandbox, or kiddy swimming pool with various substances that offer sensory experiences: sand, water, cornstarch, rice, styrofoam packing "peanuts," dried corn, buttons, flour, even mud. Bury small objects for your kids to find.

Homemade balance board

Wobble boards and rocker boards are commercially available items that are good for improving one's balance. The first item is a circular wooden disk with a rounded "bump" on the bottom. When you stand on the disk, it wobbles and you must find your balance. The second item is rectangular shaped, with a crosspiece underneath it that allows you to rock from side to side. They are available from various sports or therapy outlets (see Appendix 7).

For a frugal solution, why not try to make a reasonable facsimile, at least sturdy enough for kids? For a wobbly disk, cut a plywood disk (14 to 16 inches in diameter). Screw or glue a small rounded wooden shape (half a small wooden ball or half a golf ball might work nicely) onto the underside. The size of the ball determines the amount of wobble. A homemade rendition will likely be more crude and less lovely than a store-bought one, but all it needs to do is serve the purpose. Be careful to recess the screw and make sure that using it won't damage a floor.

For a rocking board, a rectangular piece of wood about the size of a skateboard should suffice, with some half-round doweling or other small piece of wood affixed across the middle on the underside. Or, how about an even simpler solution? An old skateboard minus the wheels and hardware can make a good rocking board. Add dowel to the bottom or just let the kids step on the upturned edges of the skateboard to make it rock. You could possibly even find an old drawer front and challenge your youngster to rock back and forth on its drawer handle; or just place a stick under a board and see how it goes for an impromptu version. The important thing is not how the thing looks, but that it provides some balance practice. Remember Joanna Rae's description of having her child walk along the rocks lining her garden (Chapter 5, "Physical education" section)? It wasn't high tech, but it fills the requirement.

Balance beam

A board an inch or two above the ground is sufficient to give our kids another kind of balance workout. Place it on two supports (phone books, perhaps, or scrap wood), to lift the board slightly off the ground. Depending on the weight of your child and the length of the board, you may want to add a piece under the middle as well.

Weighted vest

Some kids feel more "grounded" if they are wearing a little extra weight on them in the form of a weighted vest. You can buy one of these ready-made from physical therapy suppliers, or consider making your own version. Moms have told me to use a simple vest pattern or take the sleeves out of a shirt or jacket. Denim or other sturdy material is recommended. Sew some metal washers securely inside a bottom hem so that they don't show. Done. You don't need much weight, just a few ounces.

Creating your own homemade items takes time and effort but it's supremely satisfying to tailor learning games and therapy items to your individual child's needs. Also, saving money on these things may allow you more money to spend on some other aspect of your homeschooling program. Lastly, it can be fun.

Chapter 7

The Computer

Computers have figured prominently in this book. The ability to present lessons to our kids via computer programs or online websites is a singular boon to busy homeschooling parents. Parents also look to the computer to connect up with other parents. Email support lists can offer encouragement that parents can often find nowhere else. No one understands the concerns, or appreciates the small triumphs, as well as another parent who is on the same journey.

More than that, however, computers have earned an important place in the hearts and minds of our children. We have already discussed in Chapter 2 that the computer seems to work with every learning style and offers many perks that endear it to our kids – namely, it offers instant feedback, it doesn't argue with them, it repeats information as often as they need it, and doesn't complain if our kids feel the need to chatter, sing, hoot, or bounce. All of this is much more convenient than working with people, so it's no surprise that nearly every child represented in my research loves working on the computer.

In this chapter, then, you will find sections on the following aspects of computer usage:

- keyboarding
- kid safety
- internet search tips
- computerized curriculum options
- favorite websites for general teaching, general homeschooling, record keeping, etc.

Keyboarding/typing

Because of our kids' affinity to the computer and their general distaste for handwriting, the sooner our kids learn to type, the better most of them like it. Kids can learn to type in a few ways:

- while learning other things
- computer (CD-ROM) typing programs
- online tutorials
- typing manuals.

While learning other things

Youngest kids are commonly introduced to the computer via mouse-driven games, but it's not long before they graduate to games that require at least a small amount of typing in order to play them. Marietta's son is only five and just learning to print letters in a very scrawling fashion. However, she reports that "he does do *a lot* on the computer and he has been able to type long words from memory if they are game cheats like 'pepperoni pizza!'"

Some parents have found that their kids have painlessly increased their keyboarding skills (and also writing skills) through use of email and Instant Messaging (IM) over internet. Ruth reports that her son Jordan does occasional keyboarding in order to IM his friends. Because her son strongly resists formal writing, it is one good way she can encourage him in his writing.

Computer (CD-ROM) typing programs

Several families I contacted use computer programs that specifically teach keyboarding or typing. Sarah C's eight-year-old son uses a program called JumpStart Typing. One that is a bit less game-oriented but still has some nice kid-friendly features is called Typing Instructor. It offers a good basic program, but also does have a small selection of arcade-type games and provides a wide selection of music to listen to as you type (or you can turn this feature off).

The most widely used and recommended typing program, however, is the Mavis Beacon Teaches Typing program. It has been around for many years and is also probably the most widely available program. It's a particularly good choice for older children. All of the typing programs cost $30 or less. Margaret W writes:

> Michaela (11) loves typing. Her public school teachers... expressed doubt that she could learn to type fast enough to do her work during class time. When I began homeschooling two years ago, I got a copy of Mavis Beacon Teaches Typing, not even a child-oriented teaching program, and she took to it like a duck to water. She loved the lessons, and loved the games even more. I didn't have to teach her, just let her go with it and occasionally remind her to use the right fingers. By the end of last year her lessons timed her at around 25 words per minute.

Another typing program mentioned was called Timberdoodle Typing. All of the various programs that have been tried by the survey families seemed to do the job pretty well, and there are probably other good ones. For more information about some mentioned here, see Appendix 7.

Online typing courses

This avenue was somewhat disappointing. A simple Google search yields many hits on so-called free typing programs, but they are generally slow to load and offer only little dribbles of typing exercises that require paging through many annoying ads to navigate between the more useful bits. There were no free ones that seemed worth the effort to use them. One mildly useful website did offer a typing test available for free (www.learn2type.com).

Online typing programs that are downloadable for a fee are likely to be much more user friendly but none of the surveyed families revealed any experience with them. Most online programs are in the same price range as the CD-ROM programs recommended above.

Typing manuals

No one reported using a simple typing manual, but that's how most of the parents certainly learned, myself included. My mom handed me her old college typing book at the beginning of the summer I was 14, and by summer's end I had figured out typing. My mom put bits of masking tape over the typewriter keys to encourage me not to look at them, but otherwise there was no need for adult guidance.

There are several typing or keyboarding books available these days, and any decent library should have one or two on their shelves. My own city's library offers a dozen different ones. Even if you want something to own and use over a lengthy period, seeing what your library has can help you choose one you'll like. Some books are specifically for typing and others are for keyboarding, but if all you are interested in is the typing exercises, either one will do.

Final note: is it important for your child to use the correct finger placement on the keys? Years ago, I would have said yes, but both my kids use "alternative fingering" and both type like the wind. If they are learning via the "osmosis" method, it's probably best to let them type in whatever way feels comfortable, although it doesn't hurt to point out the standard finger placement if they seem willing to take it in. If they are motivated to learn in a more formal way (CD-ROM, online tutorial, or via typing manual), then part of that formal way would reasonably include starting with the proper finger placement. In the end, it's a good idea, but it needn't and shouldn't be a showstopper.

Kid safety

Here are three hints for keeping your child away from inappropriate material on the computer:

- Kid-friendly research is best done through a kid-friendly site (not Google). This ensures that your child won't accidentally access material that is not appropriate for him. Some are listed below.

- An even safer alternative for conducting research on the computer is to stay off of internet entirely and use an encyclopedia CD instead.

- Finally, and most obviously, stay close to your child to help him and monitor his activities.

A special word of warning is appropriate for our special kids with respect to online "netiquette" and safety. All children are at risk in this dangerous day of internet pedophiles and the like, and we need to be specially wary of any chat rooms our children enter. You can have a serious talk with your child and outline some hard and fast rules about not revealing any personal information, reporting anyone suspicious to you, and so forth.

A contract that you and your child can read and sign is available at www.safekids.com/contract_kid.html.

In the end though, our kids can be very naive and trusting. Nothing replaces keeping a sharp eye on your child.

Kid-safe search engines

- Ask Jeeves for kids: www.ajkids.com/
- Cyber Sleuth for kids: http://cybersleuth-kids.com/
- Yahooligans: www.yahooligans.com/

Internet search tips (for adults)
Google

Google is an excellent workhorse search tool on internet. It is fast and thorough, but to use it wisely you will want to be specific. Once accessed (www.google.com), type one or more terms to be searched. As mentioned in Chapter 4 on unit studies, if you are trying to develop a unit study on, for instance, frogs, you might want to take a shortcut by seeing what other people have already developed. Instead of typing "frog" into Google, type "frog theme unit" or "frog unit study" or even "homeschool frog" and see what you get. If you want to know about the frog's life cycle or how to dissect a frog, by all means add "life cycle" or "dissection" to your list of terms. You don't want to search through hundreds of websites.

HINT FOR SEARCHING OUT NON-US WEBSITES ON GOOGLE

For websites or webpages whose origins are other than the USA, go to the "advanced search" option. Fill in the blank for "domain" with an appropriate country suffix (for example, type ".au" for Australia, ".ca" for Canada, ".uk" for the UK, and so forth). You can also search specifically for images, or for documents, with the click of an icon.

Computerized curriculum or coursework
Full curriculum

There isn't a great deal of choice in computer-delivered homeschool curricula yet, but it's coming. The main deliverer is Alpha Omega Publications, which offers both Switched on Schoolhouse (CD-ROM) and also Classes2You (provided via web).

SWITCHED ON SCHOOLHOUSE

Switched on Schoolhouse has been around since 1997 and is currently being used by several of the families I contacted. Most have been pleased. One or two parents found a certain subject over their child's head, but with our kids' splinter skills, that's always a risk. It covers grades 3 to 12. Core subjects include Bible, language arts, math, history and geography, and science. There are also elective courses in Spanish, French, health, and a few other subjects. Courses cost in the region of $70 to $90 per course. There is a price break when you buy a five-course set. The learning approach is Christian. See their website (www.switchedonschoolhouse.com) or Appendix 7 for other contact information.

CLASSES2YOU

Classes2You was introduced in 2003 and is Alpha Omega Publications' answer to interactive learning. To the casual observer it seems similar to Switched on Schoolhouse with respect to grade levels offered and the overall approach to subject matter. As of this writing, math is not offered (they suggest you take a Switched on Schoolhouse CD-ROM math course) and there is not the range of electives (see the website www.classes2you.com/).

Individual courses via computer

There are individual subjects available both via CD-ROM and online offered by various companies, but it's a hit-or-miss proposition as to whether they will provide enough in the areas that may be important to a parent. Some of the issues you may be concerned about are:

- adequate course content
- level of explanation or teaching support
- accreditation.

Most CD-ROM software you find in computer stores are advertised as a means for strengthening skills, doing review work, or as adult (i.e. hobby) education, rather than being touted as a full academic course.

That may be adequate for your purposes, especially if you just want a framework to work from and don't mind supplementing it where needed. A few offer more rigorous content, however, and even formal testing and assigning of high school credit. Whether a given course will meet your needs depends on what you want.

The same may be said for individual online courses offered by commercial companies. My non-Asperger 15-year-old currently takes an online course that is right up his alley – Introduction to the video-gaming Industry. We accessed it from www.ed2go.com through our local city parks and recreation department and he is taking it simply for interest's sake. This is the same course that is normally accessed through colleges and universities for credit, however. One never knows.

Public school connection

For those American homeschoolers who don't mind affiliating themselves with the public education system while still educating at home, the K12 virtual school is making its way across the USA. It is still in its infancy, only serving ten or eleven states so far, but is predicted to grow substantially in the next few years. Through this program, students can still be a part of their local school district, but do their learning at home via the web. This option may appeal greatly to those who would like to get their materials (including loan of a computer) essentially for free, or for whom a complete divorce from the public school system feels too radical. K12 also offers a homeschool option that is not affiliated with the public schools and costs about $1300 per year. Both K12 programs currently offer coursework through grade seven. Grade eight and beyond is planned for the future (see www.k12.com for more information).

Also, many high schools provide their own online or computer-driven courses or offer more advanced high school courses via an arrangement with local colleges. Depending on local law or relationship with the school, your child might be able to enroll in one of these courses, either at home or through the school's computer lab. This is a particularly good choice for those parents interested in "sanctioned" or "accredited" coursework (for a listing of the many courses that are available online, see the website: www.bbc.co.uk/learning/courses/index.shtml).

General education favorite resources

This chapter would not be complete without listing a few favorite all-purpose learning or homeschooling sites. Some have been mentioned as a good resource for a particular subject, but their biggest strength is in being great in many areas simultaneously. Become familiar with these:

- Brainpop features two to four minute mini-movies, geared for grades five to eight, but many are useful for older students and adults. For younger audiences, I would suggest using the pause button often to explain things as needed, and skipping the accompanying quiz. As a visitor, you may watch two movies per day at no charge. For unlimited access, you must subscribe. Even without spending a penny, you can access experiments, comic strips, activity worksheets, timelines, and a how-to section to incorporate the subject at hand into everyday life. Subjects: English, 26 topics; health, around 60; math, about 50; science, over 100; technology (how things work), 30. Social studies topics are planned in the future:
  www.brainpop.com

- Kidcyber (Aus) is an online children's encyclopedia and a safe and interesting place for quick information, not only on Australian topics but also general topics of history, science, social studies, health, and so forth: www.kidcyber.com.au/

- Funbrain has pop-up ads when using it for free, but it has heaps of learning games for many age levels and lots of subjects. Don't miss the idiom game, Paint by Idioms: www.funbrain.com/kidcenter.html

- Enchanted Learning has an outstandingly large collection of activity sheets and little lessons:
  www.enchantedlearning.com/Home.html

- Personal Educational Press is a nice website for flash cards, worksheets, etc. You can use the ones already developed or customize your own:
  www.educationalpress.org/educationalpress/Index.asp

For websites *about* homeschooling (getting started, record-keeping, etc.), these have been very helpful:

- A to Z Home's Cool Homeschooling website: www.gomilpitas.com/homeschooling/index.htm

- About.com Homeschooling: www.homeschooling.about.com

- Free printable homeschool schedule pages (daily, weekly, monthly, yearly): www.chartjungle.com/homeschoolschedules.html

Chapter 8
Older Students

As children grow into their teens, things change. On an academic level, they progress into ever-loftier areas of knowledge and interest. They ask tougher questions now, and prepare to tackle topics such as chemistry, higher math, and other subjects that tend to put parents into a panic. How do we provide the learning they need? Will they graduate high school? Will they be ready for college or a vocation?

On a personal level, there are other changes taking place. Making friends remains a concern for the teen and even takes on increased importance, but the days of mom making all the arrangements are numbered. And of course, there are issues of increased independence, learning to drive, etc. As usual, there are lots of "whole child" issues. Additionally, our kids may be more concerned about the diagnosis of Asperger Syndrome and what it means to them.

As before, the homeschooling parent needs to keep two goals in mind – academic growth and personal growth. It's tempting for parents to fixate on the academics during this time, but there are still other big-picture items that we need to think about to help our Asperger-affected children get along in life.

This chapter attempts to handle many of these issues, both academic and personal. It's meant to be a supplement to things that have been covered early in this book, so if you started your reading with this chapter, you will want to also read the rest of this book for further hints and discussions. The remainder of this chapter will cover these areas:

- high school matters
- academic subjects

- some profiles of real teens
- "whole child" issues.

High school matters

Most homeschooling parents I surveyed didn't have clear ideas on how they would handle secondary school years when their children get to that point. About half said it was too far off to think about, and they just would have to see what life brings. Others had a sense that they would continue to homeschool throughout the high school years, but they didn't necessarily have a plan for doing so. Only one mom had things pretty well mapped out in her mind. Most only knew that they could not see their child fitting into the high school environment and felt homeschooling would remain the best choice.

There were a few families whose kids are already of high school age, however, so this chapter contains kernels of information from their experiences – what has worked or not worked for them. In a rather patchwork style then, we will cover the following topics:

- homeschooling style
- high school diplomas and other options
- building a curriculum
- entering community colleges.

Homeschooling style

The mix of homeschooling styles has changed somewhat for some of the families. Whereas they might have used informal means of education (unschooling or unit studies) more in earlier years, there now seems to be a shift toward more formal schooling choices. Part of this is due to the increased teaching demands of higher academic coursework and part is due to general parental anxiety over fulfilling graduation requirements or feeling the need for external authentication of work done toward that graduation. This wasn't the case with every family, however.

The most typical pattern of homeschooling in the high school years seems to be as follows:

1. A significant portion of coursework was done through a formal means, usually provided through a long-distance education school or accredited program. This is especially the case for subjects with a reputation for being difficult, such as higher math or science.

2. Some academic topics may still be provided through eclectic means – perhaps a grammar or vocabulary workbook has been added to beef up a weak area, or unit studies have been added to make a science course more tangible and interesting.

3. Extra "stuff" was added on a more ad hoc basis to round out a child's development, not necessarily for academic reasons. A teen may continue with piano lessons, or be doing a sport. Parents also reported continuing to work with their teens on issues such as becoming knowledgeable about Asperger Syndrome, life skills, or improving social/communication skills.

High school diplomas

The need for an actual diploma looms large on a parent's wish list for their child. But how does one get a diploma as a homeschooler? There are general homeschooling books and websites that can field this question better than I, so it will be covered only briefly here.

The important thing to know is that there are dozens and dozens of colleges and universities that will accept homeschoolers these days. If these institutions are not adamant about getting a traditional diploma, it is obviously not as all-important as we in the older generation have been led to believe. Fear about not getting an official transcript from a bona fide high school should not scare you away from homeschooling. Although having that real piece of paper is nice, there are many work-arounds or substitutes.

BUILD A HOMEMADE HIGH SCHOOL TRANSCRIPT, WITH CREDITS ASSIGNED BY THE PARENT FOR WORK DONE

If you are working on your own in true homeschooler fashion, there is nobody except you to translate your child's endeavors into high school credit. Speaking strictly from a US standpoint, a general guideline is to count 60 hours of work as one semester of work (or a half credit). A sample high school transcript is included in Appendix 6. I highly recommend the book by Cafi Cohen (2000b) where she goes into more detail on the mechanics of putting together a homemade transcript and many other matters having to do with homeschooling teenagers (not AS related, but good nonetheless). Her own website is also a great font of informative articles on homeschool teens and college (www.home schoolteenscollege.net/hsarticles.html).

TAKE TESTS FOR COLLEGE-BOUND STUDENTS

The most common of these are the SAT, or ACT, tests. SAT II tests may also be required in certain subject areas to prove proficiency and to take the place of a diploma.

TAKE CLASSES AT A JUNIOR OR COMMUNITY COLLEGE

Many community colleges are "open enrollment" and/or offer a dual enrollment program where kids who are still in their high school years may take courses and count them as credit for both high school and college. Once a student is already going to school at the community college, the issue of a formal high school diploma is probably moot, and the new body of work at community college level becomes the credential for moving on to university studies.

Australia works much the same way. Homeschooled kids who have completed year ten can typically enroll in a TAFE diploma program, then on to university. One statistic says over 60 percent of university students enter via TAFE (for further information, see the website www.home schooling.com.au/). Also see the archived newsletters on this site for information regarding such things as possibly earning youth allowance while homeschooling, sitting for the SAAT, and other items of interest to homeschooling Australian families.

In the UK, readers may want to check out the following website, which details comments, both favorable and not, from several British universities with respect to admitting homeschooled applicants: www.angelfire.com/ri2/egbertina/homeschool/england.html. For information on alternatives for taking GCSEs as a homeschooler, see www.geocities.com/Heartland/Lake/3262/gcse.html.

GENERAL EDUCATION DEVELOPMENT (GED) DIPLOMA

It's not necessary to take a GED test in lieu of getting a standard diploma, but some folks like the idea. Approximately 800,000 people take the GED test every year, and one diploma in seven earned today is via GED. If this sounds like a good idea, see contact information in Appendix 2.

ENROLL IN AN ACCREDITED PROGRAM ACCOMMODATING HOMESCHOOLERS

If you are desperate for your child to earn high school credits that will not be questioned anywhere (accredited, in other words), you need to stay affiliated with a program that can offer you that. These are fairly sparse in some countries, but a veritable new industry has evolved for this in the USA. They come in many names and flavors: correspondence programs, long-distance education programs, umbrella (cover) schools, private schools, or independent satellite (or study) programs (ISP) through private academies. Cost for the programs varies widely ($300 to $3000 per year, by my layman's research). A few correspondence schools are listed in Appendix 7.

Assuming your child fulfills the requirements of a course at one of these schools, the curriculum provider will provide official documentation upon completion (i.e. assign a credit). Completing enough credits in this manner will earn a high school diploma (USA). In other countries, the terminology is different but the results much the same. In Australia, for example, such an avenue would lead to a year ten or year twelve certificate.

TRY THE PUBLIC SCHOOLS AGAIN

Some families send their child back to regular high school for the last year or two of school. After years of homeschooling, many kids are able to cope with high school. Also, their classmates are more mature by then, so harassment and bullying is, with luck, a smaller issue. My son returned to school (a smaller private school this time) and enjoyed the experience. He was ready for it this time.

A related option is to pursue an independent study option through your local school. If the school will accommodate this, it's a good deal for them because they would get funding from your child's enrollment. Meanwhile, you would get the flexibility of homeschooling. As long as the school doesn't get too heavy handed in what they require of you with respect to testing and record keeping, it can be workable.

An offshoot of that is a charter school. Something in the order of 38 states in the USA now have a provision for charter schools. These schools are public but are run like private schools, and some are closely aligned with families who like homeschooling. That is, they will work with parents to choose a curriculum but the parent remains the primary teacher. They may have a resource center for homeschoolers, offer small classes, and may be able to advise on course selection and offer a variety of (secular) publisher's materials from which to choose. But it's not for everyone. Again, there is an element of bureaucracy and authority by public officials that some homeschoolers heartily object to. The upside is that because it's public school, you would not have to foot the bill for all the textbooks and such. Those looking for the schools to provide therapy (OT, PT, language, or social skills) might get better service by actually being on the school rolls. Again, each situation is going to be different, so you need to thoroughly research your options.

Building a curriculum

If you're operating under the auspices of an established long-distance education program or other type of school, the business of deciding what courses to take and how to record it all is pretty well established for you. For the more eclectic homeschooler, though, putting together a high school curriculum can feel pretty daunting. What makes a good high school education? How should you spend your time? How many hours of which subjects?

Similar to our discussion of scope and sequence objectives in earlier chapters, there is no one perfect answer as to what your child should learn in the high school years. Here are a few ways you can gain insight into what a typical high school curriculum might look like, however:

1.   Look at the information provided by umbrella schools and use them as models. Request catalogs and brochures, or study their websites (see Appendix 7 under "Long distance education" or "Packaged curricula").

2.   Ask your local college what it is they look for in an applicant.

3.   Look at national guidelines. A typical course curriculum for US college-bound students might look like the following: English (four years), math (three to four years), history and geography (two to three years), lab science (two to three years), visual and performing arts (one year), electives (one to three years). This list was derived from government websites. Also see the government publication *Getting Ready for College Early: A Handbook for Parents of Students in the Middle and Junior High School Years*, which is available on the internet (www.ed.gov/pubs/GettingReadyCollegeEarly/#examples). Alternatively, write for the free handbook *Preparing Your Child for College* from Consumer Information Center, Preparing Your Child for College, Pueblo, CO 81009. Or call 1-800-USA-LEARN for this and other Department of Education publications.

4.   Ask your state school department or local school authority for information on what is required for graduation and use that as a model for your own minimum requirements (if you want). Individual state requirements vary. Oklahoma, for instance, requires arts coursework rather than foreign language. California requires less science and math but more PE. Some areas require some volunteer service work. Once again, there is no magic formula. Certainly as parents of kids with AS issues, there are things I'd like to see added or substituted, but more about that in the second half of this chapter.

5.   Check out Cafi Cohen's books *And What About College?* (2000a) as well as *Homeschooling the Teen Years* (2000b), and also Rebecca Rupp's *Home Learning Year by Year* (2000).

Is college realistic?

If your child is still fairly young as you read this, your eyes may have widened when I mentioned college. Parents have told me they can't imagine their Aspie youngster ever going to college. After all, they say, my child can't sit in a classroom, can't take notes, won't do group work, and will only talk about one topic endlessly. If he can't get through a shopping mall without becoming upset, how is he going to handle a huge campus? Parents may reasonably point out "the very reason we're homeschooling is because our kid just can't cope!"

I have felt this way too. When my son was age ten and twelve, I couldn't imagine what was going to become of my rigid, sensory-defensive, ritual-following kid who was a joy to me, but who also talked on odd topics at great length, asked people's bowling average as a greeting, and didn't seem to be on the same page with others in the room. It wasn't a question of intelligence, it was all that "other stuff."

Today, at age 19, my son's doing well in his second semester at a community college. He drives his own car, bowls on two bowling leagues, and lives on his own next door to his grandparents. And he is happy. If you had told me in early teen years or before that that this would occur, it would have taken my breath away. In some ways, it still does.

The years from 16 to 18 were a period of awesome growth for my son, in that it seemed as though things started clicking. All those talks that we had had in previous years seem to have sunk in. It was as though all the bits and pieces, lessons and lectures, rehearsals and conversations, and trying new things here and there, had been like different vegetables going into a pot. And in his late teens, it all turned into a wonderful stew.

This was not a sudden awakening, but a prolonged period of the same sort of developmental growth spurts that we have all seen in our kids. It should be pointed out that my son still has AS – he still interprets things from a literal, logical, and mostly black-and-white perspective; he still craves routine and dislikes surprises; he's still not a social butterfly (neither am I) and has difficulty in some situations (such as a retail job that did not work out). But he is fitting into the world on his own terms, and I have no doubts that he has a very bright future. My only worry is that as my little duck skims around the lake with all the other ducks of the world now, not too many of those other ducks know just how far he has already traveled, nor how hard he is paddling under the surface. If they only knew, they would be as impressed with him as I am.

The paragraphs above are certainly those of a boastful parent, but I share this because I think parents need to hear the good news. Many beleaguered moms and dads become so mired in day-to-day problems of raising a special needs child that they are either afraid to hope for college (or other good things in life), or have already dismissed the idea as highly unlikely. Although there's no guarantee when it comes to our children's capabilities, and our kids all have different starting points and rates of growth anyway, still I am positive that our Asperger-affected kids go through a very long development curve, much longer than that of the typical child, and they will keep on making strides and connections well into adulthood. If your child isn't ready for college or other major life events (car, job, etc.) when other kids are, so be it. If there need to be modifications in order to make things happen, that's all right too. My point is that we mustn't shortchange our kids' futures by putting any sort of limits on it, either in terms of timelines or the goals themselves. It is our job to just keep plugging away and helping our children build on each success. Good things will happen.

If not college, then what?

Not every teen is going to want to go to college, or be able to go even if he wants to. Other options might include vocational training, or getting a job. There are dozens of books on surviving the interview process. Whichever one is chosen, parents will want to help their child rehearse an interview situation and review good body language. A terrific book for teens looking into the possibilities of life beyond school (or even instead of) is Grace Llewellyn's *Teenage Liberation Handbook* (1998). This book shows a wide variety of other options out there – mentorships, apprenticeships, volunteer work, entrepreneurial ventures, and so forth. This book was not written with Asperger Syndrome in mind, but it still might be useful.

Teaching academic subject matter

This section is meant to be a supplement to Chapter 5. We will cover:

- English (reading, writing, handwriting)
- Math (algebra, geometry, trigonometry, calculus)
- Science (biology, earth science, chemistry, physics)
- Social studies (current events, government, economics, history)
- Foreign language
- Art.

This section is to be used in conjunction with the corresponding text in Chapter 5. Although the topics covered should be of benefit to the older student, in truth many of the issues, learning materials, or suggestions in both chapters are applicable for all ages or at least can cross several grades. Because of both delays and splinter skills, not to mention the special interests of our kids, there is no straightforward equation to say that a certain child is going to fit into a certain grade. Please do swap back and forth and take what is useful to you, regardless of where you find it.

In some topic areas of advice for older students, you may find the information sparse. The survey pool of families with teenaged children was significantly smaller than the pool of those homeschooling younger aged children. I believe that is largely a reflection of the general state of things in society. Knowledge about Asperger Syndrome only began in the mid-1990s and homeschooling has not been well accepted until relatively recently. In a few years, the numbers of older homeschoolers affected by AS should increase dramatically. Meanwhile, we can be grateful for the families with teenagers now who did respond, for they are the real pioneers, treading new ground and dropping some breadcrumbs behind them so that we might all benefit from their experiences.

English
READING

Reading, phonics, and basic reading skills are usually accomplished in the younger years, but reading comprehension remains a huge issue for AS-affected students of all ages. One mom asks, "How do you get a child with Asperger Syndrome to discuss the topic you are reading about?" MJ rightly observes:

> Most reading comprehension programs are just "read a passage and answer questions about it." That doesn't teach how to comprehend better, any more than being in a class with a bunch of kids my son's age teaches him social skills. I need a step-by-step breakdown of the skills needed and how to teach them – especially things like inference, figurative language, context, catching the meaning of unfamiliar words and phrases, etc.

MJ has hit it exactly on the head. Our kids benefit greatly from concrete steps, so depending purely on "osmosis" (simply reading good authors) will not guarantee reading comprehension or ability to analyze a written work.

Why it's difficult

Suppose you enroll your teen in a literature class and the teacher asks the students to read a passage and identify the mood that the writer is attempting to convey. To give one example, an intuitive reader might sense sadness or loss from clues in the story's setting – perhaps a mention of overcast and drizzling weather; dead leaves falling from a barren winter tree; a lonely train whistle.

What would a child with AS conclude from reading the same passage? He might take the descriptions at face (literal) value, without adding emotional value. Rain is rain and winter is winter. Unless pointed out, it might not occur to our kids that there is any below-the-surface meaning to be found. Once that hurdle is cleared, an AS-affected child still needs to figure out what the hidden message is. If rain, dying leaves, and winter do not seem sad to our kids but merely a fact of nature, then what are they to think?

It's dangerous to generalize that this would be the case for all AS-affected teens, but this is the sort of disconnect I have uncovered in my own son's reading and also in his movie viewing. I have found great benefit in being very plain to my son about these things. Eventually our kids can pick up a lot of it, after they've been shown the patterns and encouraged to look for the clues. I remember one such breakthrough while watching a scene in the movie *Billy Elliot*, where Billy was dancing furiously in the alley behind his house until he got to the back wall and could go no further. My son blurted out, "I get it! They're showing us that he's come up against a brick wall in his life!" Bingo!

Suggestion 1

Use movies. They're fun, fast, and you can point out clues that authors leave. You can ask questions or make a game, but rather than trying to pull information out of your child that he may be totally unable to provide, casually give him information. Your child cannot "connect the dots" unless he's provided the dots in the first place. At some point, when he begins to get it, you may start getting more meaningful conversation.

Here are a few examples of movie comments you could make, to help your child see how authors/directors plant clues and create moods:

- *Tootsie*: "Uh-oh, look at the way Julie's father just put a sweater on Dorothy's [Dustin Hoffman's] shoulders. The director is showing that he is falling in love."

- *Nine to Five*: "I can tell the boss is mean before he even walks in. All the workers have to clear their desks and stop chatting. They act afraid of him."

- *Christmas Vacation*: "Clark's boss's desk is huge! And he keeps getting Clark's name wrong. He isn't comfortable around his employees."

- *Doc Hollywood*: "The farewell cake at Doc's old job is shaped like a rear end. I don't think Doc's coworkers respect him, do you?"

- *Grumpy Old Men*: "Hmmm, spicy food used to be off limits for John Gustafson (Jack Lemon). That Tabasco sauce he put in his eggs shows he's suddenly feeling young."

- *As Good As It Gets*: "Melvin just stepped on a crack. No one has said that he's getting better, but we see signs that he is."

Suggestion 3

Look at symbolism mathematically. While it is usually taught in a subjective way, most of it can be presented in a definitive way. For example, rain = sadness; dark = mystery; falling leaves = death, ending, or passage of time; avoiding someone's eyes = lying or hiding emotions; stuttering or talking fast = nervousness or excitement; rumbling thunder = impending trouble.

Suggestion 4

Keep working on idioms and figures of speech (see Communication Skills in this chapter). Idioms get in the way of reading comprehension just as they do spoken conversation.

Suggestion 5

Make sure your child knows that authors choose details for a reason. Almost nothing is random. Also, there are almost always three levels to a story:

- basic plot line

- the evolution or change of the main character (and sometimes other characters)

- a larger message that the author is telling about life.

You can use movies to practice identifying these three threads.

Wider reading

The younger reader often gets caught up in popular book series, but the older reader should be encouraged to stretch and read different things. *Reading Lists for College-Bound Students* (Estell, Satchwell and Wright 1990) is an excellent book, whether your child is college-bound or not. It compiles lists of suggestions from many US colleges and universities. In addition, here are a few online lists:

- http://als.lib.wi.us/Collegebound.html

- www.sms.org/books_co.html

- www.uni-mannheim.de/users/bibsplit/anglistik/aus_bks. html (Australian)

Other suggestions:

- SAT preparation: to increase vocabulary quite effortlessly, this novella is specially written to incorporate words commonly found on the SAT – www.studyhall.com/webpage2000/NOV/novela.htm

- Try audiobooks or radio theatre programs (either actually on the radio or through internet), as well as seeing plays, to increase your child's exposure to good literature.

- Short stories, and Reader's Digest condensed books, can impart the flavor of authors without great time expenditure.

- To hear poetry read by the poets themselves, treat yourself to the Academy of American Poets listening booth:

http://poetry.about.com/gi/dynamic/offsite.htm?site=ht
tp%3A%2F%2Fwww.poets.org%2Fbooth%2Fbooth.cfm

- Use Cliff Notes or literature guides. Two websites that provide literature guides for many classic novels are: http://pinkmonkey.com/ and www.sparknotes.com

- Many classics can be found in full text online: www.bartleby.com/ or www.bibliomania.com

WRITING

Reading enhances writing and writing enhances reading, so everything above also applies in writing. In addition, here are a few other suggestions.

Journal-writing is a common technique for honing writing skills. The daily writing and personal nature of it make it a great place for young writers to "take risks" and experiment with different techniques. Your child may prefer a computer journal to a notebook, however. It is also a good idea to keep a steady stock of writing topics or starters for days when nothing comes to mind.

Suggestions from parents for good writing programs include:

- *Learning to Write the Novel Way*

- *Writing Strands*

- *Painless Grammar*

- *Institute for Excellence in Writing.*

Writing websites include:

- An online writing lab from Utah Valley State College: www.uvsc.edu/owl/writing.html

- A series of helpful articles aimed at teens: http://teenwriting.about.com/library/

- *Traditional English Grammar* by Don Hardy: www.engl.niu.edu/dhardy/grammarbook/title.html

- Daily Grammar (simple rule and exercises sent daily to your computer): www.dailygrammar.com

- The Write Source site offers a writing program from kindergarten through grade 12 in a series of handbooks. No AS family I've heard from has happened to use this system, but the website is helpful for two reasons. It offers writing topics for various age groups and it also shows models of student writing at various grade levels. This is very helpful to me: www.thewritesource.com/index2.html

- *Research Strategies*, by William Badke (online book): www.acts.twu.ca/lbr/textbook.html

HANDWRITING

The goal by high school is simply legibility. Regardless of our kids' almost universal preference for using a computer, they do still need to fill out job applications and other things that require legible handwriting, so I would still insist on at least a minimum standard, and would require a few minutes of daily work toward that end. A teacher once asserted that if handwriting hadn't improved by sixth grade it never would, but my own son's progress belies that. He improved all through junior high and high school. In fact, the most improvement we ever saw was in grade 12 when, through a misunderstanding of directions, John was forced to recopy a 50-page handwritten journal. Writing a total of 100 full pages of handwritten work over a few weeks was something I would have never asked him to do, but it did improve his handwriting even at the age of 17. I'm now convinced that it is never too late.

Math

Of all academic subjects, math seems to be the most intimidating for parents. Mostly everyone I contacted is using a formal course, either through a long-distance education program, a CD-ROM curriculum (Switched on Schoolhouse), or by enrolling in local community college courses. All are viable options as is hiring a tutor. For those who would like to create their own math course, however, or supplement using materials from internet, some helpful resources are listed below.

ALGEBRA

- A review of algebra:
  www.physics.uoguelph.ca/tutorials/algebra

- An entire online algebra textbook:
  www.sosmath.com/algebra/albegra.html

- Algebra II set of lesson plans:
  www.score.kings.k12.ca.us/algebra2.html

- UK-based site for preparing for the GCSE exam:
  www.gcse.com/Maths/algmen.html

GEOMETRY

- Several geometry lessons are at:
  www.score.kings.k12.ca.us/geometry.html

- Math 129 home page:
  www.math.csusb.edu/courses/m129home.html

- An archive of geometry problems with full solutions:
  http://mathforum.org/geopow/solutions/

TRIGONOMETRY

- A basic course is at: www.sosmath.com/trig/trig.html

- UK-based site for preparing for the GCSE exam:
  www.gcse.com/Maths/teach/trig1.html

CALCULUS

- A full textbook online is available at www.pinkmonkey.com.
  You will need to register, then look under Study Guides.

Science

High school science typically includes two or three years of science, which might include biology, earth science, chemistry, or physics. The same comments listed in Chapter 5 apply here for the older student. Be mindful of safety issues, especially with chemicals and dissection tools, and also be sensitive that some subject matter in biology may seem gruesome or frightening for the child. Although one generally thinks of younger children being upset, the teenage years are also quite prone to anxiety and depression.

BIOLOGY

Since I recently prepared to homeschool my younger son's grade ten, I've been looking at biology resources particularly closely. I ended up choosing a college-level textbook. It's a reference book for me, and offers good illustrations and a CD with animations (*Biology Concepts and Connections,* by Campbell, Mitchell and Reece 1999). You can also find a great many sources on the net:

- A free online full textbook of biology by Maricopa Community College: www.emc.maricopa.edu/faculty/farabee/BIOBK/ BioBookTOC.html

- A beginner's guide to molecular biology (college level): www.rothamsted.bbsrc.ac.uk/notebook/courses/guide/

- Animal diversity web: http://animaldiversity.ummz.umich.edu/index.html

- A level biology course (UK): www.mrothery.co.uk/

- BBC's biology website: www.bbc.co.uk/learning/library/biology.shtml

EARTH SCIENCE

- Online course: www.solarviews.com

- Earth and geological sciences tutorial:

    http://jersey.uoregon.edu/~mstrick/RogueComCollege/ Rogue_index.html

CHEMISTRY

- Chem4Kids: www.chem4kids.com/

- An assessment of the best chemistry sets: http://homeschooling.about.com/cs/toppicks/tp/ chemistry.html

- General Chemistry Online (lots of resources):
  http://antoine.frostburg.edu/chem/senese/101/index.shtml

PHYSICS

- Physics Classroom – high school physics tutorial:
  www.physicsclassroom.com/Default2.html

- Online Tutorial – Learn Physics Today:
  http://library.thinkquest.org/10796/

For the auditory learner or for a change of pace, try listening to the show "Talk of the Nation Science Friday" on National Public Radio, Friday afernoons, or listen to archived programs: www.sciencefriday.com/pages/

Social studies

One of the greatest services we can do for our kids in the area of social studies is to ignite an interest in the world through various news outlets, magazines, and TV. A few parents have indicated that slipping news and politics, including political cartoons, into the daily conversation has been very helpful. Most of our kids like to understand jokes and cartoons, so this is an especially palatable way of bringing up current events.

Four of the eleven teens represented in the survey actually have a special interest in social studies – two in military history and two in geography. Now, here are some online resources to help the homeschooler:

CURRENT EVENTS

- Political cartoons:
  http://politicalhumor.about.com/library/bldailyfeed2.html

- Newspapers from all over the world:
  http://newsdirectory.com/

GOVERNMENT

- An entire tutorial on American government:
  http://go.hrw.com/hrw.nd/arbiter/pRedirect?project=
  hrwonline&siteId=695&pageId=6279

ECONOMICS

- A full online course in economics:
  http://go.hrw.com/hrw.nd/arbiter/pRedirect?project=
  hrwonline&siteId=499&pageId=3427

HISTORY

- Country Watch – information and quizzes on each country:
  www.countrywatch.com/@school/

- For the audio learner, Radio Expeditions offers audio clips
  you can hear while you view accompanying photos online
  and sometimes even watch video clips:
  www.npr.org/programs/re/archivesdate/index.html

- The History Buff – audio clips of historic speeches, news
  stories: www.historybuff.com/media/index.html

- Various Historical Topics has nice interactive material:
  www.historychannel.com

Foreign language

A couple of teen students in the survey are currently taking a course in
either Spanish or French through Switched on Schoolhouse
(CD-ROM). This option seems reasonable and modestly priced. Other
(non-Asperger) homeschooling families give high marks to the Power
Glide Language Courses (CD-ROM), and there are more languages on
offer with this system. The course does look good and, although more
expensive, offers a variety of learning techniques that may appeal to
folks of many different sorts of learning styles. You can view a sample
lesson at www.power-glide.com/products/FrenchUlt/ultimate.asp (or
click on different languages to see other samples).

As I said before, most other courses available on the market give only
a superficial exposure to the language. If this is adequate for your needs,
that's fine. You will find many that claim to be fast and easy, but learning

a language is neither in my opinion. Try your library (and inter-library loan) to sample one or more of these sorts of programs before you buy. Also see Chapter 5 for some online resources.

As an alternative option, a teen might wish to take an organized class. This might mean a return to high school for one course, or taking a language course through community college. If accreditation is not an issue, one might also try parks department or open university type courses.

Art

The older child can still benefit from hands-on art (see Chapter 5), but might like to use this as a research opportunity in art appreciation. Below are 38 artists listed in approximate date order for the older student. This could easily be a loose structure for a series of unit studies.

Here are some famous artists: Donatello, Da Vinci, Michelangelo, Raphael, Rubens, Rembrandt, Copley, Goya, Manet, Whistler, Degas, Homer, Cezanne, Rodin, Monet, Gaugin, Van Gogh, Pissarro, Seurat, Grandma Moses, Remington, Toulouse-Lautrec, Matisse, Klee, Chagall, Picasso, Hopper, Salvador Dali, Miro, Pollack, Howard Pyle, Rudolph Zallinger, Wyeth, William H. Johnson, James J. Audubon, Peter Maxx, Andy Warhol, Escher.

Some profiles of real teens

Now, let's see how some AS-affected teens and their families are coping with homeschooling during high school years.

1. Sharon's son Sam is 15 years old. During Sam's seventh and eighth grade years, Sharon put together an eclectic curriculum using things she ordered from homeschool catalogs. Beginning with grade nine, however, she enrolled him in University of Nebraska Long Distance Ed High School (they live in Louisiana). At $3500 or so per year it is not cheap, but she notes that it's only half what she would have spent at a private high school and it includes all materials. She is pleased with the coursework and the fact that Sam will have a regular four-year high school diploma at the end. Assignments are turned in at regular intervals and the school keeps track of all records. He does have

homework and has had to work into the summer to get all the work finished up, but it does not compare with the pressures of a traditional school. Writes Sharon: "He is *very* happy for the most part now that he is out from under the stress of school."

2.   Lucy's son James homeschooled from grade seven to grade ten using a correspondence course through Texas Tech University. Now at age 17, James has gone back to public school this year (in Texas) and is doing well. Lucy chose this correspondence school in part because it was always their intention that he would return to the classroom, and she wanted to ensure that all credits would transfer. All in all, she is well pleased with how everything has turned out.

3.   Sandy's two boys have been using the Open Access College system in Australia, which is a government-sanctioned, long-distance schooling option. Her older boy will continue to homeschool through graduation. However, her younger son, also with AS, has chosen to return to regular school.

4.   Katy's son Thomas, age 15, has been homeschooled since early childhood. He uses textbooks for math and science, and unit studies for history, literature, and other things. He's been working on SAT preparation this year, and plans to continue homeschooling all the way through high school. When he turns 16, he will probably enroll in some community college courses.

5.   Nedra's two teenaged sons are using the computer curriculum Switched on Schoolhouse, which is furnished through Alpha Omega Academy and provides courses through grade 12. Although it offers a diploma program, Nedra's family and other families I contacted were all using it in an eclectic way. Nedra makes the system work for her by substituting or supplementing in some areas, especially in math (she uses Singapore) and English (reading and writing).

6.   Cathy's son Daniel, now 19, used Switched on Schoolhouse for Bible, language, and history (government and economics), but also started at the local community college

and qualified for dual high school and college credits in other courses. Cathy notes: "I also gave credits for some combinations of classes taken through our homeschool enrichment program. I counted things like four sets of six cooking classes as a home economics credit – things like that."

7.   Marilyn's son Craig is 17 and has just completed grade ten. He's enrolled in an Education Association for homeschoolers in PA. The EA hires teachers for certain classes. Students attend two times per week and do homework in the off time. Marilyn maintains a portfolio type of record for Craig and keeps track of time spent doing schoolwork to determine credit earned. He has two more years of high school and it will be done in the same manner that he's been doing it so far.

"Whole child" issues

"How can we prepare our children to live functional lives on their own after school is finished?" asks Sarah G.

That's the big question, isn't it? Academic education means little if our kids can't function in the world. That means another look at "whole child" issues – life skills, self-awareness, and many other things. We handled many of the issues in Chapter 5, but the following additional suggestions may be helpful.

Communication skills

Beyond the reading and writing requirements of coursework, our kids need to continue to grow in everyday communications:

- *Phone skills.* Leaving a message on an answering machine is problematic for a few of our kids, much more so than simple phone conversation. Have your child practice this.

- *Customer service or information desks.* Make sure your teen can handle asking for information or returning a defective item.

- *Speaking to groups.* Look for opportunities with church, Scouts, or clubs. Also, homeschool groups sometimes get together for this purpose, arranging a time when students can give speeches or demonstrations for each other.

- *Working in a group.* The child that was unable to get along in a group when younger due to Asperger difficulties may be more ready by now. Look for opportunities.

- *Idioms.* This has been mentioned before, but now the older child can hold the reins. Sharon's son Sam has worked on idioms on his own with the book *Scholastic Dictionary of Idioms.* Older students can also work through Appendix 5 of this book on their own, testing themselves to see which ones they know. Or they might like to check the online resource from E. D. Hirsch's *Dictionary of Cultural Literacy,* which has an idiom section (www.bartleby.com/59/4/).

Life skills

Can my child handle everyday household tasks? This might sound like a mundane question but it's also important. Most of us have been through the motions of teaching our kids how to measure things, read a recipe, and set the oven timer. But it doesn't really mean they can cook, unless they do it often enough that it isn't a huge mental strain for them. That takes practice.

Sandy has her teen son make his own lunch every day. By doing it every day, it will soon be a "no-brainer" for him rather than a task that takes mental energy.

Cathy signed up her high school age son for several sets of cooking classes. Other families have designated a certain night that their child will cook dinner every week.

In the same manner that cooking needs to be done on a regular basis, the same might be said about laundry and general cleaning.

PERSONAL ISSUES

Some parents have revealed there are still issues of hygiene, problems of taking copious time with showers, and so forth. If there are any issues having to do with hygiene, toileting, dental care, nutrition, or general personal care that haven't been resolved in younger years, it's time to re-look at these issues. Over years of talking with Asperger families, the most reliable methods of dealing with these issues seem to be:

- using a chart or check-off list, to make sure that everything gets done

- using a timer, if necessary, to keep things moving

- using factual books (biology or health books) to bring home the importance of cleanliness, nutrition, etc.

- enlisting the help of a doctor if necessary to explain things to the child.

Alone time

Under the category of personal issues might be the fact that your son or daughter spends many hours alone in his or her room. Our kids tend to need long periods of time on their own. What I had at first mistaken as a possible sign of depression in my son turned out to be a need to decompress, process, or just relax. When I would go in his room, he would most likely be pretty cheerful in there, which reinforces the idea that for him heaps of alone time is just what he needs. Other parents have said the same thing. Marilyn reveals, "Craig needs recovery time after he's been around people so on Wednesdays and Fridays, he sleeps in and does a lot of his school work in his room." LeAnn's son requires some time each evening to work out on his step bench before bed so he can sleep better. Sharon describes her Sam as "addicted" to his headphones listening to country music. This too is probably a way of decompressing.

Does my child still have motor, body space, or sensory difficulties?

The answer is probably yes, although some traits may have faded into the background. It's time to take stock and think about which issues are ones to relax about and which should still be worked, perhaps more aggressively than ever. The decision should revolve around what is making life difficult for your child. For example, if your child never reached the goal of skipping or turning a somersault, maybe it doesn't matter once he reaches his teens. But maybe it does matter if he can't stand in line or in a crowded train car, or can't walk down a city street due to the noise.

In the end, the goal is not to make our kids emulate the rest of the world, but to help our kids to function in the world so that they can enjoy it and find success.

Social skills

Teens don't want their mommies arranging playdates for them, but they may be having difficulties managing to meet friends on their own. The easiest road to finding friends seems to be finding people with common interests. Parents can encourage participation in a group where the teen has a special interest (chess club, rocketry club, astronomy group are some examples). Such a focused group will likely work out better than a more generic group with no other stated special interest, such as a town youth group or a mixer or dance.

Some teens begin to work harder on knowing pop culture in an effort to mix with kids their own age. They might work on knowing the current music fads, for example, or get very enamored of a TV show that is popular. Katy's son Thomas (15) knows a great deal about who plays which character in the movies. Even though he doesn't really watch movies that much, he keeps up with this information, which Katy describes as "quite socially acceptable and kind of handy."

Some teens make a conscientious study of social skills about this time. My son John has gathered quite a collection of self-help books that he purchased for himself on topics such as the art of mingling, how to persuade people, working with difficult personalities, how not to be lied to, and other pop psychology sorts of topics. His favorite is a book on body language by Allan Pease, which he said was very helpful to him.

Note: some of these books are a bit adult in their topics (i.e. flirting, how people hold drinks or smoke cigarettes, etc.). Parents may want to check these books out first.

Asperger education

Closely related to social skills and communication skills is the need for our kids to understand Asperger Syndrome on a more adult level than they would have been able to in earlier years. My son has read parts of books on AS in order to understand more of what it entails. Sharon says of her 15-year-old, "Sam has read several books on AS and social skills and he applies some of what he reads to real life situations."

Books mentioned as being helpful: *Asperger's: What Does It Mean to Me?* (Faherty and Mesibov 2000) and *Asperger's, Huh?* (Schnurr and Strachan 1999).

FACIAL EXPRESSION FOR OLDER STUDENTS

In addition to resources mentioned in Chapter 5, here are some resources more geared for the older student or adult:

- This website features John Cleese and Liz Hurley, who did a BBC documentary on the human face. Here, you can read about the details of facial expressions such as angry faces, smiles, sad faces: www.bbc.co.uk/science/humanbody/humanface/exp_intro.shtml. You can take a quiz to spot a fake smile from a real one. You'll need to click around to find everything, but be sure to read about eye contact (www.bbc.co.uk/science/humanbody/humanface/exp_stare.shtml) and also about isolation, where a young man with Asperger Syndrome discusses what's difficult for him (www.bbc.co.uk/science/humanbody/humanface/exp_laurenandchris.shtml).

As you can see from my many references to go back and relook at Chapter 5, the issues for the older child are many times an extenuation of the same issues faced in younger years. The big difference is that the older student can often begin to be a partner in working them, often finding resources or in self-initiated reading. Our job as parent and teacher remains important though, in providing hands-on, explicit teaching. It's often tempting for parents of teens to step back and coast, but for our kids we cannot do that. In many ways, it's a time to re-evaluate where improvements need to be made and ensure that no time is wasted.

Driver education

My son had no desire to drive until the day he turned 16 when he suddenly announced that he wanted to learn. I was in no hurry for this, but we were situated in a small town and it seemed safer than waiting until we would be transferred back to a larger city. So we agreed to driving lessons. This was in Australia, post-homeschooling, and he took lessons through a private company employed by his high school. A homeschooling family would be able to access the same lessons by going directly through the company.

The lessons went fine, practice with us went fine, the test went fine, and he has yet to have an accident (touch wood). In talking with many adults with AS, it's safe to say that many and probably most people with Asperger Syndrome can and do learn to drive a car.

In comparing experiences with other families, my observation is that it seems that the traits and tendencies you notice in your child off the road may give you some clue as to how things are going to go on the road.

1. *The rule-based kid.* My son likes rules and takes pride in following them. He also wants to be the best at whatever he does, and is cautious by nature. This was reflected in his driving in that he had a tendency to drive too slowly at first, hug the curb, and make absolutely square corners.

2. *The either/or kid.* Some teens don't have much middle ground when it comes to driving. They drive with the brake or gas on or off with little or no ability to finesse the mid-range. Is this a gross motor issue or a feature of black-and-white thinking, or just general inexperience? I do not know. My son did not have much problem with this, possibly due to working the joystick on Microsoft Flight Simulator over the years. After many simulated crashes, he understands what happens when you just think in terms of up and down! He has also gone go-karting on several occasions, which gave him some early experience with pedals.

3. *The spatial klutz.* Some people have incredible difficulty at judging size or distances. This can translate into difficulties estimating braking distances or size of parking spaces. Is your child good at judging whether something will fit into a box, or if a bed will fit along a certain wall? Perhaps this will give you some clues as to what to expect in your child's driving.

Of equal concern is how your child will handle unplanned events. This is a challenge for most of our AS-affected kids. The first time my son missed a turn, he couldn't think how to recover, or even where he was. He drove straight for many blocks, berating himself out loud for being so stupid, rather than trying to fix the error. After that episode, we worked through steps to follow if you've missed your turn, and I also emphasized the fact that this happens to everyone. (One could also model this by missing a turn while the child is a passenger, and then going through the decision process and steps to recover.)

My son was recently pulled over by the police. He got flustered trying to find his registration and insurance papers for the officer, but that's understandable. I reminded him to calm down and look carefully, and he found them. All in all, it was a good exercise. My son now knows what to expect. He also now knows not to put funny neon lights on his car tire valves. Luckily, he just got a warning. It would have been good to do some role-playing rehearsals of this situation before being stopped by a real policeman.

Role playing is also important for knowing what to do in an accident. This should be covered in a driver's education course, but you as parent should also go through the steps with your child. Besides role playing, another help would be to devise a list of things to do in case of accident, to keep in a glove compartment.

As to where or how your child can learn to drive, the best first step is to contact or visit your local motor vehicle office. They can tell you what the requirements are, give you a handbook, and possibly even provide contact information for local driving companies.

Once you have advice from the authorities, decide who is going to provide the instruction, both theory (class or book instruction) and practice (on the road). Your most likely choices are you, your local high school (some high schools allow homeschoolers to take driver's education), or a private company. The theory portion can also be taught via an online course, a correspondence course, computer software, or as instruction by DVD. See Appendix 7 for vendors and always check to make sure whatever option you choose is legal in your area. It should be noted that none of the families in the survey reported using any of the programs, however. Buyer beware.

Chapter 9

What Else Do I Need to Know?

No doubt as you have begun homeschooling a hundred other questions have cropped up. This chapter tries to address some of the most troublesome ones. It is a collection of questions that parents offered when asked: What problems do you have? What gaps in information have you been unable to fill? What are you worried about? Needless to say, parents have some very tough questions. They are categorized as:

- socialization

- motivation

- siblings

- record keeping

- perfectionism

- keeping costs down

- diet

- medication

- general household issues

- burnout

- quitting.

Socialization

"How will your child get socialization if he doesn't go to school?" Nearly every generic homeschooling book and website devotes text to the subject of socialization. Authors discuss at length how it is a ridiculous myth to think that homeschooled kids are stuck at home, never to see the light of day or have a friend. They reassure us that homeschooled kids are, by and large, very active in outside activities – Scouts, clubs, karate classes, music lessons, volunteer work, etc.

That's all well and good, but unfortunately the question gets tougher to answer when an Asperger-affected family attempts to homeschool. People who understand just a little about AS know that our kids are by definition socially awkward and have difficulties making friends. So, the conclusion drawn by those people is that our kids should be surrounded by as many people as possible all the time – in other words, our kids should surely be in school. When they find out that we have taken the opposite approach and pulled our child out altogether, they are downright appalled. Melissa laments: "More times than I care to think about, I've heard, especially from educators, that homeschooling an AS kid would be the worst thing you could do to them."

Well, one hardly knows where to start in pointing out the fallacy of that attitude. The only simple answer I can give is to make the analogy that in the great swimming pool of socialization our kids cannot swim. Throwing them into the deep end of the pool only causes panic and grief for our kids and so it makes no sense to do that to them. However, pulling them out of the deep end, calming them down, and drying them off does make sense. Then we can walk them around to the shallow end of the pool and let them start again, gradually, and begin to teach them to swim. Of course, with this analogy, there will always be someone who says that our kids have to learn to "sink or swim." What can you do with someone like that? Most of us could point to having already spent a few unsuccessful years watching our child sink in the classroom, but it's probably fruitless to try to change people's views by just talking about it.

A lot of us have been more successful in showing skeptics, however. Family members who were once against homeschooling due to the socialization issue have become converts from seeing our kids make friends for the first time, and from seeing our kids become less stressed and angry and more sociable. This is exemplified by the changes that have occurred for Margaret's daughter. Says Margaret:

Michaela's more relaxed and capable when she's with other children [now]. The long school day of forced company with children who often scapegoated her was simply too much for her. She routinely came home in a rage, talking about wanting to punch other children for being mean to her. She became hypersensitive to the laughter of other children, assuming they were laughing at her. I feel this is because they often were. Now her contacts with other children are with kids who are taught by their mothers to be kind and considerate. Not that they're perfect, but what she encounters is more manageable, and I'm available to deal with any problems on her end with her autism in mind. Her teachers let things slide. I saw this with my own eyes. Their philosophy was "she has to learn to deal with it" so they left her to deal with it alone. I don't think a child with Aspergers needs to be thrown into constant contact she can't escape for eight hours or more every day. Talk about overload! My child is no longer full of rage. She looks forward to being with other children (she always wanted friends), and now those contacts are usually positive.

A big part of the positive growth in our kids seems to stem from finally being able to relax and then having shorter, but more positive, exposures to kids. Another aspect comes from the fact that homeschoolers can take the time to educate their kids one step at a time. From Elizabeth:

AS kids don't learn how to interact socially by being in a classroom with 25 other kids. They need to be taught skills on a more basic level. Homeschooling has given my child the opportunity to interact with children and adults of various ages and to have more consistently positive interactions. Neighborhood preschool children love having my son push them on the tire swing. Elderly widows enjoy when we stop to talk with them when we walk our dog.

As Elizabeth's experiences confirm, one of the best services we can do for our kids is to help them expand the meaning of friend to someone beyond their immediate age group. Why can't we have friends who are little kids? Old people? The neighbor lady? Actually, our kids do understand this better than the rest of society. Although onlookers may witness that our kids don't have a lot of friends their own age, many of the parents surveyed mentioned friends that are outside the same-age definition. Joanna Rae's son's very good friend is his guitar teacher's wife, whom they visit weekly. A couple of parents noted that their children enjoy playing with kids younger than themselves, and Lydia's son has been more likely to play with girls "that would kind of mother him or look out for him." There isn't anything wrong with this. When my own son would sometimes be sad at not having friends (same-age friends), I would always remind him of the many people that liked him very much and were his friends – his babysitter, the neighbors, uncles, grandparents, and so forth. It's only the institution of school that has locked people into a restrictive mindset of defining friendship in the context of same age.

Parents do persist in worrying about socialization though, and it is justified when they have a child who resists interacting with other kids at all, refuses to join groups, and rejects the chance to spend time with other people. My gut instinct is that we can't force this sort of interaction, but neither can we give up and let our child stay on his own all the time. We just have to keep plugging away, bit by bit, with short and successful interactions. A five-minute successful chat with the lady down the street is a better idea than signing up a child for a gymnastics class that he is just not ready for. I know that parents can get a bit panicky when nothing seems to work, but in most cases I think they are just being too impatient or have not laid the groundwork. I signed up my son for a very small parks department magic class once. Since he was really keen on magic at the time I thought it would work, but it didn't. My son was still pretty scarred from his previous experience in special ed class, and when we walked into that meeting room with eight or so other boys sitting around a table, it looked too much like school and my son wanted no part of it. But I was able to join a babysitting co-op that same year and have one other kid over to the house and that worked better.

Once our kids are able to join a group activity of any sort, things open up quite a bit. LeAnn writes of her son Mitch (13):

> He crossed over to Boy Scouts last year, and started karate. He's found kids he gets along with in both those activities. The friendships don't extend outside the organized activities, but at least he's happy and fairly well accepted in Scouts and karate. This makes him more positive and motivated about homeschooling and life in general.

If something like Scouts or karate is too much (and both of these activities were too much for my son), you can start smaller. Annie has done a wonderful job of creating a social opportunity for her daughter Indigo based on a special interest. She operates a "Puppy Dog Club" that gives drinks of water to dogs at the Sunday Market. Says Annie: "Thus encaptured, we question the owners about their dogs. It's a cleverly disguised social skills group." Isn't that inspired?

Annie's daughter has also been able to be involved in puppet theatre. Annie has used puppets in social stories for a few years and it evolved into her daughter being able to be with other kids for the common purpose of putting on a show. Annie noted that when her daughter was "shoulder to shoulder with living breathing peers for a common purpose, there was a noticeable growth in being able to tolerate kids being 'closer' to her. She also took a leap in her mind blindness, as…she realized she was hidden, represented symbolically for an audience… She first acknowledged that there was value in group activity."

Some of us do have problems in choreographing social experiences for our kids. One mom who suspects she may be on the AS side herself writes:

> I'm not sure I'm the best person to be teaching my son social skills. I still have to psyche myself up to use the phone. I'm really going to have to go out of my comfort zone to make sure that he has social exposure. He hasn't had any time with peers since we took him out of school, except for Sunday School and a couple of afternoons with his cousins.

Another mom has the same sorts of issues:

> Although I have not been diagnosed, I think I probably have Aspergers myself. It is easy for me to doubt myself and wonder how I can teach my boys social skills when I myself have always struggled with social skills.

Yes, these moms both need to work extra hard to get out of their comfort zones, and I'm sure they will for the sake of their kids. But again, it can be gradual and start small. Perhaps the first mom could identify a child from Sunday School who might like to come over one afternoon and see where that takes things. We don't have to have daily activities. Most of us are quite satisfied with one or two outside activities per week, and any more than that tends to cause stress.

In the end, less is more. With small steps of steady progress, our kids will be able to be more social, although it may never approach the same level of socialization as society expects and our children's awkwardness may always be misunderstood. MJ notes: "I know that I will have to deal with people who think that he can't relate well to his peers *because* he's homeschooled. *I* know that's wrong, but it's hard to have people judge me anyway." Yes it is, and yes, it will occur. Our only recourse is to spend our energies helping our kids and ignore the other people.

Motivation

Some kids are resistant to parents' efforts at homeschooling in general. A few relate a "battle of the wills" all too often. Here are some possible causes and solutions:

1. Learning style mismatch – try a different type of learning style.

2. School phobic – try "unschooling" or take a break. You may be pressing too hard and causing your child to dig in his heels or feel overwhelmed.

3. Your child rejects you as teacher – a computer curriculum or a formal syllabus can take you out of the loop so that you're not the bad guy. You can't help it if that's what the syllabus says must be done!

4. Child is testing the waters – if you are comfortable with the work you are asking him to do, stand firm. After the tantrum, require (again) that the work be done. Taking away any and all screens (TV, video games, computer) can work wonders in getting a stubborn child's attention.

5. Child just seems generally unmotivated – appeal to his intellect. According to Tony Attwood, one of the things our children generally prize is being very smart. Instead of admonishing our kids to "be good," we are better off entreating them to "do the smart thing."

6. A rewards chart for work done can work for some children, although it can also cause stress in children who obsess about whether they will earn the reward. Use sparingly.

7.   If things are going badly all the way around, look for any changes in routine that may be throwing your child off. Also, beware of fever or colds. Bad behavior or upset often occurs in the days leading up to a bout of illness.

Siblings

"How do I homeschool my AS-affected child when I've got other children, too?" There's no magic formula, but here are the techniques several moms have used. Maybe one of them will work for you:

1.   *Juggling act.* Sometimes it's tricky, especially with a toddler. Jenn explains her situation and how she handles it:

> Having a toddler at home does make homeschooling much more challenging. Trying to balance the two boys has me pulling my hair out some days… Almost every day I have to tend to the baby at some point in the middle. Manny (6) puts on a prerecorded educational program or plays a computer game until I can get back to him.

2.   *Timing.* Marietta says: "I try to do most of our schooling after 7 pm when the toddler is asleep and I can give focused attention to Robby (5)."

3.   *More the merrier.* Fionna has a four-year-old daughter in addition to Ari, her first grader. Her technique is to include her daughter as much as possible.

4.   *See no evil.* When I homeschooled John and his little brother, there were days when my boys would really wind each other up. A good solution was to separate the kids and have one work at the computer while I worked with the other at the kitchen table. It gave us all a break.

> Sandy's two boys both have AS, and for a while she homeschooled both at home: "When both boys were homeschooled we made a screen to put across the dining room table for the days when they just couldn't get along. If they didn't see each other, they coped better."

5. *Divide and conquer.* For some families, this hasn't been an issue at all. The AS-affected child is homeschooled and the other child prefers to attend regular school. This works fine for everybody.

6. *Enjoy the camaraderie.* Some parents report positive experiences of siblings working together. Says Vicki from England:

> The four years of homeschooling together was terrific – they taught each other and Stephen learned so much by having another child to talk to, play with, especially someone who understood him, understood how to play with him…and it really freed me up as well. The benefits of them being together far outweighed the days of misery when no one felt like doing school.

Eventually though, Stephen's sister wanted to try the local school. Vicki has found it harder to homeschool since then:

> The special difficulties with Stephen being on his own has been the loss of the really beneficial interaction with his sister… When his sister was around doing it with him, there was always conversation, song and interaction. Being on his own has drained me even more than having the two of them, and has proved to be the greater challenge…Next academic year, they will both be homeschooled again and we are *all* looking forward to it!

Sarah G from Las Vegas, Nevada, has also found success with siblings. She explains: "Actually, it has made things easier. If Kathryn has a difficulty understanding something, her [same age] stepsister will try to explain it to her. Sometimes having a peer explain it makes it easier to understand."

Record keeping

How does one keep records? First, check with local homeschooling law to find out what you are required to do. Add to that anything you'd like to do. The families I queried ran the gamut, from one gal who had trouble even putting an X on a calendar to show what day had been a school day to a mom who records everything on a spreadsheet that she built on her computer. Most, however, reported using just two things:

- *A place to jot down what gets done each day.* This can be a calendar with large squares; a spiral notebook; a file box of index cards; a computer file; a planner; or a journal. Pick one, keep it handy, and use it daily.

- *A place to collect things your child has done.* This is called the portfolio method; it's a fancy name and a more permanent place than – but performs the same function as – the front of your refrigerator. Some schools require that you keep a portfolio of your child's best work, whether it is a written report, a watercolor picture, a math test, or other. Parents might use file folders, a notebook, a filing cabinet, or a plastic tub. I prefer the plastic tub because not everything you'll want to save fits in a file folder. You may wish to save a videotaped presentation, a clay model, a sample of sewing, or other hard-to-file objects. If you do wish to save pieces of flat artwork that are larger than the standard sized paper, simply cut two large pieces of cardboard and tape them securely together at the bottom to make your own homemade artist's portfolio.

Some parents have difficulty keeping track of their records, but this is something that's not only important for being legal in your area, it's also of terrific benefit to you. Many parents do not feel as though they are making much progress until they look back over the previous weeks and see just what did get accomplished.

Perfectionism

Diane writes of her son Allan (11):

> Because he demands such high standards of himself, by the time he's written a word that he can live with, he, because of his difficulty concentrating, has forgotten what he planned to write…thus more frustration.

It's tough enough to cope with our own mistakes, but homeschooling a child who flips out at every error is exceedingly difficult. You may recognize one or more of these reactions in your own child when he makes a mistake on an exercise or quiz:

- erases holes in the paper

- crumples up the paper

- flies into a rage

- dissolves in a puddle of tears

- gives up

- shuts down

- refuses to give an answer for fear he might be incorrect.

When you encounter any of these reactions, forward progress is stalled, and pretty soon you find yourself walking on eggshells in order not to provoke further negative responses. When this happens day after day, it can have a sizable impact on getting anything done.

It's hard to know just where this perfectionism comes from, but the child with Asperger Syndrome seems particularly prone to it. There is a variety of techniques that can be tried, and with luck one or more of the following tactics may be effective for you.

Model good behavior

You might say, "Oops, I goofed, but that's okay," to show your child that it is not the end of the world.

Grab some clichés

When I could see that my son was upset over having an incorrect answer I posted some tried and true sayings up on the walls of our kitchen where we worked. The ones I posted were "You can't make an omelet without breaking some eggs," "If you don't make at least one mistake a day, you're not trying," and my favorite, "If you can't make a mistake, you can't make anything." Here are some additional quotes by famous people:

> Whether you think that you can or that you can't, you are usually right. (Henry Ford)

> Only those who dare to fail greatly can ever achieve greatly. (Robert Kennedy)

Take a chance and you may lose. Take not a chance and you have lost already. (Soren Kierkegaard)

Failure is the opportunity to begin again more intelligently. (Benjamin Disraeli)

Learn from the masters

Babe Ruth was not only the homerun king of baseball, he was the strikeout king. Abraham Lincoln went bankrupt and lost several elections. Thomas Edison failed to find the proper material to use as a lightbulb filament about a thousand times, but he preferred to think of it as being successful a thousand times, at determining which materials would not work. It's all in the attitude.

Make perfection sound less perfect

It always seemed a shame that even though I might be pleased if my son got 95 percent on a spelling quiz, he would still be hugely upset because he hadn't gotten 100 percent. I finally explained to him that if I were to give him a test and found that he got only half or less correct, I would know that the test was too hard for him. However, if he always got 100 percent on a test, then it was too easy for him. So, I reasoned that one or two wrong was just right. That's right, it's *good* news. That helped him a lot. Of course, he still enjoyed getting 100 percent correct, but if he got one or two wrong he would just say, "I got one wrong, but that's okay, isn't it? It means it's a good test." Our day went much smoother under these new guidelines.

Keeping costs down

"I would like to know how to keep the cost of homeschooling down. What are some creative free resources?" This book is devised to give you as many free or frugal ideas as possible because I firmly believe that you do not have to have a lot of money to homeschool your child (and that includes a child with Asperger Syndrome). What follows are the top five money-saving resources.

Library

Most people think they know what's in their local library, but they don't. Yes, there are books and magazines, but also musical CDs and cassettes, movies, books on tape, archived newspapers, and historical material on microfiche. Libraries also have databases that allow you access to professional journal articles, and usually have some computers, word copiers, and copy machines for public use.

Libraries also have meeting rooms, which are great for a homeschool group meeting or a mini-class. Libraries may have kiddie story hours, summer reading programs, contests, educational talks, and so forth. Be sure to get onto their mailing list, and check out their bulletin boards, which are frequently teeming with local announcements. If you are looking for other families of special needs kids, other families who homeschool, or both, put up your own notice.

Many libraries have display cases begging to be filled by someone with a collection of interesting items. Maybe your child has a special interest that someone else would like to see? My son was able to display his brass bell collection in our local library. The project inspired him to polish his bells, make labels for the different countries of origin, and figure out how to display them in an interesting way. The nice comments from library visitors were a great payoff for his work too.

Don't forget inter-library loan, which allows you to borrow from other area libraries. Also, libraries have a book budget to spend and welcome suggestions on what to buy. If there is a book or magazine subscription you'd like to see, ask.

Internet

This has been amply covered throughout this book, but also do try to get hold of the book *Homeschool Your Child for Free* (Gold and Zielinski 2000). It's full of great website information.

Used curriculum sales

Libraries often have book sales once or twice per year. Used bookstores often carry books useful to homeschoolers. School districts sometimes sell or give away textbooks that they no longer use. A phone call might let you know if you can get in on this good deal. Used curricula are also bought and sold online (see Appendix 2).

Your local homeschool group

If you join a homeschool group, see if they hold swap nights. Let other members know what material you are seeking. Ask if the group could buy a piece of equipment (microscope, telescope, etc.) and make it available.

You can also make your own learning tools and experiences. Some ideas are contained in this book, but you can come up with more on your own.

Diet

Jackie writes: "I am interested in special diets, if anyone has found them to be effective with Asperger Syndrome." Twenty-two surveyed families answered this particular question, and of those 12 were following a special diet. Mostly this was the gluten-free/casein-free (no wheat or dairy) diet, which is often recommended for people on the autism spectrum. In a couple of cases the family was monitoring dairy only. Some families mentioned taking dietary enzymes and/or vitamins. At least one family was vegetarian. Also, three families noted problems in getting their kids to eat at all due to finicky tendencies or oral sensitivities. Several families noted that their inroads into diet had gone much smoother after starting to homeschool. According to Ruth:

> It's easier to be gluten-free/casein-free without having to watch other children eating forbidden foods. That last time we tried it Jordan was in school and we made many errors.

And Sarah G reports:

> Kathryn is currently on the gluten-free/casein-free diet and we are seeing great improvements! I had tried the diet when she was in public school, but it didn't work because she was able to sneak food from the cafeteria or her friends and go off the diet. Now that she is older and is home, the diet is a success.

Medication

Several kids are on medications of various sorts, usually to deal with attention issues, but sometimes dealing with other problems such as anxiety or depression. At least three families reported that a child who was on Ritalin or other ADD medication was able to go off of it once they began homeschooling. This was the case for my son too. Once we reduced the amount of sensory input and overall stimulation from his day, we found that he didn't need the Ritalin.

Lucy's son is now back in school after a few years of homeschooling. He took Ritalin prior to homeschooling, nothing while homeschooling, and has begun to take Concerta (essentially time-release Ritalin) now that he is back in school. Sarah G talks about her daughter Kathryn:

> She was on Ritalin at the time we began to homeschool. After a short transitional period, we were able to take her off of the medication because there were not all the distractions that public school has so there wasn't a struggle for her attention.

A couple of parents whose children have remained on medication noted that adjusting medication sometimes had the effect of making their child extra tired or sleepy. On those days, homeschooling was an advantage in that they would simply let their child sleep in and catch up later.

General household issues

"My kids tear the house apart. I need help in how to keep the house under control and teach them to clean up after themselves." It's a special challenge to have your kids at home all day long and sometimes the house can really suffer unless you employ some tricks:

- Schedule a clean-up as part of your homeschooling day. A break between classes can be a three-minute march around the room with everyone picking up clutter.

- A daily chore chart can help too, or a points system to encourage kids to pitch in.

- You might also think about stowing away some toys or giving some away. Fill a bag for charity and incorporate that into your day as a social lesson in community living. Encourage the kids to choose items they no longer want and give those things to those less fortunate.

- It's easier to put things away if there is a definite "this goes *here*, that goes *there*" plan. Our kids can't deal with a generic command to pick up clutter or clean a room because they don't have a definite idea of what and how much and where. Be extremely specific and you might get much better results.

Burnout

"The biggest drawback to homeschooling is for me. There is no time for me now and I keep saying it will get better, but it hasn't yet and I truly worry about burnout, as I have few opportunities to recharge my own batteries."

Lack of personal time is a big issue, but it does help to realize that the early years are the worst. Most of our kids do learn to work more independently as they mature. Beyond that, moms had these suggestions. Sim G says:

> Take a little time off if you can, and then start reading the homeschool resource catalogs! This always inspires me, even if I don't actually buy anything. Reading about some other angles and approaches to various subjects in the blurbs following the product information always seems to spark a renewed enthusiasm for me to jump back in.

Joanna Rae:

> Well, I'm learning to turn "those" weeks into good weeks by just letting go. We're doing a lot of playing at the local pond and just following his lead. He always comes back to what he's learning and usually has done some percolating in the meantime. I'm the one who has to learn to honor his process. Sigh.

Margaret W says: "The hardest thing for me is patience, day in and day out. Scheduling only four days a week helps, because some days she just can't focus... I use the fifth day as catch up."

And from me – read the works of John Holt, John Taylor Gatto, and other inspirational educators who write thoughtfully on what education really is. Other choices might be Grace Llewellyn, David and Micki Colfax, David Guterson, and Cafi Cohen. Every time I read the words of these people, I get excited again and seem to remember where it is that I am going. And, they also help me relax about the whole thing.

Other suggestions include: take a day "off" and have fun with your child; unschool a while; go on vacation; take a walk, with or without your child; hire a sitter; journal about what you are trying to do and why; soak in the tub; watch a funny movie.

Quitting

In the course of this book's research, four children of the 40 or so represented stopped homeschooling at some point. Two have been mentioned previously. They both began homeschooling for safety reasons (due to bullying and threat of physical harm). In the case of the boy we heard about in Chapter 1, homeschooling stopped an intensely stressful school situation that drove a junior high schooler close to suicide. After two years of positive and successful homeschooling experiences he was able to return to school (high school this time) and is now doing well.

A second boy, profiled in Chapter 3, wanted to stop homeschooling because he missed his "friends" (even though some were no more than bullies and he was lured into frequent fights). Against his parents' better judgment, he recently returned to school. He is currently one incident away from being expelled, and his mother expects she will be homeschooling him again soon.

The other two are girls. In Emma's case (now 13), homeschooling saved her from an unsuccessful school situation, but her adoptive father Keith found that academic learning stalled after six months, in spite of his best efforts. She grew unwilling to work, and the whole thing became extremely frustrating for both of them. Eventually, it was discovered that what had been suspected to be an autistic disorder was really fetal alcohol syndrome, which went far in explaining the cognitive and behavioral issues she was having. A proper diagnosis and a highly structured Montessori-based system was the next step. She has since aged out of that program and is now in a special education program at public school with lots of supports, and is doing well. Keith is glad he homeschooled Emma, though. He explains:

> It gave her time to catch her breath and fill in some missing spots in her learning…The knowledge I picked up concerning her behavioral delays, her auditory processing problems, her memory processing problems, and her still existing gaps were invaluable

when it came time to rewrite her IEP. I could tell them whether their goals were realistic or simplistic because I knew exactly what she could and couldn't do...I think if I had a regret it would be that I didn't know about Montessori soon enough. She needed some time to get away from the whole school environment, but when she started to not work for me, I think we lost about a half a year by not getting her into something like Montessori.

Sue S decided to make a change for her daughter Penny (11) after three years in a homeschool-like charter school program. Sue taught Penny at home under the school's guidance, also enrolling her at the school's resource center where she could take a course or two with other students in the same program. Sue ran into two problems. First, the resource center courses had the same fatal flaws for Penny as traditional classroom setups. Sue writes:

Penny's getting less social as time goes on. She's had a lot of sort of failures at her charter school, of trying classes and then not wanting to stay in them because of her Asperger issues (too much noise; too many kids; too much of a lecture blah-blah-blah approach for her to take it all in, etc.). She's also had failures at trying to make friends there. She gets shut down a lot by kids her own age who...don't want to include her. She's getting to where she doesn't like people and she's pretty vocal about that. So I see her going from being socially delayed to possibly becoming antisocial.

The charter school was unwilling to provide Penny an in-class aide and, although Sue could have forced the issue legally, there was another problem too:

As she's gotten more into puberty, she's more oppositional with me and less willing to sit down and do anything that resembles schoolwork. She's happiest just being left to her own devices, playing on the computer for hours on end. Some of the things she does on the computer have educational value – she's started a wolf lovers' guild on Neopets [online game group] and she IMs [does instant messaging] with her little computer friends from across the country and she can write web pages. So she does a lot of writing online. She also writes cartoons and draws a lot. And she is happy to study science books about things that interest her –

usually we get a stack of books about a different animal each week at the library. But it is harder and harder over time to get her to sit down with me to do math or read some social studies or even just to read for pleasure.

Sue decided that rather than pushing for an aide at the charter school and then still having to butt heads with her daughter at home, she would look around the district again to see if options had improved. She was happy to find a small year-round special education class geared specifically for high functioning autistic students that hadn't been available before. After minor transitional issues, Penny is flourishing there.

Sue, like the others, is happy for having had the experience of homeschooling. It was a better option than others available at the time, and it has given her a level of insight into Penny's learning that she couldn't have acquired in any other way. She is open to the idea of homeschooling again, and anticipates that the junior high years might be a mix of special education and homeschool. If she does homeschool again, she will use more of a structured approach with some behavior modification. In a letter to me she wrote:

> I feel very in tune with the premise of your first book, Lise, that we are sort of "hitchhiking" a ride with this special ed program for right now, and it will probably be a ride that will work for the rest of this school year and for next year. After that, who knows?

Chapter 10
Final Thoughts

This book is about finding one's own path. But while the families represented here have all traveled different roads, they have also trod the same ground in places too. Here are some views many families have noticed along the way:

- Our kids have "on" days and "off" days.

- Lots of families instinctively fall into a pattern of working four days and leaving the fifth day more relaxed, or having a quiet day after a busy one.

- Our kids' days flow more smoothly with some predictability. Set a schedule that is firm enough to provide comforting structure, but loose enough to account for inevitable changes.

- Giving your child a small amount of choice can do wonders.

- Our kids become more sociable when they feel less threatened.

- Several modest successes beat one big failure.

- A happy playdate with just one other kid teaches more than a miserable playdate with ten kids.

- Ten math problems set before the child is an uphill climb. One problem (and then another and another until you get to ten) is the same distance, but downhill.

- Too much sensory input can cause panic. Just a little one day and a little more the next will increase the threshold.

A potpourri of quotes

Since I've been talking a great deal, it's time to let some of the 40 families say a few final things:

> I am absolutely thrilled with our experience. The biggest benefits (wow, how do I choose?) would be the closeness of our family, the reduction of stress, the freedom to go where we want, learn what we want, and do what we want. The drawbacks are really minor – loss of public school services (which weren't all that great anyway) and the public misconceptions. No regrets at all. (Fionna – Ari, 7)

> Even though it is hard, I believe homeschooling is the very best way to preserve my son's childhood and make it a happy one. If he was in school, his deficits would be a constant focus, he would be teased, he would in general be made to feel more different than he already is. With homeschooling, we can focus on my son's strengths, and gently ease into social situations as he is ready. We work on his deficits throughout our day in a natural fashion. He is a happy, exuberant child with amazing self-esteem. I believe homeschooling will allow him to grow to adulthood with those qualities still intact. (Marietta – Robby, 5)

> My daughter needs one-on-one instruction. I've found that if I'm too far away from her (more than five feet) she doesn't "hear" what I've said to her. If you're going to engage her attention you have to be close, efficient with words, flexible and willing to try again with different phrasing if she didn't get it. Once she's got it, it's hers and she blossoms, but you have to make sure she gets it. An inclusion classroom with 30 other students, a dozen of them with learning disabilities, was not the place for her to learn. (Margaret W – Michaela, 11)

> In terms of AS – it is definitely worthwhile. I've seen my child blossom at home – he's becoming more social and can focus on the things he's really interested. He is more "grounded" and sure of himself. No regrets yet! (Marie – Michael, 6)

> I would say that so far homeschooling has been a challenging but positive experience. On the upside, I don't have to guess any more what his day was like, why he might be upset, etc. I also love to see him learn something new, and I know that he's not getting lost in

a crowd. On the downside, homeschooling takes a lot of time. And as selfish as this may sound, it's difficult not to get a break from him. I know we made the right decision, though, at least for now. (Jenn B – Manny, 6)

It is worthwhile because I have researched schools/programs in our area. We the parents are the only ones who can give her the one on one attention/therapy that she needs. I know in the long run it will give her the best chance to live a "normal" life in our society. (Jamie – Autumn, 3)

My son loves being homeschooled and I love that it has been such a positive experience for him. The biggest difficulty with public school was the teasing/harassing he experienced during unsupervised times (e.g., recess, bathroom breaks, lunch, etc.). The taunting was beginning to impact his perception of who he was and he was depressed. Homeschooling has given him a new outlook on life and given him many positive social interactions, while continuing to challenge him intellectually. (Elizabeth – Eric, 11)

I'd have to admit that I entered homeschooling kicking and screaming but that I've slowly seen the benefits more-and-more with each passing year. (LeAnn – Mitch, 13)

A big regret I have is ever being involved in the black hole of special education. I wish I had embraced homeschooling as a first option. (Annie – Indigo, 10)

Probably the biggest benefit to homeschooling Mitch has been his general mental attitude… I sure haven't been SuperMom (anything but!!!) but I think just being away from the teasing, bullying, etc. that many AS kids experience in public school has been helpful for him. In my local AS support group, I've seen kids who have been broken down by the school system start to develop better self-concepts when they are finally brought home to be educated. (LeAnn)

I have been happy with my decision to homeschool. I have seen enormous improvement in Kathryn since beginning to homeschool. Her social skills have improved a great deal. She is able to function in a group setting with little difference from her peers. I love the closeness it has developed between Kathryn and me. As she enters her teens, we have a close relationship that I don't see in families that are using the public school system. I honestly cannot think of any drawbacks and I have no regrets. (Sarah G – Kathryn, 12)

The biggest benefit I see is the ability to tailor my teaching methods to his strengths and weaknesses without having to take into account the needs of a whole class full of students. Also, I think he will be better off socially, he will be able to pick who he associates with more. Next year he'll be in 6th grade, which is middle school in the public school. Middle school is the worst time period for teasing and bullying, and I'm glad he won't have to be exposed to all of that. (MJ – Peter, 11)

Craig needs recovery time after he's been around people so on Wednesdays and Fridays, he sleeps in and does a lot of his school work in his room. (Marilyn – Craig, 17)

I believe homeschooling is a very viable option for some situations. It is definitely worth considering for the mental well being of the child *and* his family! (Diana R – Neal, 12)

There is not just one way, one therapy/treatment, or one person that knows everything. Take the time to research and set up a game plan. Keep researching because that game plan will change as your child grows up. Do not be afraid to change doctors, therapists, or therapies. Also, it is OK to blaze your own trail. You are the parent and you do know what is best for your child! (Jamie – Autumn, 3)

[Parents need to know] that you don't have to work on everything at once! Homeschooling is a process… Your child will continue to learn and progress through *all* your homeschooling time, and they will have advanced far more than they would have in school. (Marietta – Robby, 5)

From my personal perspective, there is no doubt in my mind that the three years that I homeschooled my son were the absolutely most critical three years. They made all the difference. Homeschooling took him off of a predetermined pathway of failure, permanent special education, likely behavior problems, depression, and who knows what? In three years we were able to start again, and this time with some sensitivity and the hope of success. We also looked at diet issues, got rid of medication he no longer needed, and bolstered both his academic ability and his confidence.

I recently asked John, who is now 19 and taking freshman courses at a community college, if he had any regrets about having been homeschooled and what he thought of it. With his usual economy of words, he said, "No regrets. It was great." I asked if he would have changed anything, and he said, "No, nothing." I asked what his favorite parts were, and he said, "I liked it all."

I'm not sure if my interview skills need work, or if John felt I'd already written enough on the subject and he had little to add. One thing that he did do was to compare his various school experiences. He told me that homeschooling was far better than all of his public school experiences, but that he had enjoyed his private school experiences the most.

If you thought that I would be wounded to find out that my homeschool efforts didn't win top prize, you would be mistaken. It only confirms to me the importance of the years that we did homeschool because it was only during homeschooling that he was allowed the time and focus to bring himself up to a level where he could, finally, not only survive in a regular school, but also come to enjoy it. We could have homeschooled all the way through, but he wanted to go back to try school again, and he was now able to reach that goal. What could be better? If he had wanted to homeschool through high school, or if I had firmly felt that he was not ready to tackle a more traditional school setting, we would have set a different goal.

The bottom line is that I am at peace that we started homeschooling for the right reasons. I'm convinced that we stopped for the right reasons too, and were always ready to fall back to homeschooling if things hadn't worked out.

It seems that a large percentage of families that turn to homeschooling initially do so from negative reasons – desperation, dissatisfaction, or fear – because the public school options are usually so out of step with what works for the child with Asperger Syndrome. Reasons for homeschooling take on a more positive glow shortly after families start, however, when they begin to see their child relax, blossom, and excel. Scores of families have been so impressed with the results of home education that they plan to continue for several years, but even for those who later choose other options homeschooling has still been of benefit.

It has offered breathing room, has allowed families to be more selective and to have more options, and the experience has made parents intimately connected with how their child learns and exactly what it is that their child needs. In that way, parents will always be better advocates for having homeschooled, even if they return to the public schools because their child is more ready to cope or more appropriate options are now available.

In the end, homeschooling is not a panacea, but it's an option worth considering, and it just could be one of the best decisions you will ever make for your special child. Good luck with whatever you decide.

Appendix 1

Asperger Resources

General autism/Asperger Syndrome information
Australia

Autism Association of South Australia
PO Box 339
Fullerton
South Australia 5063
Tel: (08) 8379 6976
Email: aasa@adelaide.on.net
Website: www.span.com.au/autism/

Autism Association Queensland, Inc.
PO Box 363
Sunnybank
Queensland 4109
Tel: (07) 3273 0000
Email: mailbox@autismqld.asn.au
Website: www.uq.net.au/~zzacook/aaq/

Autism Victoria
PO Box 235
Ashburton
Victoria 3147
Tel: (03) 9885 0533
Email: autismav@vicnet.net.au
Website: http://home.vicnet.net.au/~autism/

Canada

Autism Society Manitoba
825 Sherbrook Street
Winnipeg
Manitoba R3A 1M5
Tel: (204) 783-9563
Email: asm@escape.ca
Website: www.hsc.mb.ca/autismprogram/autism_society_monitoba.htm

Autism Society of Ontario
1 Greensboro Drive, Suite 306
Etobicoke
Ontario M9W 1C8
Tel: (416) 246-9592
Email: mail@autismsociety.on.ca
Website: www.autismsociety.on.ca/

Child and Family Canada
Website: www.cfc-efc.ca/
Has an online library of 1300 documents on various child development issues.

UK

National Autistic Society (NAS)
393 City Road
London EC1V 1NG
Autism Helpline: (0870) 600 8585
Tel: (0)20 7833 2299
Email: nas@nas.org.uk
Website: www.oneworld.org/autism_uk

USA

Autism Society of America (ASA)
7910 Woodmont Avenue, Suite 300
Bethesday, MD 20814-3015
Tel: (800) 3AUTISM or (301) 657-0881
Website: www.autism-society.org

CHIP
U.S. Dept. of Health and Human Services
Tel: (877) 543-7669
Website: www.insurekidsnow.gov/
Contact to find your state's program of Children's Health Insurance.

On-Line Asperger Information and Support (OASIS)
Website: www.udel.edu/bkirby/asperger/

Advocacy and legal
Australia

Disability Information and Resource Centre (DIRC) South Australia
195 Gilles Street
Adelaide
South Australia 5000
Tel: (08) 8223 7522
Email: dirc@dircsa.org.au
Website: www.dircsa.org.au/pub/docs/links.htm#Index
An excellent resource with links to agencies throughout Australia.

Queensland Disability Information and Awareness Line (DIAL)
3rd Floor, 75 Williams Street
Brisbane
Tel: (07) 3224 8444 or 1800 177 120
Email:dial@disability.qld.gov.au

Canada

B.C. Self-Advocacy Foundation
3rd Floor, 30 East 6th Avenue
Vancouver
BC V5T 4P4
Tel: (604) 875-1119
Email: gschiller@bacl.org
Website: www.vcn.bc.ca/bacl/bcsaf.html

Canadian Association for Community Living
Kinsmen Building
York University
4700 Keele Street
Toronto
Ontario M3J 1P3
Tel: (416) 661-9611
Email: info@cacl.ca
Website: www.cacl.ca/english/index.html

UK

Advocacy Service Manager
National Autistic Society
393 City Road
London EC1V 1NG
Education Advocacy Line: 0800 358 8667
Tribunal Support Scheme: 0800 358 8668
Email: advocacy@nas.org.uk

USA

Amicus for Children, Inc.
1023 Old Swede Road
Douglassville, PA 19518
Tel: (610) 689-4226
Email: amicusforchildren@att.net
Website: www.amicusforchildren.org/

Wrightslaw
Email: webmaster@wrightslaw.com
Website: www.wrightslaw.com
Note: this site, while commercial, provides useful articles on special
education law.

Homeschool Resources

National support organizations for homeschoolers
Australia
A to Z Home's Cool
Website: www.gomilpitas.com/homeschooling/regional/australia.htm

Homeschooling Supplies
PO Box 688
Werribee
Victoria 3030
Tel: (03) 9742 7524
Email: office@homeschooling.com.au
Website: www.homeschooling.com.au/

Canada
Association of Canadian Home-Based Education (ACHBE)
c/o J. Campbell
PO Box 34148
RPO Fort Richmond
Winnipeg
Manitoba R3T 5T5
(Please include SASE or $1 if you require a written response)
Email: homeschool-ca-admin@flora.org
Website: www.flora.org/homeschool-ca/achbe/

Canadian Home Based Learning resource page
Website: www.flora.org/homeschool-ca/

New Zealand
Homeschooling Federation of New Zealand
PO Box 41226
St. Lukes
Auckland
Website: www.homeschooling.org.nz/

UK
Education Otherwise
PO Box 7420
London N9 9SG
UK Helpline: 0870 730 0074
Website: www.education-otherwise.org/

Home Education Advisory Service
PO Box 98
Welwyn Garden City
Herts AL8 6AN
Tel: 01707 371854
Email: admin@heas.org.uk
Website: www.heas.org.uk

USA
National Challenged Homeschoolers Association (NATHHAN)
Tel: (206) 857-4257
Website: www.nathhan.com/

National Home Education Network (NHEN)
PO Box 41067
Long Beach, CA 90853
Email: info@nhen.org
Website: http://nhen.org/

Online support groups for homeschooling autistic or Asperger children

AS-HFA-homeschool
http://groups.yahoo.com/group/AS-HFA-homeschool/

Aspergers Homeschool
http://groups.yahoo.com/group/AspergersHomeschool/

Aut-2B-Home
http://www.weirdkids.com/autism/aut2bhome.html

Aut-home-fam
http://groups.yahoo.com/group/aut-home-fam/

AutismUnschool
http://groups.yahoo.com/group/AutismUnschool/

HomeschoolingAspies
http://groups.yahoo.com/group/HomeschoolingAspies/

Homeschooling Kids with Disabilities
http://groups.yahoo.com/group/hkwd/

Parents Rearing and Education Autistic Children in Christian Homes
http://groups.yahoo.com/group/PREACCH/

General homeschooling resources

frugal_homeschooling (chat with other homeschoolers)
Website: http://groups.yahoo.com/group/frugal_homeschooling/

GED
Tel: (202) 939-9490 or (800) 626-9433

Website: www.acenet.Edu/calec/ged/intro-TT.cfm (general info)
www.acenet.Edu/calec/ged/disability-accom-TT.cfm (for disabled
test-takers)

homeschool_stuff (free sharing of resources, mostly web-based things)
Website: http://groups.yahoo.com/group/homeschool_stuff/

Recycled_Learning_Homeschool (sell and buy homeschooling
materials)
Website: http://groups.yahoo.com/group/Recycled_Learning_Homeschool/

Australia

Australian Unschoolers (not Asperger related) (esp. New South Wales)
Website: http://groups.yahoo.com/group/australianunschoolers/

Christian Homeschooling in Australia (not Asperger related)
Website: http://groups.yahoo.com/group/ChristianHomeschoolinginAustralia/

Eclectic Homeschoolers in Australia (not Asperger related)
Website: http://groups.yahoo.com/group/EACHE/

Canada

h-l Victoria (Home learners hotline, Victoria)
Website: http://groups.yahoo.com/group/hl-victoria/

HomeSchool_In_Quebec (not Asperger related)
Website: http://groups.yahoo.com/group/HomeSchool_In_Quebec/

hs-nb (Homeschool in New Brunswick) (not Asperger related)
Website: http://groups.yahoo.com/group/hs-nb/

Appendix 3

Social Skills

The following social skills are the sorts of things our children typically struggle with. Decide which items apply to your child and introduce them through real-life experiences, stories, puppets, games, discussion, role playing, or other.

In some ways, everything seems like a social skill, so it's easy for this list to swell. Best of luck as you devise your own list or work with this one.

Being in a group. What is teamwork? Can everybody be in charge? How do we join a group? Discuss playing fair, accepting group decisions.

Being lost or losing things. How can we keep from getting lost? What should we do if we do become lost?

Being on the bus. Do we sit or stand? Talk to driver?

Body movements. Going through a door politely. Shaking hands. Pointing a finger. Following a pointing finger with your eyes. Common gestures.

Body space. Hugs – too tight? Should you ask first? Whom may you hug? The mailman? A stranger? Who might hug you?

Cars. Seatbelts. Parking lot (car park) safety. Crossing the street, traffic lights, noisy trucks, car horns. Sounds and smells.

Clothes. Dressing for the weather. Why do we change clothes every day?

Dealing with animals. Will they bite? Do you tease them? Feed them?

Dealing with special people. Babies – should we pick them up? Old people. People in wheelchairs or with canes.

Elevators, escalators. Is it safe? How long is the ride? Getting on and off.

Emotions. What does happy look like? Angry? Surprised? Afraid? Confused? Embarrassed? Excited? Worried? Sad? Proud? Startled?

Fire and smoke. Fire alarms and smoke alarms. What do they sound like? What do they mean? What should we do?

Food issues. Table manners. Table conversation.

Handling upset. What upsets us? What does anger look and feel like? Using words instead of actions. What words? Expressing anger, asking for help. Calming techniques – slow breathing; counting to ten; taking a walk.

Hygiene. Nose blowing. Sneezing/coughing. Washing.

Lying. What is lying? Fact versus opinion.

Making a friend. Making a friendly face – what does it look like? How do we sit if we want to make friends?

Making choices. For example, flavors of ice-cream, etc. There is no wrong answer. If we choose one, we can't have the other – next time we can change our choice.

Making conversation. What topics might be good? Not good? How do we tell if someone wants to be friends? What are some nice greetings?

Mistakes. Is it okay to make mistakes? Should we laugh at someone's mistake? What if someone laughs at our mistake?

Ordering food. So many choices! Small, medium, large, what might be asked? What if they do not have what you order?

Ownership and respecting people's things. Who owns it? If you find it, is it yours? Asking to borrow something. How long do you keep it?

Phone skills. Calling someone. Leaving a message. Taking a message.

Public bathrooms. Why are they extra noisy?

Special occasions. Birthdays – someone else's? Our own? Christmas or other holidays – special events, noise, what to expect.

Special places. Movies. Bowling. Swimming. Shopping. Museums. Library. A stranger's house.

Voices. Indoor voices and outdoor voices. How/when to whisper.

Waiting. Waiting in line – where might we have to wait in line? For example, grocery store, movies, amusement parks.

What is a friend? Do they give things to you? Share? Do they take turns with you? Offer to help? Walk with you? What is not a friend?

Winning and losing. Learning to say "Good game!" and "Better luck next time." For the winner, learning to say "You played well."

Appendix 4
Facial Expressions

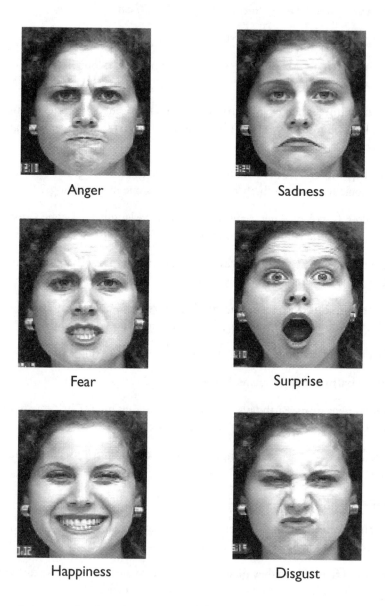

Anger

Sadness

Fear

Surprise

Happiness

Disgust

Permission to print these images granted by Prof. Jeffrey Cohn, Department of Psychology, University of Pittsburgh.

Appendix 5

Idioms

All bark and no bite
All eyes up front
Are you up for it?
At my wit's end
At the end of my rope
Back to square one
Bad apple
Bad seed
Birds of a feather
Burning the candle at both ends
Buy a clue
Call someone on the carpet
Carry on
Champing at the bit
Cheeky
Chill out
Chuck a wobbly (Aus)
Combing through my notes
Cop out
Couch potato
Crocodile tears
Cry wolf
Cut someone a break
Dark cloud on the horizon
Dark look
Dirty look
Don't count your chickens
Don't push it
Don't push my buttons
Don't put words in my mouth
Don't rock the boat
Don't yank my chain

Double-edged sword
Drop your eyes
Dropping a hint
Eagle-eye
Eat your heart out
Elbow-grease
Fast-burner
First cab off the rank (Aus)
Fix your gaze
Flu shot (Aus) / flu jab (UK)
Frog in your throat
Gag order
Get a grip
Get one's nose out of joint
Get your kicks
Give her a hand
Give in
Give out
Give them a big hand!
Give up
Glass is half empty
Glass jaw
Glued to the TV
Gobsmacked (UK)
Gun shy
Have a try (US) / have a go (Aus)
Have your cake and eat it too
He can't carry it off
He's green
Head in the sand
Hit the nail on the head
Hop to it

In a funk
I've got your number
John Doe
John Q. Public
Johnny-come-lately
Jump right on it
Keep your eyeballs peeled
Keep your shirt on
Kick someone out
Kick the bucket
Lend me a hand
Lend me your ear
Let the cat out of the bag
Lift your spirits
Like a chicken with your head cut off
Like a cut snake (Aus)
Like water off a duck
Loan shark
Lost in thought
Lower your voice
Lucky stiff
Mary Sunshine
May I have your name?
Mutton dressed as lamb (UK, Aus)
Nose up in the air
Off-base
On the wrong side of the bed
Paint yourself into a corner
Pot luck (US) / plate dinner (Aus)
Pull any punches
Pull your leg
Put a sock in it
Put on your thinking cap
Put some wellie into it (UK)
Raise a question
Raise your voice
Rat on someone
Read between the lines
Read someone's face
Read the fine print
Roll with the punches
Rub someone up the wrong way

Scream your head off
Seven ways to Sunday
Shattered
She won't stand for it
Silver lining
Sink your teeth into it
Sit down
Sit up
Skin and bones
Sleep on it
Smell a rat
Smell trouble
Smoko (Aus)
Sour grapes
Splitting hairs
Spot something
Standing order
Stay on your toes
Stick to it
Stick together
Stop on a dime (US)
Take a powder
Take a stab at
Take for granted
That takes guts
The cat's got your tongue
Thick-skinned or thin-skinned
Throw a fit
Throw someone a look
Tie one on
Turn the other cheek
Uncle Sam
Under his thumb
Under the table
Up a creek without a paddle
Up a tree
Wear your heart on your sleeve
Wet behind the ears
What are you trying to pull?
What does it stand for?
Wrap it up
You have a lot on your plate

Appendix 6

Sample High School Transcript (US)

Name: _____ Birth Date: _____

Address: _____ SS#: _____

City, State & Zip code:_____ Gender: _____

Phone: _____ Name of Parent(s): _____

Name Used: _____ GPA: _____Class Rank: _1_ out of _1_

SAT Scores: _____ Test Date: _____ Graduation Date: _____

Grade/ School/ School Year	Course taken	Grade	Credits Earned	Grade/ School/ School Year	Course taken	Grade	Credits Earned

Key to Schools attended:

_____

_____

_____

Total Accumulation of Credits Earned

School Year	English	Math	Science	Social Studies	PE Health	Foreign Language	Electives

Oakwood High School Secondary School Record

Name: _____Daniel Sample_____ Birth Date: __01/00/1984__

Address: _____1234 Big Oak Lane_____ SS#: ___123-45-6789___

City, State & Zip code:__Yourtown, TX, 00000__ Gender: __M__

Phone: _123-456-7890_ Name of Parent(s): __Don S. and Cathy Sample__

Name Used: __Daniel Sample__ GPA: _3.83_ Class Rank: _1_ out of _1_

SAT Scores: _1340 Verbal 650, Math 690_

Test Date: _06/01/01_ Graduation Date: __16/02__

Grade/ Location	Year	Course Title	Final		Yearly Cumulative Totals	
			Grade	Credit	Credits	GPA
8/B		Algebra I (Honors) :H :J	88	1.0		
9/C		English I	79	1.0		
9/C		Geometry (Honors) :H	86	1.0		
9/C	97–98	Biology (Honors) :H	89	1.0		
9/C	98–99	Geography	89	1.0		
9/C		Health	100	0.5		
9/C		PE	96	0.5		
9/C		Bible I	88	1.0		
					7.0	3.79

10/C		English II	81	1.0		
10/C		Algebra II (Honors) :H	88	1.0		
10/C		Chemistry (Honors) :H	92	1.0		
10/C	99–00	World History	82	1.0		
10/C		PE – Athletics	95	0.5		
10/C		Journalism	100	1.0		
10/C		Bible	93	1.0	6.5	3.85
11/O		American Literature	82	1.0		
11/O		Speech	100	0.5		
11/O		Trig (Honors) :H	93	0.5		
11/M		Plane Trig: D :H :R	A	1.0		
11/O		Physics (Honors) :H	90	1.0		
11/O	00–01	US History	85	1.0		
11/C		PE – Athletics	100	1.0		
11/O		Oil Painting	100	0.5		
11/O		Drama	100	0.5		
11/O		Intro Logic	100	0.5		
11/O		Bible	86	1.0	8.5	3.86
12/O		British Literature	P	P		
12/M		An. Geom. :D :H	P	P		
12/M		Gen. Physics :D :H	B	1.0		
12/O	01–02	Government/Econ	P	P		
12/O		PE – Athletics	100	0.5		
12/M		Comp. Literacy :D	A	1.0		
12/O		Cooking	100	0.5		
12/O		Bible	P	P		
					4.0/P	3.83

Grade Scale: A 90–100; B 80–89; C 70–79; D 64–69; F<64; P Course in Progress

Weight for 1-credit courses: A=4; B=3; C=2; D=1; F=0

Weight for Honors/College Courses: A=5; B=4; C=3

Location of Schools

Code	School Name and Address
B	Byrd Jr. High School, 1000 W. Wherever Rd., Downtownville, TX, 00000
C	ChristWay Academy, 123 N. Cedar Ridge, Downtownville, TX, 00000
M	Mountain View Community College, 1234 W. Elm Ave., Town, TX, 00000
O	Oakwood High School, 1234 Big Oak Lane, Yourtown, TX, 00000

Special Explanation Code

The list of codes can be found after a colon following the course name (above).

Code	Explanation
D	A college course taken for which high school & college credit is awarded.
H	An honors course.
J	A high school course satisfactorily completed prior to grade 9.
R	A course completed in summer school.

Additional Remarks about Student:

Signed: _____ Date: _____

Books, Software, DVDs, Games, Toys

Long distance education

AUSTRALIA

Australian Correspondence Schools
PO Box 2092
Nerang MDC
QLD 4211
Australia
Tel: (07) 5530 4855
Website: www.acs.edu.au/

USA

Stanford University
EPGY (Education Program for Gifted Youth)
Ventura Hall
Stanford University
Stanford, CA 94305-4115
USA
Tel: (800) 372-EPGY

Texas Tech K-12 Option
Outreach and Extended Studies
Texas Tech University
PO Box 42191
Lubbock, TX 79409-2191
USA
Catalog request tel: 800-MY COURSE
Website: www.dce.ttu.edu/K12

University of Nebraska-Lincoln Independent Study High School
PO Box 839400
Lincoln, NE 68583-9400
USA
Tel: (402) 472-2175
Website: http://nebraskahs.unl.edu/

Assessment tests

Bob Jones University Press
5731Greenville, SC 29614
USA
Tel: (800) 845-5731
Website: www.bjup.com/services/testing/academic_testing.itbs-tap.html
Iowa Test of Basic Skills, Stanford Achievement Test, and others

Family Learning Organization of Washington
PO Box 7247
Spokane, WA 99207-0247
USA
Tel: (800) 405-TEST
Website: www.familylearning.org
Iowa Test of Basic Skills, and others

McGuffey Academy
2213 Spur Trail
Grapevine, TX 76051
USA
Tel: (817) 481-7008
Website: www.mcguffeyhomeschool.com/
Stanford Achievement Test, and others

Homeschool book suppliers
AUSTRALIA
Homeschool Supplies (Aust)
Website: www.homeschooling.com.au/

CANADA

A+ Books
Box 2375
St. Marys
Ontario N4X 1A2
Tel: (519) 284-2804
Website: http://aplusbooks.safeshopper.com/index.html334

USA

Great Homeschool Books
Shepherd's Nook
554-D Ritchie Hwy
Severna Park, MD 21146
Tel: (410) 544-7800
Website: www.greathomeschoolbooks.com/
Carries a lot of books and programs (Saxon, WrapUps, Easy Grammar, and more). One-stop shopping.

Homeschool Supercenter
1129 Tamiami Trail 3N
Port Charlotte, FL 33953
Tel: (800) 230-0020
Website: info@homeschoolsupercenter.com

Packaged curricula

A Beka
Alpha Omega Publications
300 N. McKemy Avenue
Chandler, AS 85226
USA
Tel: (800) 622-3070
Website: www.home-schooling.com

Core Curriculum (secular and others)
14503 S. Tamiami Trail
North Port, FL 34287
USA
Tel: (888) 689-4626
Website: http://core-curriculum.com/index.php

Oak Meadow School
PO Box 740
Putney, VT 05346
USA
Tel: (802) 387-2021
Website: www.oakmeadow.com

Sonlight Curriculum
8042 South Grant Way
Littleton, CO 80122
USA
Tel: (303) 730-6292
Website: www.sonlight.com

Switched on Schoolhouse (see Alpha Omega Publications, above)

Competitions

National Geography Bee: annual competition, for US kids, grades 4 to 8
National Geographic Society
1145 17th St. NW
Washington, DC 20036-4688
Website: www.nationalgeographic.com/society/ngp/geobee/gasics.html

Scripps Howard National Spelling Bee, for US kids, grade 8 and under
Scripps Howard National Spelling Bee
PO Box 371541
Pittsburgh, PA 15251-7541
Website: www.spellingbee.com

Driver education

Australia

Index of driving schools, plus free tutorial and license information
Website: www.driving-school.com.au/index.asp

Canada

Young Drivers
One James St S., Suite 300
Hamilton
Ontario L8P 4R5
Canada
Tel: (905) 529-5501
Website: www.yd.com/YoungDrivers/
You can also take a free learner's permit test on this site.

UK

"Driving Test Pass 2002/2003" CD-ROM
This is inexpensive at about £9 and gives you ten free tries before it asks you to register. Read about it.
Website: http://software.reviewindex.co.uk/reviews_uk/B00006LSW6.html

USA

ONLINE

TeenDriver.Com
Tel: (800) 482-6593
Website: http://teendrivingcourse.com/
Not approved in all states (see website).

SOFTWARE

"Driver Ed in a Box" is software that claims to have all the materials and essential tools for parents to train teens to drive collision free. They state that it is valid for every state, although some states may have additional requirements. Do check this aspect out for your state.
Website: www.driveredtraining.com/

"Rules of the Road" DVD you play in a regular DVD player (or in a computer). You use your remote to make choices when the DVD comes to a decision point and asks you what to do, or if you want to change your view.
Tel: (314) 569-1771
Email: Jamie@JumbyBayStudios.com
Website: www.gooddriverdvd.com/

Foreign language

Power-Glide Language Courses

988 Cedar Avenue
Provo, UT 84604
USA
Tel: (800) 596-0910
Website: www.power-glide.com

Ultimate French, Living Language Series
Ultimate French: Basic-Intermediate

Book/Cassette Package
Published by Living Language
(order through any bookstore)

Handwriting resources

Handwriting Without Tears

8802 Quiet Stream Ct
Potomac, MD 20854
USA
Tel: (301) 983-8409

Math

Cuisenaire Rods

ETA/Cuisenaire
500 Greenview Court
Vernon Hills, IL 60061
USA
Tel: (800) 445-5985
Website: www.etacuisenaire.com/index.htm
This company sells hundreds of manipulatives, including Pattern Blocks

Learning Wrap-Ups

1660 West Gordon Ave #4
Layton, UT 84041
USA
Tel: (800) 992-4966
Website: www.learningwrapups.com/aboutLW.asp

Math-U-See
6601 E. Mill Plain Blvd
Vancouver, QA 98661
Tel: (360) 750-9050
Website: www.mathusee.com

Miquon Math
Sonlight Curriculum
8042 South Grant Way
Littleton, CO 80122
USA
Tel: (303) 730-6292
Website: www.sonlight.com/miquon.html
Also available through many other suppliers

Pattern Blocks
ETA/Cuisenaire
500 Greenview Court
Vernon Hills
IL 60061
USA
Tel: (800) 445-5985
Website: www.etacuisenaire.com

Ray's Arithmetic
Mott Media
112 E. Ellen St
Fenton, MI 48430
USA
Website: www.mottmedia.com/rays.html

Saxon Math
Saxon Publishers
1320 W. Lindsey St
Norman, OK 73069
USA
Tel: (800) 284-7019
Website: www.saxonpub.com

Singapore Math
19363 Willamette Drive #237
West Linn, OR 97068
USA
Tel: (503) 727-5473
Website: www.singaporemath.com

Touch Math
6760 Corporate Drive
Colorado Springs, CO 80919
Website: www.touchmath.com

Music
Suzuki method

AUSTRALIA
Suzuki Talent Education Association of Australia (NSW) Inc.
PO Box 134
St. Paul's
NSW 2031
Tel: (02) 9399 9888

UK
British Suzuki Institute
39 High Street
Wheathampstead
Herts AL4 8BB
Tel: (44) 1582 832424
Website: www.stour.force9.co.uk/esa/countries.britain.html

USA
Suzuki Association of the Americas
PO Box 17310
Boulder, CO 80308
Tel: (303) 444 0948
Website: www.suzukiassociation.org/

Physical education/movement

Brain Gym ($9.95) and *Brain Gym Teacher's Guide* ($19.95) by Paul E. Dennison and Gail E. Dennison. This is a series of 26 specially designed exercises to stimulate the flow of information along neural pathways and increase learning in your child.
Website: www.braingym.com/html/our_products.html

Available from:

AUSTRALIA

Summerfields Booksellers
PO Box 1809
Coffs Harbour
NSW 2450
Tel: 61 (02) 6651 4652

NEW ZEALAND

Glenys Leadbeater
14 Joyce Street
Papakura
Auckland 1703
Tel: (64) 9 299 8878

SOUTH AFRICA

Brain Dynamics
PO Box 44389
Linden
2104 Gauteng
Tel: 02711 888 5434

UK

Body Balance Books
12 Golder's Rise
Hendon
London NW4 2HR
Tel: (44) 20 8202 9747

USA/CANADA

Edu-Kinesthetics, Inc.
PO Box 3395
Ventura, CA 93006-3395
Tel: (805) 650-3303

Wobble Board
These come in various sizes and types and prices start at around $30 and are available from fitness stores. Available from stores that sell fitness gear.

Kangaroo Hopper (toy) ($9.95)
Mondo, USA
This is a sturdy vinyl ball with handles, approx. 16.5 inches tall and suitable for ages 3 to 8. Balls such as this are available in many toy stores worldwide. Similar brands are called Fun Hop or Sport Ball Hoppers.

Reading resources

Explode the Code
Educators Publishing Service
PO Box 9031
Cambridge, MA 02139-9031
USA
Tel: (800) 435-7728
Also available from many homeschool suppliers

Harvey's Grammar
Mott Media
112 E. Ellen St
Fenton, MI 48430
USA
Website: www.mottmedia.com/harvey.html

Hooked on Phonics
Gateway Educational Products
2900 S. Harbor Blvd
Santa Ana, CA 92704-6429
USA
Tel: (800) 616-4004

Painless Grammar
Barron's Educational Series, Inc.
250 Wireless Boulevard
Hauppage, NY 11788-3917
USA
Tel: (516) 434-3311
Email: info@barronseduc.com
Website: www.barronseduc.com

Phonics Pathways
Dorbooks
Tel: (800) 852-4890
Email: info@dorbooks.com
Website: www.dorbooks.com/about.html

Science
Edmund Scientific
Tel: (800) 728-6999
Website: http://scientificsonline.com/default.asp?

Home Training Tools
546 S 18th St W
Suite B
Billings, MT 59102
USA
Tel: (800) 860-6272
Website: www.hometrainingtools.com/

Typing/keyboarding resources
JumpStart Typing
CD-ROM
Order from any software store or
Website: www.knowledgeadventure.com/home/

Mavis Beacon Teaches Typing
Tel: (800) 895-0277
Website: www.broderbund.com/SubCategory.asp?CID=249

Typing Instructor
Timberdoodle Company
1520 E. Spencer Lake Road
Shelton, WA 98584
Tel: (360) 426-0672
Website: www.timberdoodle.com/index.asp?PageAction=VIEWPROD&
ProdID=136

Appendix 8

Finances of Homeschooling

Below, our family finances are bared to you, not because I'm a financial exhibitionist but because I really want to show you step by step how we figured out that I could be a stay-at-home mom and we wouldn't starve. Keep in mind that the numbers are rough, based on 1990 figures and in US dollars. It won't translate well to today's costs, but it is the process that is important. Here's what we did.

Step one

Start by calculating how much money that paycheck is really bringing in.

After taxes

Although my yearly income was roughly $46,000, federal taxes immediately whittled that down to $38,800, and after state taxes the paycheck was closer to $36,800. My retirement fund took up $2800. That left us with $34,000. Medicare tax was around $700. Now the paycheck I was thinking about cutting was down to $33,300.

After expenses

Going to work always entails some overhead expenses, but you may be chagrined to see just how very much expense is involved. Consider work clothes, extra schooling, briefcases or tools, and transportation. Daycare took two large bites but there were many items that added up to considerable expense:

- Before and after-school care (Chris) – $60/wk × 50 = $3000

- Daycare (Chris's brother) – $90/wk × 50 = $4500

- Gasoline to work and back – $10/wk × 50= $500

- Daily lunches – $25/wk × 50 = $1250

- Business clothes, shoes, nylons, purses, jewelry, dry cleaning – $650

- Office extras (coffee fund, gifts, office parties, business lunches) – $500

- Vending machines – $10/wk × 50 = $500

- Fast food dinners (because I was too tired to cook) – $30/wk × 50 = $1500

- Total work-related expenses = $12,400

My paycheck was now looking more like $20,900 in real income, quite a comedown from the original $46,000. It was depressing to think that my fat paycheck and hard work yielded so little, but on the upside it seemed easier to cope with losing my paycheck when it was now less than half its original size. It redoubled our conviction to become a single-income family. Now the question became, could we make up a $20,900 loss?

Step two

Look for gains you can make. One nice part about reducing family income is that it often reduces one's tax bracket. In our case, my husband got to keep about 5 percent more of his paycheck, resulting in something like $1350 that he didn't have to pay to Uncle Sam. We then looked at some money-saving strategies. A top priority was paying off credit cards because interest payments alone were eating $100 per month out of our income (sad, but true). Luckily, one bonus of leaving my job was that I got back my retirement fund contributions. That lump sum was enough to pay off our credit card bills, which would save another $1200 in interest we no longer had to pay. We refinanced our house loan for a savings of about $3000 per year. The dollar cost for me to stay home was now looking more like $15,350 instead of the original $46,000. When my husband got the opportunity to work shift work ($4000 gain) and we knew a promotion was not too far off ($2000), we felt we could make it. I resigned my job and came home.

Step three

Economize. This aspect may amaze you the most. It's shocking how much economizing can be done if you put your mind to it. Could you cancel cable or satellite TV options? Contrary to popular belief, these are not necessities. Can you drop magazine subscriptions? Shop for cheaper insurance or better long-distance rates? Cut the kids' hair yourself? (Given the tactile sensitivities and stress triggers of many kids with Asperger's Syndrome, haircutting at home is often a less frightening option than a salon cut anyway.) These are just a few cost-cutting hints.

Step four

Be flexible. Our ways may not work for you, but maybe some other options would. You might decide to sell a car or motorcycle, move to a more modest neighborhood, or ask your parents for your inheritance early. You might look into debt consolidation loans, running a home-based business, or putting some things on hold, such as family vacation or college night classes.

Step five

Have faith. I'm pleased to tell you the happy ending to this story. After I quit work and we trembled through a brief adjustment period, everything went smoothly. We survived. In fact, we not only survived but we soon reached a firmer economic standing than we'd ever had before. Our bills were fewer, our needs were simpler, our debts were non-existent, we had less clutter around the house (because we bought less), and our priorities were straight. Man cannot live on bread alone, but how many of us really need this year's model car?

Bibliography

Armstrong, T. (2000) *In Their Own Way*. New York: J.P. Tarcher.

Attwood, T. (1998) *Asperger's Syndrome: A Guide for Parents and Professionals*. London: Jessica Kingsley Publishers.

Basham, P. (2001) "Home Schooling: From the Extreme to the Mainstream." *Public Policy Sources. Vancouver: Fraser Institute.*

Bendt, V. (1994) *How To Create Your Own Unit Study*. Tampa, FL: Common Sense Press.

Bernstein, R. (1997) *Phonics Activities for Reading Success*. New York: Center for Applied Research in Education.

Brainerd, L. (2002) *Homeschooling Your Gifted Child (Language Arts for the Middle School Years)*. New York: Learning Express.

Campbell, N.A., Mitchell, L.G., and Reece, J.B. (1999) *Biology Concepts and Connections*, 3rd Edition. Menlo Park, CA: Addison Wesley Longman.

Cheatum, B. and Hammond, A. (2000) *Physical Activities for Improving Children's Learning and Behavior (A Guide to Sensory Motor Development)*. Champaign, IL: Human Kinetics Books.

Cohen, C. (2000a) *And What About College? How Homeschooling Leads to Admissions to the Best Colleges and Universities*, 2nd Edition. Cambridge, MA: Holt Associates.

Cohen, C. (2000b) *Homeschooling the Teen Years: Your Complete Guide to Successfully Homeschooling the 13- to 18-Year-Old*. Roseville, CA: Prima Publishing.

Colfax, D. and Colfax, M. (1988) *Homeschooling for Excellence*. New York: Warner Books.

Elliot, R. and Hamilton, L. (1997) *Painless Grammar*. Hauppage: Barron's.

Estell, D., Satchwell, M.L. and Wright, P.S. (1990) *Reading Lists for College-Bound Students*. New York: Prentice-Hall.

Faherty, C. and Mesibov, G.B. (2000) *Asperger's: What Does It Mean to Me?* Arlington, TX: Future Horizons

Field, C. (1998) *A Field Guide to Home Schooling (A Practical Guide for Parents)*. Grand Rapids, MI: Baker Book House Company.

Freeman, S. and Dake, L. (1997) *Teach me Language: A Language Manual for Children with Autism, Asperger's Syndrome and Related Developmental Disorders*. Lyndon, WA: SFK Books.

Gardner, H. (1993) *Multiple Intelligences: The Theory in Practice.* New York: Basic Books

Gatto, J.T. (2002) *A Different Kind of Teacher.* Berkeley, CA: Berkeley Hills Books.

Gold, L. and Zielinski, J.M. (2000) *Homeschool Your Child for Free.* London: Prima.

Gray, C. *The New Social Story Book.* Arlington, TX: Future Horizons.

Greene, R. (2001) *The Explosive Child: A New Approach for Understanding and Parenting Easily Frustrated, Chronically Inflexible Children.* New York: HarperCollins.

Holt, J. (1982) *How Children Fail.* New York: Delta Publishing.

Jansson-Verkassalo, E., Ceponiene, R., Kielinen, M., Suominen, K., Jantti, C., Linna, S., Moilanan, I. and Naatanen, R. (2003) 'Deficient Auditory Processing in Children with Asperger Syndrome, as Indexed by Event-Related Potentials.' *Neuroscience Letters 338*, 3, 197.

Kaye, P. (1995) *Games for Writing.* New York: The Noonday Press.

Llewellyn, G. (1998) *Teenage Liberation Handbook: How to Quit School and Get a Real Education.* Eugene, OR: Lowry House.

McAfee, J. (2001) *Navigating the Social World: A Curriculum for Individuals with Asperger's Syndrome, High Functioning Autism, and Related Disorders.* Arlington, TX: Future Horizons.

Mannix, D. (2000a) *Social Skills Activities for Special Children.* San Francisco, CA: Jossey-Bass.

Mannix, D. (2000b) *Life Skills Activities for Special Children.* San Francisco, CA: Jossey-Bass.

Maslow, A. (1987) *Motivation and Personality.* Harlow: Addison Wesley Longman.

National Center For Education Statistics (2000) Table 53: Children 0 to 21 years old served in federally supported programs for the disabled, by type of disability: 1976–77 to 1998–99. http://nces.ed.gov/pubs2001/digest/dt053.asp

Nowicki, S. and Duke, M. (1992) *Helping The Child Who Doesn't Fit In.* Atlanta, GA: Peachtree Publishers.

Nowicki, S. and Duke, M. (2002) *Will I Ever Fit In (The Breakthrough Program for Conquering Adult Dyssemia).* New York: Free Press.

Pyles, L. (2001) *Hitchhiking through Asperger Syndrome.* London: Jessica Kingsley Publishers.

Rosner, J. (1993) *Helping Children Overcome Learning Difficulties.* New York: Walker.

Rupp, R. (2000) *Home Learning Year by Year: How to Design a Homeschool Curriculum from Preschool Through High School.* New York: Three Rivers Press.

Schnurr, R. and Strachan, J. (1999) *Asperger's, Huh? A Child's Perspective.* Gloucester, Ontario: Anisor Publishing.

Tobias, C. (1998) *The Way They Learn.* Colorado Springs, CO: Focus on the Family Publishing.

Index